Positive
Child Guidance

Early Childhood Educators—Select from these other 1990 Delmar publications for the most current coverage of issues:

The World of Child Development: Conception to Adolescence, by George S. Morrison.

Early Childhood Experiences in Language Arts: Emerging Literacy, 4th Edition, by Jeanne M. Machado.

Creative Activities for Young Children, 4th Edition, by Mary Mayesky.

Creative Resources for the Early Childhood Classroom, by Judy Herr and Yvonne Libby.

Math and Science for Young Children, by Rosalind Charlesworth and Karen K. Lind.

Early Childhood Education: A Workbook for Administrators, by Dorothy Hewes and Barbara Hartman.

Infants and Toddlers: Curriculum and Teaching, 2nd Edition, by LaVisa Cam Wilson.

A Practical Guide to Solving Preschool Behavior Problems, 2nd Edition, by Eva Essa.

Administration of Schools for Young Children, 3rd Edition, by Phillis and Donald Click.

Developing and Administering a Child Care Center, 2nd Edition, by Dorothy June Sciarra and Anne G. Dorsey.

Developmental Evaluations of Software for Young Children, by Sue Haugland and Dan Shade.

Positive
Child Guidance
Darla Ferris Miller

DELMAR PUBLISHERS INC.®

NOTICE TO THE READER

Cover illustration by: Dahl Taylor

Delmar Staff

Associate Editor: Jay Whitney
Managing Editor: Gerry East
Project Editor: Marlene McHugh Pratt
Production Coordinator: Larry Main
Design Coordinator: Susan C. Mathews

For information, address Delmar Publishers Inc.
2 Computer Drive West, Box 15-015, Albany, New York 12212

Copyright © 1990 by Delmar Publishers Inc.

Printed in the United States of America
Published simultaneously in Canada
by Nelson Canada,
A division of The Thomson Corporation

10 9 8 7 6 5 4

Library of Congress Cataloging-in-Publication Data
Miller, Darla Ferris.
    Positive child guidance / Darla Ferris Miller.
        p.   cm.
    Includes index.
    ISBN 0-8273-3383-8 (pbk.).—ISBN 0-8273-3384-6 (instructor's guide)
    1. Child rearing—United States. 2. Child development—United
States. 3. Child psychology—United States. 4. Parenting—United
States. I. Title.
HQ769.M5325   1990
649'.1—dc20
                                                        89-11772
                                                            CIP

Dedication

This book was inspired by and is dedicated to my father, Roy Merk Ferris (1918–1987). "Papa Roy" did not live to see the book completed, but he had great interest in and enthusiasm for its writing. Because he grew up the youngest child of a troubled single parent during the Great Depression, Papa Roy spent much of his adult life struggling to learn how to be a good parent and to let his children know that he loved them. When he read the beginning draft of this book, his eyes got a bit misty, and he said, "You've said some important things in here. I'm really proud of you." Of course, no child ever outgrows the need to know she has made her parents proud.

As my husband, Tommy Miller, and I have reared our own two daughters, we have come to realize that no mother or father ever outgrows the struggle to learn how to be a good parent or to let their own children know that they are loved.

About the Author

Darla Ferris Miller has spent more than two decades working in the areas of child care, development and education. She holds a doctorate in Early Childhood Education, Texas and Mississippi Teaching Credentials, and an American Montessori Society Preprimary Certification. In Dr. Miller's current role as Assistant Dean of Instruction at North Harris County College, South Campus, she oversees the Child Care and Development program and serves as an outspoken advocate for children and families in the region and state.

Since its inception, Dr. Miller has served as Board of Directors President for Initiatives for Children, a non-profit organization that administers hundreds of thousands of dollars in private and publicly funded grants and provides child care resource and referral to more than fifty area corporations. She has served as President and Affiliate Representative for North Harris County Association for the Education of Young Children, has been a teacher and director in child care, and is the author of *First Steps Toward Cultural Difference: Socialization in Infant/Toddler Day Care*, published by Child Welfare League of America.

Contents

Contents

Preface

One of the most pressing concerns of people who care for young children is child guidance—the process of establishing and maintaining responsible, productive, and cooperative behaviors in children. It takes a great deal of time, effort, and persistence over many years for children to develop the skills they need to become considerate and self-disciplined members of society. Knowledge of the natural processes of child development and good judgment on the part of adult caregivers greatly helps this process.

The development of self-discipline and self-control in children is neither accidental nor easy. Competent, well-behaved children do not "just happen." Dedication and skill on the part of parents, early educators, and caregivers is required for highly effective guidance. Effective guidance is necessary to prevent or eliminate behavior problems, so that learning can take place, children can be safe, child-to-child aggression will be minimized, and a foundation can be built for children's future participation in society.

This book was written specifically for those adults who make an invaluable contribution to society by caring for and teaching the youngest and most vulnerable members of society—our children. The book is intended as a road map to guide adults as they strive to meet the developmental needs of children from infancy through early childhood. Every child has unique needs. Therefore, no single guidance strategy will be appropriate for all children at all ages. This book addresses typical characteristics and needs of children as they proceed through chronological and developmental stages. It provides a broad range of practical, effective, and flexible guidance strategies based on principles of straightforward communication and assertiveness. The underlying theme is that of respect for the dignity and human rights of the infant and young child.

Much writing in the area of child guidance has focused only on behaviorist learning theory—a view that all behavior can be explained as the result of *externally* reinforced (or rewarded) learning and that, because a real understanding of the *internal* workings of the human mind is impossible, it is therefore irrelevant. A key problem with exclusive reliance on behavior modification—ignoring negative behaviors and reinforcing positive behaviors—is that it may be carried out in an aloof or manipulative manner.

Additionally, rewarding children for behaving a certain way raises several sticky issues. Because human beings of all ages are infinitely complex, the praise or prize that reinforces one child may embarrass, bore, or alienate another. Doling out privileges and prizes may place an adult in the role of a stingy Santa Claus rather than that of a democratic guide and role model, and may stimulate competition rather than cooperation among children. Doling out attention and praise as reinforcement risks implying to children that compliance is a condition for affection, that only "good" children are loved.

Another problem that undermines the effectiveness of behavior modification as a sole strategy for guidance is the contemporary child's frequent exposure to many different adults and settings. Even intermittent reinforcement of a behavior through attention from children or other adults can undo an attempt by a caregiver to eliminate that behavior by ignoring it. The behaviorist attempts to control the child's behavior by controlling the child's environment. This is a very helpful tool for guidance in specific situations, but not a feasible overall plan for child guidance.

Strategies for child guidance should not rely only on methods for external control, but rather must stimulate the development of internal mechanisms and motivations for self-control. In this way children can be encouraged to become independent and self-directed, rather than dependent and other-directed as they grow toward adolescence and adulthood and begin making more and more critical choices about what to do and how to behave.

Because imitation, or modeling, is a key avenue for early child learning, *how* adults cope with the stress and frustration of handling children's misbehaviors is critical. Children tend to do what we do rather than what we say to do. The purpose of child guidance is to support and direct the growth of effective life skills rather than only to bring about the immediate control of annoying behaviors.

Positive, persistent assertiveness is considerably more painstaking and time-consuming than bullying and intimidating children into compliance by scolding, screaming, or spanking. And it definitely requires a great deal more thought and effort than giving up responsibility for children's behavior, indulging their every whim and assuming that maturation will somehow automatically bring discipline and self-control.

In child guidance—as in much of our instant, drive-thru, disposable culture of expedience—the slower, more difficult method has special value. In spite of the added skill and effort required to carry out positive, assertive discipline, its impact on the child's personal growth and on the early childhood setting make it a worthwhile method. Positive, assertive discipline bolsters self-esteem, nurtures cooperativeness, and models socially-acceptable coping skills.

The early-childhood program is a training ground in which very young people acquire and practice the skills needed for effective living. The personal characteristics and capabilities needed for survival in an autocracy or anarchy are very different from those needed for participation in a democracy. In a democratic country, early child guidance should begin the development of self-respect, awareness of and consideration for the rights of others, and recognition that persons of all ages, colors, and creeds should be treated with equal dignity, although each may have very different roles and responsibilities.

The ultimate goal of child guidance is the child's development of responsibility, self-confidence, and self-control. Inner discipline, based on an intrinsic desire to be a cooperative community member, is more functional to adult life in a democracy than sole reliance on external discipline based on an artificially contrived desire to gain rewards and avoid punishments. And, of course, there is no place in any democracy for laissez-faire anarchy in which people wantonly trample the rights of others in their quest for self-gratification.

This book outlines practical, workable steps for creating a cooperative, respectful community of children and adults. Behavior modification will be addressed, not as the foundation of child guidance, but as a single, carefully-placed stone in a solid structure of active guidance. Maturation will be addressed, not as an excuse to relinquish responsibility for child behavior, but as a powerful tool for understanding and responding appropriately to various stages of child behavior. The method presented is one of assertive and respectful enforcement of cooperatively developed rules and persistent protection of individual rights.

Aggression, passivity, and manipulativeness are identified as hindrances to positive child guidance. They trigger negativeness, even rebellion, in children, and they model behaviors that are hindrances to successful participation in democratic community life. The role of the adult, in this book, is that of one who seeks not to gain control over children but rather to guide them effectively while setting for them an immediate and tangible example of appropriate coping and assertive negotiation.

In this model, the adult not only guards the safety and individual rights of children, but also stimulates their development of inner control by creating a functioning democratic community of children and adults. Positive child guidance means guiding children as firmly as necessary, as gently as possible, and always with respect.

This book is intended as a lively, poignant, warm, and very human look at the process of adults guiding, managing, and coping with children's behavior—and children trying to deal with their own emerging needs and feelings as well as with persistent adult expectations. Although the book is readable, and at times even funny, it is based on a solid theoretical foundation built from the empirical study of social and emotional development in infants, toddlers, and young children.

Acknowledgments

I am indebted to many colleagues, friends, and family members who gave endless encouragement, assistance, and guidance during the writing of this text. I especially owe thanks to Cynde Miller, Lynne Aiken, Rod Smalley, Gary Peters, Denny Kaltreider, Patty Knowlton, Wilmer Roberts, Sandra Couch, Pam Anderson, and Robert Jordan for the sensitive and beautiful photographs included in these pages. (The children, families, and teachers of Montessori Country Day School and Heights Montessori School, both of Houston, Texas, were most kind in granting permission for photographs to be taken.)

I thank Michelle Miller, Julianne Pederson, Karen Burkhardt, and Marge Ellison for precise and tireless proofreading. Additionally, the content of this text has been inspired and informed by numerous dedicated child advocates such as Dr. Joan Wyde, Dr. Sharlene Peters, Pat Phipps, Sallie Cochran, Sue Thornton, Rene Merrell, Mary Beth Gaertner, Grace Hively, Joni Mceuen, and Lisa Valentine.

I also thank Kathleen Rowland, Dr. Peggy Emerson, Dr. Jeanette Phillips, Dr. Mark Ginsburg, Dr. Joe McMillian, and Dr. Larry Phillips, professional mentors who have guided my own professional development and indirectly made this writing possible.

The people of Delmar Publishers, Inc. have been of great assistance. In particular I owe a debt to Jay Whitney, Marlene Pratt, and Brett Peabody. I also offer my sincere appreciation to the early childhood experts listed below who reviewed this book and contributed a great deal to its readability and usefulness by critiquing it and by adding their own ideas and suggestions.

The reviewers of this text include: Elaine Jones, Plano, TX; Sue Haugland, Cape Girardeau, MO; Jo Ann Wood, San Antonio, TX; Sharon McClusky, Portland, OR; Cindy Nail, Anderson, SC; Rebecca Reid, Cobleskill, NY; and Mary Ann Cortin, Minneapolis, MN.

Section 1

What Is Positive Child Guidance?

Figure 1–1 Every child represents a new beginning, full of bright possibility. *(Photo courtesy of Evolee Farris)*

1

Introduction

OBJECTIVES
This chapter will assist you in:

- Identifying contemporary practices in child care.
- Defining responsibility for healthy childrearing.
- Recognizing the purpose of child guidance.
- Stating the criteria for creating early-childhood rules.
- Describing the optimum early environment for long-term development.

NEW ROLES AND RESPONSIBILITIES IN CHILD REARING

It's 7:00 a.m. Monday morning. Across the country, from bustling cities to tiny rural communities, families are struggling to begin their workday. In millions of homes and apartments, parents hurry to feed and dress babies and young children, then buckle them into car seats, and head for a variety of child care arrangements. They range from Grandma's house to registered family-day homes to proprietary and government-funded day-care centers. The world is changing, but children are always children. Whether Mommy is a full-time homemaker or a business executive makes little difference to a toddler who plops in the middle of the floor and cries because he doesn't want oatmeal for breakfast. Child guidance is a challenging task for any parent, but if parents work outside the home, managing their children's behavior may be more complicated, and parents may rely a great deal on child-care workers to support their children's social and emotional development.

Practical, day-to-day responsibility for guiding the next generation is shifting from parents alone to parents and early-childhood personnel working together. Today there are fewer traditional, two-parent, single-earner families, and rapidly increasing numbers of dual-earner couples, single parents, and other arrangements of employed households with young children. At the same time that family structures are changing, more and more research has surfaced highlighting the critical importance of early experiences for the long-term development of a child's personality, character, values, and social competence (Adlam, 1977; Anyon, 1983; Bandura, 1975; and Cook-Gumperz, 1973). Never before has there been such acute awareness of the impact early caregivers have on young lives. Never before has there been such need for people outside the family to assume major involvement in the process of child rearing.

Years ago, "babysitting" was a custodial time-out from the real business of child rearing (which was most often handled by mothers). Because "babysitting" represented only a brief interruption from day-to-day caregiving, any untrained but reasonably responsible teenager or adult could be relied on to sit with the baby or child for a short time, just to assure that the child was safe and that basic physical needs were met. Now, however, about half of all babies and young children live in homes where the adults in the family work part- or full-time outside the home. Child care is no longer a brief interruption from routine caregiving but, rather, a major portion of it. Many children spend most of their waking hours in some form of child care by someone other than parents, from as early as the first weeks of life.

These changes place new pressures on parents and on early childhood professionals. Working mothers must face the stress of juggling family and career obligations. Fathers find that modern lifestyles present a new level of paternal involvement in caring for and managing young children. Child-care workers find that more and more is expected of them by parents who depend on paid caregivers to be skillful in supporting wholesome growth and development in the children. Even parents who are full-time homemakers find that contemporary lifestyles bring new stresses and strains to child rearing. Many feel that their toddlers and preschoolers benefit from participating in professional early-childhood programs, even if a parent is home full time and child care is not absolutely necessary.

In today's world, many children do not spend the first years of their lives sheltered in cocoon-like home settings. They are up with the alarm clock, their days are structured and scheduled, they come in contact with many caregivers, and they must learn to get along with other young children in groups. Modern parents need help in developing the skill they need to guide young children effectively and prevent behavior problems, because they may have limitations in their flexibility and time to deal with a tantruming toddler who refuses to get dressed or a pouting preschooler who insists that everyone in the whole world hates her. They also need support with guidance so that behavior problems do not place additional strain on family-life structures that may already be stretched thin simply from the stresses of contemporary living.

Early-childhood professionals need help in developing effective

Figure 1–2 For many families child care is a way of life, so parents and child care providers must work together to assure effective child guidance. *(Photo courtesy of Pam Anderson)*

child-guidance strategies so that they can truly meet the social and emotional needs of the children in their care, so that they provide much needed support to family life, and so that they can assume a reasonable portion of the responsibility for teaching the next generation how to be responsible, cooperative, competent citizens. Teachers and caregivers can never replace the important role of caring parents. Parents have an irreplaceable impact on their children's lives simply because of the emotional bonds that are a part of being a family. While caregivers must never compete with or infringe upon this special parent/child relationship, they can be a tremendous support to both children and their families.

We are all responsible for the well-being and guidance of children. In past centuries, children were thought to be their parents' property. In Western Europe only a century-and-a-half ago, babies were not considered to be real persons. It was not even thought necessary to report their deaths (Aries, 1962). In a modern democracy, however, children are not viewed as property of their parents, but rather as human beings with inalienable rights. Governmental agencies hold responsibility for the welfare and guidance of young children because children are the future citizens of the country. Failure to address early needs later costs government millions of tax dollars in remedial education, indigent support, and crime. Business and industry hold responsibility for the welfare of young children because they will be the work force of the future, and competitiveness in world markets depends on the availability of competent, cooperative, responsible workers. Communities, churches, schools, and everyone else are responsible because good citizenship obligates us to look to the future well-being of humanity rather than just our own immediate interests.

Throughout the country there is growing recognition that investing efforts and resources to better the lives of children is not only humane, but also very cost effective. Children are open to ideas and experiences and it is possible to bring about meaningful changes in their lives and to have real influence on their long-term development of values and character traits. Adults, on the other hand, tend to be more rigidly set in their habits and potentials. If adults are to live in a democracy, then we must begin by helping children learn personal responsibility and respect for others so that they will know how to function cooperatively as adults.

SHORT-TERM OBJECTIVES FOR CHILD GUIDANCE

The short-term objective for child guidance is deceptively simple. Children will be helped to follow the same basic rules for decent and responsible behavior that are applicable to all persons living in a democracy. In order to accomplish this, the adult will assure that the following criteria are used to monitor the appropriateness of children's day-to-day behaviors:

1. Behavior can be allowed only if it does not infringe on the rights of others.
2. Behavior can be allowed only if it does not present a clear risk of harm to oneself or to anyone else.
3. Behavior can be allowed only if it would not unnecessarily damage the environment or animals, objects, or materials in the environment.

In order to communicate these rules effectively, to translate them to the comprehension level of young children, they must be greatly oversimplified. By oversimplifying them, young children can be helped to make sense of what may seem to them to be an endless number of unrelated little rules. By lumping rules into three basic categories, one can help young children to remember and understand the basic guidelines for appropriate behavior—be kind, be safe, and be neat. These ground rules can be stated as reminders before more specific and practical instructions are given. For example:

- Be kind! Wait for your turn.
- Be safe! Go down the slide feet first.
- Be neat! Put your paper towel in the trash can.

Stating the guidelines for appropriate behavior is easy. Evaluating real behaviors in real children is a great deal more difficult. A very well-coordinated five-year-old is leaning back on two legs of his chair. Does this behavior infringe on the rights of others? (For example, is the walkway between tables blocked for other children?) Does this behavior risk an accident? (Could the child fall? If he fell, would he hit soft carpeting or a cement floor?) Does it appear that equipment could be damaged by this behavior? (How sturdy is the chair? Are breakable things nearby?) Personal judgment, practical experience, and knowledge of individual children and their capabilities will determine how different adults answer these questions and how they go about setting rules and enforcing discipline.

What are the rights of children? Children have a right not to be hurt. Adults should be very conscientious about protecting every child's right not to be hit, kicked, bitten, or shoved. It is never okay to allow a child to be kicked because she did it first and "deserved to get a taste of her own medicine." It is never okay to bite a toddler back "so that he will learn what biting feels like." An old cliche that happens to be true is—"Two wrongs don't make a right." The only thing that revenge really does is set the stage for more hurtful behavior. Adults should monitor children carefully and consistently so that aggression can be prevented or interrupted immediately when it does occur.

Children also have a right to avoid unnecessary discomfort. They have a right to eat lunch peacefully without an unnerving noise level caused by children around them screaming and yelling. They have a right to listen to a story without being squashed by others who are struggling to see the pictures. And, they have a right to build sand castles without getting sand in their eyes because gleeful playmates are shoveling sand into the air just for the fun of it. Although all young children begin with a kind of thinking that limits them to a self-centered (or egocentric) view of the world, adults can help children begin to recognize that others have feelings. In time children begin to get a sense of what it feels like to be someone else. A one-year-old may try to give her pacifier to an older child who is crying, or a pre-schooler may run to tell a teacher that his friend got pushed off the swing. Adults who are consistently sensitive to the comfort needs of children set an emotional tone in which children are much more inclined to be sensitive to each other.

Children also have a right to their possessions. Adults sometimes impose very strange views of sharing on children. In the adult world, government provides very precise laws related to possession and ownership. Law forbids others from tampering with one's possessions with-

Figure 1–3 Young children appreciate pleasant and comfortable surroundings.*(Photo courtesy of Cynde Miller)*

out permission. Even social customs follow the same rule. If I take a cart in a grocery store and begin doing my shopping, it would be extremely rude and surprising for another shopper to snatch that cart away and dump my groceries because she wanted "a turn" with the cart. I would greatly appreciate a store manager (authority figure) who intervened politely but assertively and redirected the offending shopper to other available carts. Oddly enough, a child in preschool who complains because another child grabbed the tricycle or snatched the container of crayons he was using is often not helped but instead chided for "tattling" and for "not sharing."

A child's personal possessions are her own, and no one, not even a parent or teacher, should tamper with them without asking the child or at least letting the child know—"I'm going to put your sweater away now." Objects that are available for shared use belong to the person using them at any given time (until, of course, that use infringes on the rights of others). In a home setting, if one child is watching television, another should not be allowed to march in and change channels without asking. In a group setting, a puzzle belongs to the child who chose to work with it, and no one else should be allowed to touch that puzzle without permission from the child who chose it first. Sharing is only really sharing if it is voluntary. (Involuntary sharing is something we adults affectionately refer to as taxation.)

Another right children have is the right to fairness. Fairness is a concept that emerges slowly in children during the preschool and early elementary years. Even before that concept is well-developed, however, children deserve fair treatment and they need to observe role models of integrity and fairness. If one child is allowed to have a picture book during naptime, it is unfair to deny that privilege to another child without some logical reason or explanation.

By the time children are about kindergarten age, they can sometimes be heard proclaiming loudly, "Hey, that's not fair." Although their logic is still rather limited, and their actual concept of fairness may be hazy, they are likely to complain if the action of an adult or another child appears to them to be blatantly unequal or out of compliance with a rule. Sometimes, if an adult carries out a disciplinary action that appears arbitrary and capricious to a child, the child will immediately begin enforcing that action on other children, partly as revenge and partly in imitation of the adult. For example, if an angry teacher yanks a child's lunchbox out of her hand and says that it isn't time for lunch yet, the child may immediately yank away another child's lunchbox, angrily repeating the same lecture about it not being time for lunch yet.

How does one distinguish the difference between enforcing prudent safety rules and being overprotective? Just about every interesting activity or environment has some element of risk. Imagine for a moment trying to create an environment that had absolutely no possibility for any kind of accident. Unfortunately, a child could potentially misuse, fall off of, throw, choke on, or bump into just about any kind of equipment or material that could be named. The only perfectly safe environment would be a padded cell—and some child would probably find a way to get hurt there. Of course, a padded cell would not offer many opportunities for exploration and skill development. So, in an interesting, challenging environment, safety is always a matter of compromise. The difficulty for many teachers and parents seems to be in deciding what level of compromise is acceptable and reasonable, and what is not.

Children feel a sense of pride and dignity when they succeed in mastering a difficult challenge that has a bit of risk involved. No baby ever learned to walk without risking a fall, and no child ever learned to jump off a step, climb a tree, roller skate, or ride a bicycle without risking a bump or bruise. Some pediatricians assume that if a child makes it through early childhood without so much as a broken finger, then he or she has been overprotected. The acceptability of risk must be weighed against the severity of possible outcomes. If the worst thing that could reasonably result from a behavior is a two-foot fall onto a thick gymnastic mat, then the risk seems very acceptable. If the child could possibly fall ten feet onto brick pavement, then there is a clear risk of harm; that kind of accident could result in serious or permanent injury to the child.

Adults must be diligent about safety for young children. Environments in which young children play should be checked and double checked routinely for hazardous equipment, toxic plants or substances, and dangerous but tempting situations. Then, but only then, adults can step back and allow children the latitude to negotiate challenges independently, under a watchful eye, rather than hovering control.

Why should children to be involved in maintaining and protecting their environment? In order to learn, children need the freedom to make mistakes, to know that it is really not so awful to break a glass or spill paint on a shirt. Most things can be restored or replaced. Stained clothes will soon be forgotten, but a child's first painting may be treasured for many years, and the benefit of the experience of painting may stay with a child for the rest of her life.

While it is essential to keep a reasonable perspective about neatness, one cannot lose sight of the fact that responsibility, manners, and good citizenship require one to have respect for his or her surroundings. We all share the resources of this planet and have an obligation, therefore, to use them wisely and well. Early child guidance prepares children for good citizenship. For example, when a child remembers to use one paper towel at a time and then throw it away, she is preparing for membership in adult society where everyone benefits if forests cut for paper mills are replanted, water used in factories is cleaned before being dumped, and fish and game are taken according to lawful limits and seasons.

In the first years of life, children can gradually learn to take only what they need, use it with care, and restore it or put it away when they have finished using it. Toys, games, and learning materials should be arranged in an orderly manner on low shelves to be accessible to children. Even a very young child can learn to replace a puzzle if it has its own place on a shelf or in a simple puzzle rack. (A stack of ten heavy puzzles crammed on a shelf makes it difficult or impossible for a child to select and take any but the top puzzle.) There should be no more materials available at any one time than children can deal with. And, adults must set an example for care of the environment and assist children consistently in learning that things are easier to find if they are always returned to the same spot.

Figure 1–4 Responsibility and independence develop when children learn to care for their environment. *(Photo courtesy of Robert Jordan)*

Children should be stopped firmly but kindly when their behavior is damaging to the environment. For example, while playing outdoors, children may innocently break limbs off shrubs, smash birds' eggs, or peel bark off trees. Teaching children about nature and the value of plants and animals assists them in building respect for living things and responsibility for their own actions. Indoors, children playfully smash riding toys into table legs and stuff tissues down the sink drain just to see what happens. These actions should immediately be interrupted in an understanding but matter-of-fact way. If the child is shown how tables are built, sanded smooth, and painted or how pipes bring water into and out of our homes, he will be more likely to understand and care for his environment.

LONG-TERM GOALS FOR CHILD GUIDANCE

Children are not simply lumps of clay to be shaped by caregivers. Children are born with individual potentials and personality traits. However, they are profoundly influenced by the people, experiences, and events they encounter, especially in the first years of their lives. Instead of being passively shaped by adults, children are actively involved in the experiences that have impact on their development. Children also have direct impact on the behavior of the adults with whom they interact. Adults behave differently with different children, in part because the actions and appearances of the children trigger different emotions and tactics in the adults. Children appear to be born with individual and distinctive behavioral patterns (Thomas, Chess, and Birch, 1970; Chess 1977; Thomas and Chess, 1977; and Rutter, 1978). These clusters of personality traits are referred to as *temperament*. The temperament of an infant or child has an influence on how adults will care for her. Also, the quality and style of the care that adults provide has a strong influence on her continually developing temperament. She affects her parents and they affect her—both change and are changed by their interactions.

Furthermore, even if different children's behavior is similar, their appearances may trigger different adult reactions. A thin, frail infant girl may evoke more protective, nurturing behavior in adults than a loud, robust infant boy, who may evoke more roughhousing and active playfulness in caregivers. A child who appears defiant may be treated sternly, while a child who appears contrite may be treated indulgently after an identical incident. A cycle begins in which the child anticipates a certain kind of interaction with others and behaves accordingly, actually triggering the expected interaction. What began as incidental action and reaction settles eventually into habit, attitude, and personality. The bottom line is, of course, that early experiences make a difference in children's lives.

If adults play a role in shaping children's future lives, the long-term goal for child guidance must be to equip children with the skills and attitudes they need for happy, responsible, and productive adult life. The early childhood setting, whether in the home or in a child-care center, is a miniature community in which children develop and practice the rudimentary skills they will need to cope with the larger community they encounter as they go through school, then finally the big, wide world when they are grown. Child guidance builds a foundation on which everything else in the child's life is built—social interaction with others, academic learning, and personal development. Guidance transforms the embryonic infant into a full-fledged, functioning member of society.

All I Really Need to Know I Learned in Kindergarten

Most of what I really need to know about how to live and what to do and how to be I learned in kindergarten. Wisdom was not at the top of the graduate school mountain, but there in the sandpile at Sunday school. These are the things I learned:

Share everything.
Play fair.
Don't hit people.
Put things back where you found them.
Clean up your own mess.
Don't take things that aren't yours.
Say you're sorry when you hurt somebody.
Wash your hands before you eat.
Flush.
Warm cookies and cold milk are good for you.
Live a balanced life—learn some and think some and draw and paint and sing and dance and play and work every day some.
Take a nap every afternoon.
When you go out into the world, watch out for traffic, hold hands and stick together.
Be aware of wonder.

Reprinted by permission. Robert L. Fulghum, *All I Really Need to Know I Learned in Kindergarten*. (New York: Villard Books, a Division of Random House, Inc., 1986).

What kind of early environment enhances children's long-term development? High-quality early childhood settings look so simple that it is easy to underestimate the importance of the interactions there. A wonderful environment for young children is mellow and playful. Children follow their own curiosity as they freely but respectfully explore objects, toys, and materials in the environment. They move about, chatter peacefully, laugh, and occasionally argue as they explore human social interactions and learn reasonable limits. A home environment where children are expected to be seen and not heard or a formal school environment with pupils sitting rigidly and silently following teacher's instructions or listening to lectures are not examples of optimum early environments.

The rote memorization of abstract concepts through workbooks, flash cards, and ditto sheets is definitely something young children can accomplish, but it is also totally unrelated to their level of brain development and, therefore, rather meaningless for them. Even a very young child can memorize and repeat chants or rhymes, but he is unlikely to have a clue as to their meaning. If too much time is spent in such questionable ventures as rote memorization, the loss of time for more wholesome experiences can interfere with the really essential business of early childhood—healthy development of the whole child, socially, emotionally, and physically as well as in practical thinking and problem solving.

Properly matching early childhood settings to the natural stages of growth and development seen in infants, toddlers, and young children has been termed *developmentally appropriate practice*. Detailed information about developmentally appropriate practice can be obtained through the National Association for the Education of Young Children (Bredekamp, 1987). (Further description of methods to "set the stage" for positive behavior by creating a developmentally appropriate early childhood environment is provided in Chapter 5.)

In family settings where parents feel strong bonds of love and attachment to their child, they will quite naturally respond to that child's cries and smiles when she needs attention or care. A healthy, well-developing baby or child gives many signals or cues to indicate what he needs, and a sensitive, caring parent uses trial and error to discover what will work to stop the child's crying and to keep the child happy and comfortable. This same give-and-take can be the heart of group care. However, if an adult sees child care as a tedious chore that can be made easier by ignoring children's cries and refusing to become emotionally attached to them, then nature's way of assuring that children's needs are met falls apart.

Because early experiences are so important to healthy development, child care outside the family takes on special significance. The first question parents should ask as they examine child care alternatives is, "Are the adults in this setting warm, nurturing, and emotionally available to the children?" And, because modeling (or imitating) and first-hand experience, rather than direct teaching, are the major avenues for learning in young children; the next crucial questions parents might ask are, "Do I want my child to absorb the personality traits,

Figure 1–5 Affection and attention foster the long-term development of children's potential to become competent, confident, cooperative people. *(Photo courtesy of Lynne Aiken, Heights Montessori School)*

communication styles, and problem-solving behaviors of the adults here?" and, "Do these adult role models set an example for the characteristics that I value most and want cultivated in my child?"

Children — Our Investment in the Future

In some child-care situations where working conditions are stressful (if not grueling), pay bottom-of-the-barrel, training inadequate, and staff turnover never ending, how many teachers/caregivers will be able to function consistently at a level parents want their children to emulate? Parents, early educators, and public-policy makers are becoming acutely aware of the significance of early experience on long-term development. Too often in past years it was assumed that child care need be little more than a kindly but custodial parking lot for youngsters. Growing evidence from the study of human development indicates that the first years of life may be the most, rather than the least, critical years in a child's emotional, physical, and intellectual growth.

Child-care centers, preschools, mother's-day-out programs, and other early childhood settings have the potential to help parents carve a better future for children and for society in general. To do so, however, they must have financial resources, support, and high expectations from their communities. The child-care industry must come to be viewed as an integral part of the country's public and private educational system, as well as a needed service for the survival of contemporary families.

SUMMARY

The world is changing, but children have the same essential needs for nurturing and guidance. Contemporary family life brings special stresses and strains to children and families. Most young children receive at least some of their early care and teaching from adults other than their own parents. Training in child guidance for parents and professional caregivers can equip them with the skills they need to improve the quality of life for children and their families.

Assuring the healthy growth and development of the next generation should be a major concern for everyone. The future of the world will be affected by whether or not children today learn to respect the rights of others and grow to be responsible, competent citizens.

The basic rules for responsible human behavior are simple—be kind (respect the rights of others), be safe (take only reasonable risks), and be neat (protect and maintain the environment). Children have a right to be protected from aggression, to avoid unnecessary discomfort, to know that no one will be allowed to tamper with their personal possessions without permission, and to be assured fair treatment.

Risk is an integral part of human life. The purpose of rules for safety is to define acceptable levels of risk and forbid activities that present a clear risk of serious or permanent injury. Coping with and mastering difficult challenges fosters one's self-esteem and sense of personal dignity.

Responsible citizenship in any community (adult or child) requires one to respect and care for environmental surroundings. Teaching children about science and nature helps them to refrain from thoughtlessly damaging the environment and to become more sensitive to maintaining the things they use. Children should gain daily practice in taking only what they need, properly using what they take, and then restoring or returning things when they are through.

Early child-care experiences affect a child's long-term development. Children learn by imitating the behaviors and attitudes of others. Child care takes on critical importance because the personal attributes of adult caregivers and teachers may be absorbed by babies and young children. While they are definitely not lumps of clay ready for passive molding, young children are profoundly influenced by the adults who care for and teach them.

Children learn best in a relaxed environment where play and curiosity are encouraged. Early development is fostered by freedom within reasonable limits to explore a safe but interesting environment.

PRACTICAL APPLICATION/DISCUSSION

The Spoiled Child—Myth or Reality?

It is a glorious day at the park. Bright sunshine is radiating just enough warmth to balance a flag-snapping breeze. This sudden evidence of spring has drawn families and children outdoors like a magnet. Sitting on the grass alongside a large sandbox is a cluster of grown-ups who are laughing and talking as they watch their youngsters squealing and running or digging eagerly in the sand. Al and Tamara's four-year-old son, Joel, makes gleeful whooping sounds as he chases his two-year-old brother, Eddy, with a wriggling bug he has found in the sand. Eddy screeches and dives onto his dad for protection as his mother beseeches Joel to "stop being so wild."

As he skids to a stop, Joel inadvertently smashes into a double stroller holding the Rodriguez twins. While Al escorts his boys back to their buckets and shovels, Tamara bends down with Elena Rodriguez to make sure the one-year-old twin girls are okay.

Several other parents have stopped talking and are watching attentively as Elena adjusts the little girls in their stroller and smooths their crisp, red dresses with identical embroidered collars.

Other mothers are amazed that the twins haven't cried. Tamara takes one little girl by the hand and says, "Shall we get them out and let them play for a while?"

"Oh, no," says Elena, "They would get filthy. They know that they have to stay in the stroller." Al comments that his boys were never that "good." They would have pitched a fit to get out and get right in the middle of the dirt.

Several other parents chime in with awestruck comments about how good the twins are. Elena responds, "I knew that with twins and me working they had better not get spoiled. In the day-care center I use, they are very strict about not spoiling the kids. They only pick up the babies to change and feed them. The babies cried for a few days right at first, but now they're just no trouble at all."

The conversation about Elena's twins trails off as other parents scatter to chase after straying toddlers and to respond to their children's cries of, "Watch me," "Push me in the swing again," and, "Look at my sand castle." As Tamara rushes to Eddy to remind him not to eat sand, she feels a surge of envy for Elena and her "good" babies who are never any trouble.

Questions for Discussion:

1. What do people really mean when they label babies either "spoiled" or "good"?

2. What appear to be Elena's priorities and values in caring for her children? What are her daughters learning about their role in the world?

3. Why do you think the staff in Elena's day-care center were opposed to holding, rocking, and playing with babies?

4. How do you feel about Al and Tamara's relationship with their children?

5. List, in order of importance, the ten characteristics you personally value and admire most in a person. (For example, 1. Is kind; 2. Has a sense of humor; 3. Is full of energy and enthusiasm....) Are these the same characteristics caregivers are expected to model in their interactions with babies and young children?

6. List the ten characteristics you like least in a person. Are these characteristics that caregivers routinely avoid modeling in their interactions with youngsters?

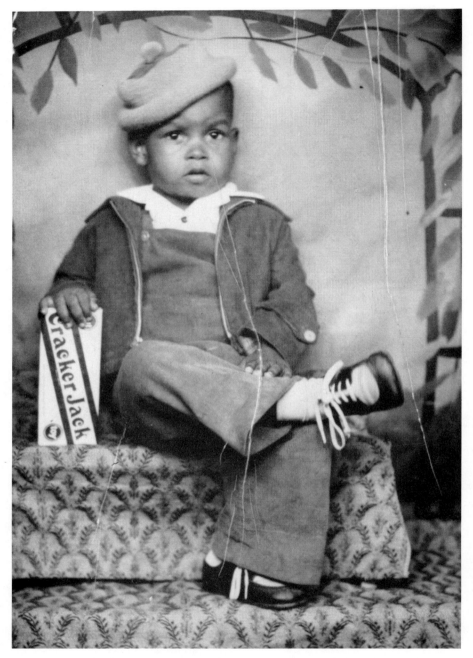

Figure 2–1 Day-by-day, every young child is in the process of creating the adult he or she will someday become. *(Photo courtesy of Wilmer Roberts and Karen Burkhardt)*

2

Beliefs About Child Guidance

OBJECTIVES
  This chapter will assist you in:

  • Recognizing historical events related to beliefs about children.
  • Outlining the child's role in society.
  • Identifying the role of child guidance in a democracy.
  • Listing changes in disciplinary strategies over time.
  • Outlining tenets of various folk ideologies of child guidance.
  • Recognizing cultural differences that affect child rearing.

- Identifying behaviorist approaches to guidance.
- Identifying maturationist approaches to guidance.
- Identifying developmental interactionist approaches to guidance.

HISTORICAL PERSPECTIVES

Child-care and guidance practices have changed drastically through the years. Many child-care traditions from the past would seem strange, even cruel, to modern parents. For example, swaddling, the snug wrapping of infants in strips of cloth or blankets, is an ancient custom that persisted for centuries in many parts of the world. While snugly wrapping newborns in blankets is considered to be a very appropriate tradition in most modern cultures, the old practice of swaddling was intended to control the baby's movement and was routinely continued until the child was old enough to walk. John Locke (1699) described the customary child care of his day:

> . . .rolled and swathed, ten or a dozen times round; then blanket upon blanket, mantle upon that; its little neck pinned down to one posture; its head more than it frequently needs, triple-crowned like a young page, with covering upon covering; its legs and arms as if to prevent that kindly stretching which we rather ought to promote. . .the former bundled up, the latter pinned down; and how the poor thing lies on the nurses lap, a miserable little pinioned captive (cited in Cunnington and Beck, p. 103).

In western Europe during the first half of the eighteenth century, infants were not only seen as somehow less human than older people, but also as somewhat expendable. A wealthy mother usually sent her newborn infant to the care of a hired wet nurse, who was expected to breast-feed and care for the child, often at the expense of the life of the wet nurse's own infant. Infant mortality rates reportedly reached as high as eighty percent in some situations as wet-nurse mothers, in order to assure their livelihood, gave birth to stimulate the production of breast milk, then sent their own infants to poorly maintained foundling homes (Weiser, 1982).

The writings of Rousseau toward the end of the eighteenth century both influenced and reflected a change in the cultural perception of childhood. He insisted that "everything is good as it comes from the hands of the Author of Nature" (Rousseau, 1893, p. 1). He argued that rather than an evil creature who must have sin beaten out of him, the young child was born good and innocent. He believed that the harsh discipline techniques of that day, which were intended to provide the child salvation from original sin, tainted the child rather than provided healthy, normal growth. Rousseau's prescription for child care included breast-feeding by the natural mother, fresh air, loose clothing, and a minimum of interference from adults.

Certain tribes of Native Americans in the 1900s particularly valued physical toughness in their children. To build up the child's resistance, newborns were plunged into cold water several times at birth, regardless of the weather. Their version of swaddling was to fasten the baby securely onto a cradle-board that could be conveniently hung inside the lodge, from a tree branch, from a saddle-bow, or wherever family members were clustered. Babies were not released from the confines of cradle-boards until they were able to walk (Weiser, 1982).

American mothers of European descent sent their infants and young children to the neighborhood widow or spinster for care and teaching. In these "dame schools," a baby might nap on a quilt in a corner of the kitchen while older children practiced reading from the New Testament (Weiser, 1982). Farm and slave children were valued as a source of free labor. Toddlers barely able to walk were assigned chores and held accountable for them.

By the early 1900s, momentum had begun to build promoting the scientific study of the development of children and the dissemination of pertinent information to parents. Some of the writings of that day foretold future trends in thinking about young children. For example, a book produced by The Institute of Child Welfare at the University of

Figure 2–2 The early 1900s marked a change in our thinking about children. *(Photo courtesy of Evolee Ferris)*

Minnesota in 1930 warned parents that children's personal characteristics were not necessarily inborn:

> As a matter of fact, the modern study of young children is indicating that such traits are in large part due to the manner in which the child is treated by adults and other children, rather than to inheritance. The parent who has the ideal of complete and unquestioning obedience, and who is forceful and consistent enough to obtain it, is likely to have a child who, when he goes to school, distresses a good teacher and delights a poor one by always doing what he is told and furthermore by always waiting to be told what to do. His whole attitude is that of finding out what authority requires and then complying, an attitude which, if maintained, is apt to result in incompetence, inefficiency, and unhappiness in adulthood (Faegre & Anderson, 1930, pp. 4–5).

MODERN THINKING ABOUT CHILD GUIDANCE

During the twentieth century, ideas about children were influenced by two world wars, periods of economic depression and prosperity, and by growing scientific interest in child development research. At the end of

Figure 2–3 Montessori saw children as our hope for a future world free of war and poverty. *(Photo courtesy of Evolee Ferris)*

World War II, Maria Montessori wrote such books as *Peace and Education* (1971) and *Reconstruction in Education* (1968) to express her view that the hope for world peace lay in a new education for young children. Montessori (1942) wrote:

> Certainly we cannot achieve it [peace] by attempting to unite all these people who are so different, but it can be achieved if we begin with the child. When the child is born he has no special language, he has no special religion, he has not any national or racial prejudice. It is men [sic] who have acquired all these things (p. 6).

In the late 1940s and into the 1950s researchers began to unlock some of the mysteries of early learning. The common belief that experiences of the first years of life were inconsequential to later development was pushed aside by more complex theories explaining the development of intelligence and personality that placed greater emphasis on early social interaction and physical exploration of one's environment (Harlow, 1959; Erikson, 1963; Piaget, 1952, 1962, 1963, 1968, 1970; Skinner, 1953; and Wolff, 1963.) In the 1960s, research into the learning processes of children from birth to school age flourished, and an estimated 23-million books on child rearing were sold during the mid 1970s (Clarke-Stewart, 1978). Clearly, there has been a mushrooming growth of parental as well as scientific interest in the processes of child growth and development.

The Child in Society

Children occupy a very special niche in our society. They are dressed in fancy clothing, photographed, given many colorful objects made especially for children (toys), fed special foods from tiny glass jars, and equipped with elaborate contraptions designed for sitting, swinging, strolling, eating, and crawling. Compared to previous cultures, children today are pampered and indulged. A bright-eyed baby decked out in several yards of lace, scented, leak-proof disposable diapers, and a huge bonnet will bring oohs and ahhs from shoppers in a supermarket and comments such as, "Oh, isn't it adorable! Look at its little shoes and its tiny earrings."

The practice of referring to infants (and sometimes toddlers) with impersonal pronouns is fairly common. The use of such descriptors as "it" and "thing" in reference to children gives a subtle indication that they are not perceived as real persons. When asked about the use of impersonal references for babies, people often respond that "it" is used since the baby's sex may not be known. Interestingly, in discussing older children and adults, even if that person's gender is not known, it would be considered highly inappropriate to refer to that person (a salesperson, a mail carrier, or an acquaintance's teenager) as an "it."

Several centuries ago, impersonal references to children were even

Figure 2–4 A contemporary baby finds herself the center of attention. *(Photo courtesy of Debby Reilley)*

more extensive. It was common for children to be referred to as "it" well into early childhood—"in this age [birth to seven years] it cannot talk well or form its words perfectly, for its teeth are not yet well arranged or firmly implanted" (*Le Grand Proprietaire*, 1556, cited in Aries, 1962, p. 21).

At the present time, in spite of indications that infants may generally be seen as somewhat less than fully human, we place a great deal more emphasis on the value and importance of individual children's lives than was evident in the past. For example, a recent newspaper account of an alleged brutal child-abuse murder quoted a district attorney explaining to shocked citizens why the murder victim, a two-year-old boy, had been given back to his biological mother after having been removed since early infancy for neglect—"Most reasonable people . . . might say the decision to put it [the child] back was probably a bad call . . . " (*The Houston Post*, 1987).

Children today are not only valued but are usually expected to have a fairly carefree existence, in contrast to the earlier use of child labor. In recent decades, young children have generally been allowed to spend a good portion of their days playing, fooling around, romping in the sunshine, and just occupying themselves (sometimes in front of a television set). Child care has brought new levels of structure to many children's lives. In many early childhood programs, this structure has enriched children's lives and assisted in their development of healthy and productive habits. In other child-care settings, children spend a considerable amount of time sitting, waiting, being berated, standing in line, and taking part in activities that are initiated and controlled by adults and are carried out by lockstep groups of children.

Since many affluent parents are having fewer children, and waiting until their professional careers are well established before having them, there is new pressure on some children to live up to the "fast lane" expectations of their parents. In the push for super babies and superior children, many youngsters may be given gymnastics, music lessons, dance lessons, tutoring, and yoga before they ever start kindergarten. Their lives may become so full of "enrichment" activities that they run out of time to lie in the clover and watch clouds go by.

The young child's role in contemporary society includes that of sometimes being seen as a pet or a possession, rather than as a person, and generally being indulged, pampered, forgotten, rushed, herded, pushed, stimulated, and valued. The growing knowledge of and emphasis on early childhood has put youngsters on a pedestal. But, of course, being on a pedestal has distinct disadvantages as well as advantages—being on a pedestal means that every move one makes is watched, judged, and managed. Early childhood experts have growing concern that children are not being allowed the freedom to "just be children."

Figure 2–5 In dual-career families, fathers may take a more active role in the day-to-day care and guidance of children.

Preparation for Participation in a Democracy

Settings where young children live, work, and play (whether in a home or a child-care facility) function as their small version of the world. As has been previously discussed, interaction in familial, educational, and caregiving communities helps children learn how to participate later in adult community life.

Child guidance is the process by which adults help children learn appropriate ways to function as part of a group. In an *autocracy*, people would only need to learn blind obedience in order to function appropriately. People are dominated by a dictator who demands submission. In an *anarchy*, one could follow one's own desires and interests. Chaos prevails because no one governs. In a *democracy*, however, educated, responsible citizens are needed to provide effective self-governance through active participation.

The guidance practices carried out by adults can help children learn how to participate in a democracy by developing:

- A concept of citizenship—being cooperative, having a sense of fair play, and respecting the rights of others.
- Initiative and self-reliance—being a self-starter, a lifelong learner, and a creative problem solver.
- Responsible work habits—having established habits of promptness, effort, and pride.
- A sense of loyalty—recognizing that sometimes one's own immediate interests and desires must be pushed aside for the good of the whole community.

Modern researchers only recently, during the 1970s and 1980s, began studying how various approaches in early childhood programs affect children's development of characteristics, attitudes, and values. However, some educators have focused on personal development and citizenship as a part of early learning and guidance for more than a hundred years. John Dewey wrote dozens of books describing his theories of learning as a part of daily living. His world-famous school, which included preschool and kindergarten, was specifically designed to foster the characteristics that are essential for living in a democracy. His school opened in 1894 (Dewey, 1966).

It is essential for those parents, caregivers, and teachers who supervise young children to recognize that guidance is not just a process for getting children to behave appropriately today, but rather a process for helping children learn to live happy, productive lives. Guidance strategies cannot be judged only by how expedient they are at the moment, but also by how effective they are in instilling functional living skills that relate to the "real" world.

In a democracy, people have rights. If I break a law by driving in excess of a speed limit, I still have rights. A police officer is authorized to use only as much force as is appropriate and necessary to stop me. He or she is forbidden to hurt me, harass me, or humiliate me as a punishment for what I did. In fact, many police officers patiently persist with recalcitrant "perpetrators" by politely but firmly insisting, "I don't mean to offend you, sir, but you were breaking the law. May I see your license?"

If officers of the law behaved the way some adults do in handling misbehaving children, we would be shocked. Imagine an officer yanking a driver out of the car, angrily shaking the driver while yelling at him or her, and snapping, "If you ever do this again, I'll use a paddle on you and you won't be able to sit down for a week!" We would probably feel very angry and misused.

Children feel that same way. It takes time and practice for children to grasp rules, but they can learn to be good citizens by the same technique that our judicial system is supposed to use—by consistent persistence and by guiding as firmly as necessary but as respectfully as possible.

The Strain of Changing Disciplinary Traditions

Changing one's methods of dealing with misbehaving children is not easy. During our own childhoods, we absorbed a great deal of unconscious information about how adults and children are expected to interact. It is as if we had mental video tapes of disciplinary interactions stored unconsciously but ready for instant replay at any time. Without thinking, we sometimes hear the voices of our parents and teachers as we scold the young children in our care. However, the disciplinary methods that were appropriate and functional generations ago may be inappropriate and nonfunctional in preparing today's children for life in the next century.

The world is changing at an astonishing rate. As it changes, children need different kinds of experiences to prepare them for the future. A hundred years ago, children were not expected to prepare for a technological world where adaptability and flexibility were more valued than adherence to set routines. Minorities and females were not expected to prepare for the likelihood that they would be competing ambitiously in the business world. And females were not expected to prepare for the distinct possibility that they would, at some time or other, function as head of household and sole breadwinner.

Once we recognize the necessity for updating strategies for guiding and teaching children, it can be difficult to change our old habits.

Figure 2–6 A hundred years ago, a strong back and a willing attitude were generally considered to be all one needed to make a living—success in today's world requires a complicated set of skills and attitudes. *(Photo courtesy of Evolee Ferris)*

Unfortunately, we adults experience confusion and stress when the methods for dealing with children that begin to seem logical and right intellectually do not match the methods we experienced and lived in our own childhoods. Beliefs cannot be turned on and off like a light switch. Instead, they must be studied and practiced for years. "Beliefs are altered primarily by experience, learning over a long period of time, and confidence in the authority of someone considered more knowledgeable (Costley & Todd, 1987)."

Human beings, adults and children alike, are influenced by life experiences. But, as human beings we also have the ability to make choices, to take control of our lives, and even to make unexpected changes in our life itinerary. We are not merely leaves floating in the stream of life. Instead, we are fish, strongly influenced by currents and tides, but free to swim upstream if we have the strength and motivation. We can choose to break old habits and establish new ones, but it is not easy and it requires stamina, determination, and a great deal of persistent practice over time.

CULTURAL INFLUENCES ON CHILD REARING

The ideas that we take for granted about the nature of infancy and childhood are different from those held by others in different places in the world and at different times in history. Current views about early childhood are not universal and have not always existed. By carefully examining our own beliefs and assumptions about children, we can recognize and put into perspective biases that interfere with effective child guidance.

Child-care practices have been strikingly different over time for various social classes. A long period of protected childhood has largely been a luxury of the middle and upper classes, and views of infancy have fluctuated according to cultural and class settings. (Bremmer, 1970; Cole, 1950; Froebel, 1887; Glubok, 1969; McGraw, 1941; Osborn 1980; Rousseau, 1893; and Ulich, 1954).

Much of what is written about childrearing, infant care, and early day-care curriculum is intended to present a generic model for quality care. That assumes, of course, that all parents hold a similar idea about what kind of care is good and right for babies and young children. There is growing evidence, however, that the importance of strategies for guiding young children is varied for parents from different backgrounds, and parents have very diverse ideas about what is and is not appropriate for guiding and disciplining children.

People from different cultural and economic backgrounds often hold starkly contrasting views about what proper child care really is. Methods of caring for and educating young children routinely expected by families in one community may shock and repel families in another community—and vice versa.

A mother in one cultural setting may be astonished that a mother in another setting still allows her two-year-old to nurse at the breast, while the nursing mother may be horrified that the first mother allows her two-year-old to eat candy and drink soda. In some settings, people expect infants to be taken everywhere the parents go. They think that is good for babies. In other settings, people expect infants to be left safely at home in their cribs with a "babysitter." They think that is best for babies.

Routines considered very desirable by one parent may be seen as inane by another. Guidance strategies believed by some early childhood educators to be essential to healthy growth may be considered inhumane or manipulative by others. Some people believe misbehaving children should be spanked. Some people believe children should be made to sit in a chair for a few minutes for punishment. Some people don't like either of those two ideas.

Figure 2–7 Cultural differences influence our attitudes about children. *(Photo courtesy of Gary Peters)*

What some consider to be essential experiences for effective early learning others consider utter nonsense. Some people think infants can be made to learn at an accelerated pace by being shown flash cards of letters and numbers. Others think no child of any age should be subjected to flash cards. Social workers, early educators, and child-care professionals often feel the tension among these opposing views and sometimes are snagged unknowingly by their own culturally biased assumptions.

Cultural perceptions of desirable and appropriate care for children reflect the perceptions and beliefs of a person at a given time and place in history. The socialization of a new generation reflects the goals, philosophies, and values of the parent generation related to their specific social and economic circumstances. In other words, culture plays a key role in defining acceptable methods for dealing with children. Cultural bias is inescapable. In order to create a supportive and pluralistic cultural environment, however, cultural differences must be understood, accepted, and respected. They must also sometimes be compromised when strong evidence emerges indicating that a culturally based tradition is harmful or ineffective in reaching desired goals.

Preparing Children for the Realities of an Adult World

From earliest childhood, children take in information about the roles and relationships of people and things in their environment. Consciously or unconsciously adults are teaching children indirect lessons as a part of every interaction they have with children.

For example, a frustrated father at a gas station vending machine explained to his toddler patiently over and over that the machine is broken and he has no more money, so he cannot get M&Ms for her. After the little girl falls on the floor kicking and screaming for M&Ms, the father finds an attendant and insists that the machine be opened so that his daughter can have the candy she wants. The tiny girl has learned two important lessons—sometimes authority figures do not tell the whole truth, and, if you make enough fuss, people sometimes find a way to get you what you want.

On one hand, we adults could rationalize any kind of harsh or careless behavior with children by explaining that we are simply preparing children for the "real" world. On the other hand, we could attempt to prepare children for what we believe would be a better world. Research into a phenomenon called self-fulfilling prophecy indicates that the expectation that something will occur actually increases the chances that it will occur (Rosenthal & Jacobson, 1968).

If children, therefore, grow up expecting to be treated with respect and fairness, they may actually behave in a way that evokes that treatment. If children grow up expecting to be treated harshly and unfairly, their behavior may trigger that response from others. The self-fulfilling prophesy may also occur because we are attracted to people and situations that match those of our childhoods. An abused child may feel familiar and comfortable with the idea that someone who says he loves you can also beat and hurt you "for your own good." That child may consequently grow up and marry an abusing spouse. People tend to be drawn toward that which is familiar and repelled from that which seems strange and unfamiliar.

How Young Children Learn About Their Role in the World

From birth to school age, children develop basic assumptions about how the world works and their role in that world. Children glean different sets of perceptions from different settings.

A. If the child's early childhood environment is rigid and children are herded through the day with no allowance for individual choice, they learn that the world is impassive and individuals cannot make a difference.

Example 1. Children are all required to sit at a long table. They are told and shown exactly how to glue precut pieces of a Santa Claus face onto a paper plate. If a child does this differently than the adult intends, the adult makes the child do it over or the adult does it herself and puts the child's name on it.

If, on the other hand, the environment is flexible and geared to individual needs, choices, and responsibilities, children learn that the world is malleable and with persistence and effort they can have impact on the world around them.

Example 2. Christmas craft materials such as paper plates, glue, glitter, cotton balls, and bits of colored construction paper are available in the art center. Children are not shown an adult model to copy, but rather are encouraged to use their own imaginations to create Christmas, Hanukkah, or other seasonal decorations. When they are finished, the children each responsibly clean up the materials they used. Unique differences in the finished products are recognized and honored and all are displayed with pride.

B. If early authority figures are aloof from the children and control them by issuing steady streams of imperative commands (Be quiet. Sit up straight. Stand in line. Don't talk.), children develop a perception of authority figures as omnipotent powers to be obeyed without question, enemies to be rebelled against, obstacles to be avoided, or irrelevant annoyances to be ignored.

Example 1. The adult attempts to maintain total control by having children do everything in unison. They must all sit and wait passively while the adult has children come up, one-by-one, to the front of the class to point out letters of the alphabet or say numbers. Children must all line up to wash hands and use the toilet at the same time. Even if their food becomes stone cold, no child is allowed to eat lunch until *all* are given the signal to begin together. Children may even be required to stand in straight lines on the playground and do calisthenics for exercise (rather than running and playing freely). The adult imagines that no learning is taking place unless he is in charge and the children are quiet, controlled, and attentive.

If caring adults are warm and involved with children and use assertive communication and positive guidance to direct children's behavior, children develop a perception of authority figures as dependable and resourceful allies, persons to rely on for protection, and to cooperate with.

Example 2. The adult structures the environment and the schedule to encourage children to function independently and individually, as well as part of a cohesive group. Children choose learning materials from learning centers and work at their own pace during large, uninterrupted periods of time. They generally use the restroom according to their own body needs, rather than group routines. Transitions from one activity to the next are flexible rather than abrupt. If a child finishes lunch earlier than others, she can throw away her trash, sponge off her area of the table, and then curl up and look at picture books until it is time for nap.

C. If adults treat children as underlings with few rights and are careless, degrading, or threatening in their treatment of children, children learn to treat others with rudeness and aggression and fail to develop self-respect.

Example 1. Adults often talk to each other as if the children weren't even present, sometimes laughing at or making fun of individual children. Adults order children around without saying "Please" or "Thank you." Punishment is meted out according to the adults' moods and whims rather than based on fair and consistent rules. The adults act as if they are above rules.

If adults treat children with respect and concern for their comfort, dignity, and basic human rights, children learn to expect politeness and civility in their dealings with others, and they learn to function with confidence and self-esteem.

Example 2. Adults behave as if children are the focal point of the environment and adults are facilitators or helpers. Adults are careful not to talk about children in a critical or humiliating way. Adults maintain a role of clear adult leadership while treating children with dignity and respect. All discipline is based on fair, consistent rules, and adults also show respect for class rules. If children are not allowed to eat, adults don't walk around in front of them drinking coffee and eating a doughnut. If an adult has to stand in a chair to change a light bulb, he explains why it was necessary for him to break a class rule about standing on furniture.

D. If an early childhood environment offers prepackaged curriculum kits, ditto sheets, and rote memorization as learning, children come to see learning as something irrelevant and external that is imposed by authority figures.

Example 1. The adult stands over children, telling them exactly what to do and what will result from each action. Adults see "free play" as recess, fun but a waste of valuable time. Adults believe that children have little capacity or interest in learning and must be taught directly through adult-controlled and educationally preplanned initiatives.

If early curriculum is individualized, discovery-oriented, and based on developmentally appropriate practice, children come to see learning as something actively sought after and knowledge as something one can create. Their learning is spurred by intrinsic curiosity rather than only by pressure from parents and teachers.

Example 2. Adults point out to children the possibilities of various materials and how to use them safely and appropriately, but they allow children to explore freely and to make spontaneous discoveries on their own. Adults trust children's ability to learn on their own as well as with adult assistance and direction.

E. If early role models limit their verbal communication to clipped criticism and commands, children, who are in the most formative period of their lives for language development, may be discouraged in the development of a level of vocabulary, grammar, and expression that is necessary for school success later.

Example 1. Adults use worn out cliches, sarcastic overstatements, and meaningless threats. They say things like, "Move, or you're really going to get it!" "Shut up and sit down!" "Hush, I don't want to hear your voice!" "Everybody freeze this instant." "You'd better straighten up and get your act together." These imperative commands don't require any thinking—only blind obedience.

If early role models are articulate, accurate, and expressive in their verbal communication with children, and if they are responsive and supportive of children's attempts to express themselves, children can blossom in their development of linguistically elaborate communication skills, which form the basis for all later academic learning.

Example 2. Adults use meaningful statements of cause and effect, descriptions of actual events or consequences, and expressions of honest feelings. The adult's words are relevant to the actual situation. Children are expected to think, understand, predict, and evaluate actions and reactions. Children are exposed to a descriptive and elaborate vocabulary through the adult expressions. Adults say things such as, "If you stand at the top of the slide, you may fall down." "If you hurt Genevieve, she may not want to play with you next time." "People have to wash their hands after they use the toilet to keep from spreading germs." "You must walk slowly and quietly here in the library because other people are trying to read." "I feel really sad when I see all the blooms pulled off our pretty petunia."

F. If early caregivers stereotype children by gender, ethnicity, or other characteristics, children build false assumptions about their limitations in the world.

Example 1. Adults may only select boys to act out the role of the fire marshal in a song or skit, totally ignoring girls who have their hands raised. Picture books are used that only show one ethnic, cultural, regional, or economic background. Adults take it for granted that all children celebrate Christmas and Easter. A particularly tall three-year-old is expected to behave more responsibly than a particularly tiny five-year-old. Children are singled out and treated differently according to how they look, how they dress, or what their parent's do for a living.

If early caregivers see all children as unique individuals who can be helped to reach their own special potential, the children develop high expectations for themselves and the self-esteem needed to master challenges they set for themselves.

Example 2. Children are all seen as unique and valuable individuals. Books, puppets, and dolls are multicultural. Children are helped to appreciate various cultures through food, music, and holiday celebrations that expose them to many perspectives. Adults respect and help the children learn about religious and ethnic differences in children and their families. Girls and boys are expected to participate fully in all activities, and girls are especially encouraged to be competent and confident.

Figure 2–8 Even very young children are learning about their roles and responsibilities within a social environment.

When does learning begin? Learning is important and possible for human beings at all stages, from birth to death. However, during the earliest years of life, people are in a particularly fertile period for learning (Bruner, 1978a, 1978b). In the first half-dozen years of children's lives, they take in a great deal of information about the cultural beliefs and values of their parents and early caregivers. After that they begin to absorb cultural perceptions from other children as well as from formal schooling, books, television, movies, records, popular role models, and folk heroes.

Because child care plays such an important role in the lives of so many children today, parents (and everyone else who cares about the next generation) should look carefully at the kind of social and emotional nurturance child-care settings provide children.

Parent Expectations Related to Social and Economic Backgrounds

A basic survival mechanism for the species is the process whereby adults recreate for children miniature communities that reflect and represent the adults' perceptions of the larger adult community. For example, if parents perceive that their own successful participation in the society hinges on being obedient and taking orders or taking control and giving orders, then they will expect their children to be exposed to imperative commands. If, on the other hand, parents perceive that giving and taking orders are inappropriate in their own adult dealings, then they will probably feel more comfortable with their children being allowed to negotiate and make compromises, rather than being told what to do (Miller, 1986).

Parents who endure long hours of crushing boredom in repetitive jobs may see nothing wrong with their children being pressured early in life to sit still for long periods without complaining or resisting. These adults may also be very tolerant of rowdy "cutting loose" behavior when it is the children's free-play time, because work and play are totally separate and unrelated in the adult's lives.

If extreme financial limitations in a community cause parents to depend for their very survival on cohesion, cooperation, and frequent help from their relatives and neighbors, then it is likely that they will expect their children at an early age to accept major responsibility for chores like tending farm animals, cooking, cleaning, or taking care of younger children. If these parents are expected in their jobs to follow set procedures and are not encouraged to think or evaluate, then it is natural that they will expect rote memorization rather than creative thinking as the core to their children's learning.

If parents perceive that the world is full of hard knocks, unfair practices, and personal insults, then they may unconsciously toughen their children for survival by exposing them early to a world that is harsh and not always fair or logical. The children learn early that they will not always get whatever they want when they want it (Cook-Gumperz, 1973).

At the opposite extreme, parents with abundant financial resources and stimulating jobs live in a very different world and thus expect a very different environment for their children. Their work may be creative and self-directed. Their hobbies may also be creative and self-directed and require as much concentration and effort as their work, so that there is not a clear distinction between work and play for them. These parents probably expect a creative environment for their children in which children can initiate their own self-fulfilling activities through innovative thinking and active involvement. Children are expected to master challenges simply for the fun of it.

Because comfort and individuality are priorities in this cultural viewpoint, a young child would probably not be expected to care for younger siblings. That would be someone else's responsibility. Parents may expect their children's desires to be met quickly and fully. Parents would unconsciously condition children to be prepared for a world in which they will expect to be treated fairly and respectfully (perhaps even preferentially) and to get what they want much of the time.

Our culture includes many variations of adult life other than the two extremes described here. Parents, caregivers, and teachers approach their work with children from many different cultural perspectives. One cultural perspective is not necessarily any better than any other. However, it is clear that early experiences prepare children to fit into existing cultural settings.

Unfortunately, preparation for one cultural setting may make it difficult for a child to function in a totally different cultural setting (Lubeck, 1985). The child conditioned to obedience and rote memorization may be very confused and overwhelmed if she, as an adult, finds herself in a situation that requires initiative, innovation, and creative problem solving. And, a child who has been conditioned to a pliable world where he always has his needs met immediately may be cruelly unprepared for adversity in a tough, unfair "real world" situation. Ideally, all children from all settings could have enough multicultural exposure to various perceptions of the world that they could learn the skills to function in whatever setting they choose or find themselves in, and not be limited to functioning in only one strata in the diverse cultural rainbow available. The day is long since gone when children could be reared to stay in the community of their birth, to live their entire lives, and to die without ever venturing out into the larger world and dealing with people whose perceptions are quite different.

Understanding Cultural Differences

Cultural differences affect the way a person perceives or thinks about things. Almost every aspect of human existence is to some extent affected by culture. Culture defines for us what is right and what is wrong, our values, our day-to-day behavior, our relationships with others, and our perception of our own worth.

Religion, ethnic customs, political affiliations, gender roles, social rituals, food preparation, literature, art, and music all express cultural uniqueness and serve to pass cultural traditions from one generation to the next. Cultural pluralism is a term used to describe the process of accepting and honoring cultural differences. If the concept of cultural pluralism is made an integral part of the first years of children's lives, they may be better able as they grow up to avoid being pulled into struggles with racial hatred, prejudice, or the stereotyping of individuals based on gender, religion, ethnic origin, age, or handicapping conditions.

Honoring cultural differences involves recognition and respect. While few people openly admit to prejudice, most of us consciously or unconsciously lump people together to some extent. Boys are aggressive, the French are romantic, Southern whites are prejudiced against blacks, overweight people are jolly and good hearted. Some generaliza-

Figure 2–9 Cultural pluralism means accepting, honoring, and celebrating cultural differences. *(Photo courtesy of Rod Smalley)*

tions are patently untrue, others revolve around some kernel of truth, but all generalizations have exceptions. There are boys who are gentle and nonaggressive, French lovers who are clods, Southern whites who fight for racial equality, and overweight people who are crabby and mean.

Respect means being given the opportunity to be seen as a unique individual rather than as a stereotypical caricature of some larger group. Underneath all the cultural and physical differences, we are all just people. We all put on our pants (or pantyhose) the same way—one leg at a time! We all want food, comfort, security, fulfillment, and, most of all, the sense of belonging that comes with being loved and respected.

It is possible to urge children to better behavior and more functional habits while clearly letting them know that we accept and respect them as they are. Sometimes adults label children by saying things like, "Vanessa, you are being so bad. Look how good Jeremy is." This sets an example for stereotyping people whose appearance or behavior is different. We can say instead, "Vanessa, hitting hurts. Use words instead of hitting, please." This way, an unacceptable behavior can be identified without lumping Vanessa into the category of "bad people."

By age three, children can recognize and identify different skin colors (Katz, 1982; Landreth and Johnson, 1953; Morland, 1972; Parrillo, 1985; and Werner and Evans, 1971). They are very sensitive to subtle nonverbal as well as verbal indications from adults as to the meaning and importance of differences in people. Adults may unconsciously show a more solicitous way of responding to people who are of similar ethnic and religious backgrounds while at the same time inadvertently snubbing those whose background is different.

Ethnicity and religion are not the only characteristics that generate prejudice. Some of us have difficulty showing warmth and respect for children whose parents behave in a way that is foreign to us, live a lifestyle we disapprove of, or are unappealing to us because of hygiene or style of dress. Some of us are obvious in our preference of girls over boys or boys over girls. We make comments such as, "The boys can go first because all the girls want to do is talk," or, "You boys go on and find something to do. The girls just want to play by themselves without you causing trouble."

In order to provide a multicultural and nonsexist environment for young children, adults must consider all aspects of cultural exposure—foods, books, toys, songs, rhymes, television shows, language, and clothing. Children can be helped to know and understand traditions of their own heritage as well as to know and honor the traditions of other cultures. They can have dolls that are male and female as well as black, white, and brown. They can be exposed to books, songs, and television shows that show girls tackling adventurous challenges and boys expressing feelings. Doll-house furniture can be combined with blocks, and men's dress-up clothing can be mixed with dishes and doll beds.

Young children can be exposed to terms like police officer, mail carrier, and milk deliverer rather than policeman, mailman, and milkman. Teachers, doctors, nurses, and secretaries can be referred to as "he or she" rather than in a stereotypical way implying that all doctors are men and all secretaries are women. Children can learn nursery rhymes and songs in Spanish or Swahili as well as in English. Foods can be offered that sensitize children to regional and national dishes, ways of preparing foods, and food-related traditions and rituals.

The purpose of multicultural, nonsexist exposure for children is not to force children into any specific mold, but rather to enhance their respect for others who are different and to empower them to be whatever they have the talent and motivation to become. By fully appreciating differences in others and by recognizing that different does not necessarily mean inferior, children may become stronger in their own beliefs and traditions and more resistant to peer pressure for conformity.

Children who have disgust for or fear of differences in others may be cruel in their treatment of handicapped or ethnically different peers. They may also be very vulnerable in adolescence to popular peers who insist that anyone is a "nerd" who doesn't conform to group standards—smoking, drinking, taking drugs, participating in premarital sex, or driving at illegal speeds. Sometimes it takes a great deal of courage to be different and to know that being different is okay.

PHILOSOPHIES OF GUIDANCE

Culture plays an important role in shaping parents', teachers', and caregivers' philosophies about children and childrearing. A person's philosophy affects his or her perception of children, how they learn, what their intentions are, and why they behave as they do. Ideas about child guidance that immediately seem logical and appropriate or sound ridiculous have been filtered by the set of beliefs and assumptions that make up one's philosophy. Although parents, teachers, or caregivers may think that they have no particular philosophy, it is likely that they simply have never really analyzed how their beliefs compare with those held by others. Some people may mistakenly assume that everyone in the world naturally shares their underlying beliefs about how things should be and why they are as they are. Because the process of acquiring appropriate behavior is a learning process, just as surely as the process of learning to read and write, it is essential to explore various philosophies related to how and why learning takes place.

The Nature-Versus-Nurture Controversy

One of the oldest debates related to children is the old nature-versus-nurture controversy. People who believe in "nature" believe that children become whatever they become based on heredity, inborn traits, and inner motivation. People who believe in "nurture" believe that children become whatever they become based on parental guidance, teaching effectiveness, television, and other external influences.

Whenever adults compare children, they can hardly resist venturing opinions about how children grow to be so different. Some will say, "Jennifer was born to be a little terror! She's just like her dad, never still for a minute," or, "Rahul will undoubtedly be a talented musician. He has inherited musical ability from both sides of his family." These people emphasize the importance of children's internal nature in their development. They believe that children are predestined at birth to certain talents and personality traits because of genetic inheritance or inborn characteristics. Others disagree. They say things like, "Of course Ming Li was potty trained so early. Her day-care teachers have trained hundreds of toddlers. They know how to do it," or, "If that were my child, he wouldn't be whining and sucking his thumb. His parents must be overindulgent or he wouldn't behave that way." These people emphasize the importance of external nurturing in the development of children. They believe that children are all born pretty much the same and their differences evolve because of differences in their treatment and teaching.

In past decades, cultural perceptions dictated that personality and potential were inborn. Some people even worried that an adopted child could carry a "bad seed." While human nature is such that parents and teachers are often tempted to take credit for accomplishments and exemplary behavior, they have routinely blamed failures and unacceptable behaviors on either the inborn traits of the child or on his or her conscious choice to be bad.

As research into human learning mushroomed during the past twenty years, a dawning awareness blossomed in parents and care-givers of the role of environment (everything and everyone the child encounters) in child development. The pendulum swung to the extreme opposite direction from blaming fate for child behaviors to attempting to manipulate children artificially, speeding the process of development and even attempting to create "better babies."

In the early 1980s, a popular trend began that was referred to as the "super-baby phenomenon." As many parents had only one or two children well after both parents' careers were established, they placed more and more emphasis on the optimum development of the child or children they had. People bought or made flash cards with abstract number concepts, names of famous composers, and anatomy terms to use in stimulating their infants. Some parents began to fear that their toddler would be left behind if she were not enrolled in baby gymnastics, French tutoring, and violin lessons by the age of two. Guilt became a national pastime for trend-setting parents.

Perhaps in the 1990s, the pendulum will settle to a middle ground, where popular culture encourages adults to recognize and appreciate the uniqueness of every individual child and his or her natural rate of development but also to take seriously the critically important role of wholesome experiences and interactions for the child's development to his or her fullest potential.

Cognitive stimulation may be to psychic development much like food is to physical development. If enough food is not available, development will be stunted. However, forcing as much food as possible on a child is probably equally destructive. Making appropriate quantities of developmentally appropriate foods (or learning experiences) available while respecting the child's hunger (or readiness for learning) makes a great deal of sense.

Lately, educators place more emphasis on the range of philosophies that underlie various theoretical explanations of the origin of human intelligence and personality. These experts trace the ancient nature-versus-nurture controversy and add a new interactionist point of view that assumes a reciprocal relationship between "nature" and "nurturing."

If human thinking could be neatly separated into simple categories, we would find three contrasting views:

- The behaviorists believe that behavior and learning result from external forces such as reinforcement and punishment.
- The maturationists believe that behavior and learning hinge on internal processes such as physiological maturation and intrinsic motivation.
- The developmental interactionists believe that behavior and learning result from complex and dynamic reciprocal interactions involving both internal processes and external forces.

The Behaviorist Approach

The behaviorists incorporate the seventeenth-century tradition of John Locke, who viewed the newborn's mind as a *tabula rasa*, or empty slate. These theorists—the behaviorists, positivists, and empiricists—believe that human learning comes from outside the learner; the environment accounts for nearly all that a person becomes.

Watson (1930), Skinner (1953, 1974), and others theorized that human beings are really products of their environments. People become scholars or cat burglars, not because of their genetic makeup or by choice, but because their environment has conditioned them to behave as they do. Subscription to this view also has powerful implications for parents and educators. It implies that human beings can be molded or shaped by the controlling of environmental experiences. This view also shifts emphasis away from focus on human will and predisposition.

Behaviorists view the development of appropriate behavior as the responsibility of the adult. The adult is responsible to identify and select specific behavior goals for the child. Then the adult observes the child and monitors any spontaneous behaviors that are slightly closer to the desired goal behavior, reinforcing each subsequent step closer to the desired goal by giving praise, treats, or tokens (that can be traded later for special prizes or privileges). The adult maneuvers the child's surroundings in order to modify (or change) specific behaviors in the child.

Behaviorists leave nothing to chance. They choose goal behaviors, select reinforcers, and even plan a reinforcement schedule of when, how often, and under exactly what circumstances reinforcers will be given. Behaviorist views are all focused on the idea that learning is an *external* process, that learning takes place in the child as a result of influences from the child's environment. Child guidance is seen as an adult-directed process.

The Maturationist Approach

From a point of view opposite to that of the behaviorists, the maturationists borrow from the tradition of Plato. These maturationists, innatists, or nativists believe that learning emerges from within. These educators and philosophers theorize that human beings are born to be whatever they become. The human infant in this conception is like the rose bud, naturally unfolding into a preordained blossom as long as it is kept healthy.

Well into the 1920s and the 1930s, Arnold Gesell, a researcher at Yale, maintained that children's external environment did not control developmental outcomes. He claimed that children's own genetic and biological characteristics determined their intelligence and personality (Gesell, 1940). The maturationists view the development of appropriate behavior as a natural process like the unfolding of a rose bud. They believe that as long as basic needs are met, the child will automatically develop the social skills, the intelligence, and the physical control necessary for the child to behave properly. They see the role of the adult as that of a facilitator. The adult studies children, carefully observing and monitoring their behaviors and abilities. When there is a problem, the adult steps in to help the child understand what has happened in a specific situation and to help the child resolve the problem as independently as possible.

Maturationists perceive that learning comes from inside the child. They believe that the processes of learning cannot be rushed. Adults view themselves as role models, guides, and consultants. They believe children are ultimately responsible for their own decision to behave properly. Personality and growth traits inherited genetically and the child's own willpower play an important role in the maturationists views about how children learn to behave appropriately. The maturationists see the development of proper behavior as a child-directed process.

Obviously, this type of perception has broad implications for parents and educators concerned with guiding children. If early experiences are relatively inconsequential to one's later development, adults need only be concerned with providing the basic necessities for safety and health, custodial care, in the earliest years. This view implies that growth and learning proceed according to internal rules of physiological growth and as a result of personal decision making, in spite of specific environmental circumstances.

The Developmental Interactionist Approach

Debate over the previous two contrasting views of human learning (the nature-versus-nurture controversy) has been complicated recently by a growing body of research compiled in the past three decades by the developmental interactionists, who believe that human learning results from the interaction between the learner and his or her environment.

The work of Piaget (1952, 1962, 1963, 1970, 1983), Chomsky (1965), Kohlberg (1966), Hunt (1976), Bloom (1964), Kagan (1962, 1971, 1978), and White (1973, 1975, 1979) made it clear that environmental factors influence human development, but the research also supports the importance of individual readiness, personal learning styles, and reciprocal interaction as a part of the process.

This new stream of thought gained scientific credibility and is now recognized to be neither a maturational nor a behaviorist view of learning. Piaget (1952), for example, termed himself a constructionist or cognitive interactionist (developmental interactionist). He asserted that infants are born with predispositions to certain kinds of thought and behavior but that they must create their own knowledge through stages of interaction with the environment. Play is the word we use to refer to this early exploratory interaction with the environment.

White (1975) said that newborn children come into the world with an internal structure that sets an upper limit to their potential, but

Figure 2–10 Each child is a unique individual, influenced by both heredity and environment. *(Photo courtesy of Cynde Miller)*

that the internal structure is not a guarantee of any level of development or learning. The child is programmed to learn, but without stimulation and reinforcement from the environment no learning can take place. This way of thinking about young children creates pressure on parents and day-care providers to produce high-quality early experiences so that optimum stimuli can be made available.

White (1975) further emphasized the importance of early environments by stating: "To begin to look at a child's educational development when he is two years of age is already much too late, particularly in the area of social skills and attitudes (p. 4)."

Lorenz (1966), Hess (1972), von Frisch (1974), and Lamb (1978, 1981) are *ethologists*, researchers who study behaviors in terms of natural processes and in natural settings. They refined the idea of sensitive periods for learning in which environmental stimuli can have a maximum impact on a child's learning. Hunt (1976) described what he called the "match." He said that a match must be created between a child's level of readiness and the exact level of difficulty or discrepancy in a specific learning situation in order for optimum learning to take place. If interactions in the environment are too difficult, children become frustrated and discouraged. If they are too easy, children become bored. Children actively seek out materials and activities that match their own level. They enjoy and learn well from an environment that offers a fairly wide range of difficulty in which they are allowed the freedom to choose toys, games, and interactions that are matched to their own ability level as well as the freedom to reject materials or activities that seem too easy or too difficult.

In terms of child guidance, the interactionists believe that children can only learn to behave appropriately when they have inner maturity as well as suitable external influences. Adults must study children and plan carefully, but they must also focus on the child's own interests and abilities. Some areas of child guidance seem more responsive to external control and some areas to internal control. Mindless habits a child really wants to change can probably be treated quickly and effectively through behaviorist strategies. More general problems that seem to have more deep-rooted emotional causes are probably best treated with maturationist support of the natural processes of maturation and exploration of the child's inner motives.

The interactionist approach integrates the processes for inner and outer development. Interactionists see child guidance, not as an adult-directed or a child-directed process, but rather as an interaction in which either can lead or follow. It is like a waltz with give-and-take, leading and following. The adult respects the child's interests and abilities but is also not afraid to take control when necessary. The child feels free to express herself but also knows and respects clearly defined limits. The interactionist approach offers the best of both worlds—nature and nurture.

Which Philosophy Is Right?

Within any group of people who care for and teach young children there will be many successful and effective adults who tend to lean a bit toward either a more maturationist or a more behaviorist view of early growth and development. Generally, however, a predominant view in the field of early childhood education revolves around the belief that early development results from the interaction between children's inner capacity and motivation and their external environment.

Two basic assumptions that build a foundation for the procedures throughout this book are the beliefs that:

- Babies and children develop skills and concepts by interacting (playing and living) in a stimulating and supportive environment.
- The way children interact in their environment is triggered by their particular stage of development as well as their own interests and motives.

In other words, one might say that healthy, well-developed children come into the world preprogrammed to learn (Chomsky, 1965). They will automatically be motivated to explore the physical properties of the environment around them by using their senses. They will seek human social contact, and they will quickly absorb any language they hear. If these components of the environment are abundantly available, the interactions that ensue will foster development in a healthy and natural way. A child who comes into the world without all of the normal physical processes in full force may need special stimulation in one or more of the environmental areas listed above to maximize his or her potential for development.

Tragically, however, even an infant who is perfectly healthy at birth may eventually suffer from the effects of a hostile or nonnurturing environment. Lack of a healthy emotional environment can cause:

- Failure-to-thrive syndrome.
- Marasmus (a severe condition of underweight and poor health).
- Developmental delay.
- Permanent mental retardation.
- Death.

Any of the above can afflict potentially normal, healthy children if they are deprived of the essential elements of a normal environment. They need nurturing human contact, a sense of being wanted and accepted, the opportunity to share thoughts and feelings in verbal or nonverbal communication with others, and exposure to interesting things to explore by seeing, touching, tasting, feeling, smelling, and moving around.

The development of an intelligent, responsible human being is not an automatic internal process that takes place in spite of environmental factors, and it is not an external process of molding a pliable child into a predetermined shape chosen by parents and teachers. It is a lively process of give-and-take in which children explore their boundaries and limits. Sometimes they accommodate to adult expectations, and sometimes, quite naturally, they resist. Children come equipped with individual personalities, likes, dislikes, interests, and motives. The role of the adult is to guide, assertively and respectfully, never forgetting that even the youngest child is truly a person with all the rights befitting any other human being (even the right to be negative and recalcitrant on occasion). *In the developmental interactionist perspective, child guidance is intended to give children feedback about the realities of their world, to allow them choices within reasonable limits, and to help them confront the logical consequences of their own actions.*

SUMMARY

Child-care and guidance practices changed dramatically through the years. By the early 1900s, momentum began to build promoting the scientific study of the development of children and the dissemination of pertinent information to parents. During this century, ideas about children were influenced by two world wars, periods of economic depression and prosperity, and the changing role of women in the workforce, as well as by growing scientific interest in child development research.

Recent studies affirm the special importance of environmental factors during the first years of life. Parents who depend on help from others in rearing their children want to be assured that their children will receive proper guidance. They want to be assured that their children will be helped to develop the social and emotional skills necessary for living responsible, successful, and fulfilling adult lives.

Settings where children live, work, and play (whether homes or child-care facilities) function as a small representation of the world for young children. Children can learn how to function in a democracy by experiencing democratic rules and respectful interactions early in life. Adults may have difficulty changing old habit patterns in dealing with children, but change is possible with motivation and practice.

People from different cultural and economic backgrounds often hold starkly contrasting views about the parameters of proper child care.

Early in life, children develop basic assumptions about how the world works and their role in that world. They learn more from modeling and practicing than from direct instruction. The earliest years are a particularly fertile period for learning.

A basic survival mechanism for the species is the process whereby adults recreate for children miniature communities that reflect the perceived day-to-day realities, values, and assumptions of the parent generation. An adult's cultural background will determine to a large extent what seems logical, appropriate, and reasonable in dealing with children.

Honoring cultural differences involves recognition and respect for the appearances, customs, and beliefs of others. The purpose of multicultural, nonsexist exposure for children is not to force children into any specific mold, but rather to enhance their respect for others and to heighten their own self-esteem in areas where they may feel different.

One of the oldest debates related to children is disagreement over how children develop personality and intelligence—the nature-versus-nurture controversy. Contemporary educators identify three philosophical perspectives—the behaviorists, the maturationists, and the developmental (cognitive) interactionists.

The developmental interactionist view assumes that external environment and internal processes of development and motivation interact to determine a child's development of personality and intelligence.

PRACTICAL APPLICATION/DISCUSSION

Bringing Home a Baby Bumblebee

In a medium-sized neighborhood day-care center, a group of preschool children cluster around their teacher and sing with her. They snatch invisible bumblebees from the air and pretend to trap the them in their clasped hands as they sing:

> I'm bringing home a baby bumblebee. Won't my mommy be so proud of me.
> I'm bringing home a baby bumblebee—bzzz bzzz bzzz bzzz. Ouch! [slap] He stung me!

In another part of town, in a day-care center located in a tiny, frayed building that is part of a low-income housing project, a group of children sit on chairs around long, wobbly tables as they enthusiastically sing:

> I'm bringing home a baby bumblebee. Won't my mama be sur-

prised of me. I'm bringing home a baby bumblebee—bzzz bzzz bzzz bzzz. Ouch! [slap] He stung me! [They giggle and bounce in their chairs as they scrub their hands together.] I'm squashing up the baby bumblebee. Now there's bumblebee blood all over me. [Their song deteriorates into squeals of delight as they vigorously rub their own and each other's clothes.] I'm wiping off the blood of the bumblebee. Now there's no more blood all over me.

In still another part of town, in a tastefully decorated private preschool, a third group of children sit cross-legged in a circle on soft carpeting singing happily with their teacher:

I'm bringing home a baby bumblebee. Won't my daddy be so proud of me.

I'm opening up the window carefully, so my bee can fly away free—bzzz bzzz bzzz bzzz. Bye bye, baby bumblebee.

Questions for Discussion

1. Do you think that songs parents and child-care workers teach children help pass cultural perceptions from one generation to the next?

2. What are your own cultural perceptions of children? Do you see children as innocent and pure, to be protected from anything violent, scary, or disgusting? Do you see children as regular people who enjoy raucous humor and vicarious aggression? Do you see children as "born sinners" who sometimes can have evil or cruel impulses?

3. Compare versions of songs and stories you have heard. Do the different versions reflect cultural perceptions of children?

4. Why do you think the third teacher in the example above replaced the word mommy or mama with the word daddy?

5. How are songs and stories used by adults to instill in children an awareness of cultural values?

6. Identify a song or story you would feel uncomfortable using with children. How would you change it? Why?

Section 2

What Can I Expect from Children?

Figure 3–1 Children see the world differently from the way we adults do. *(Photo courtesy of Montessori Country Day School)*

3

Understanding Children's Behavior

Growing Comprehension of Language
Using Words to Express Feelings and Needs
Learning How to Be a Friend
Accepting Responsibility
Following Rules
Developing a Clear Self-Concept
Schoolagers (5–12 Years)
Growing Ability to Think Logically
Becoming a Capable Listener
Dealing with Authority Figures
Analyzing and Creating Rules
A Sense of Fairness
A Need to Belong
Becoming Productive
Controlling Impulses
Maintaining Self-Esteem

OBJECTIVES

This chapter will assist you in:

- Recognizing typical ages and stages of early childhood.
- Identifying developmental milestones that affect behavior.
- Identifying relationships between maturation and guidance strategies.
- Outlining changes over time in adult/child relationships.
- Tracing the development of positive self-esteem.

TYPICAL AGES AND STAGES

The most important thing to remember when considering the typical ages and stages of childhood is that no child is completely "typical"— every child is unique. Although typical or average patterns can be identified, real children have individual patterns and rates of development that may be normal but not at all average. The most valid reason for comparing a child's rate of development to standard rates is to be alert to any consistent pattern of differences, or "red flags," that indicate a need for professional screening and possibly the need for therapeutic intervention.

Sometimes, by comparing a child's individual behaviors to typical behaviors, we can better understand the child, recognize that the child is only going through a normal phase, and anticipate phases that the child will soon be entering. Adults are often comforted to know that many children at a certain age behave the same way as the child they are dealing with. Babies shy away from strangers, toddlers become stubbornly assertive, preschoolers worry about who is or is not their best friend at any given moment, and schoolagers reject everything that isn't considered "cool" by their friends. Adults are also relieved to realize that most children tend to outgrow whatever phase is at issue, regardless of how adults try to respond to it.

Typical behaviors tend to be fairly consistently clustered together and in a sequential order. Therefore, a child's behaviors might be matched to those at a specific age level, although her chronological age may actually be younger or older than that listed. A seven-year-old who is developmentally delayed may show a wide range of typical toddler behaviors. However, a gifted four-year-old who can already read may behave a bit like a schoolager in some behaviors but like a preschooler, or even a toddler, in other behaviors. The value of assessing each child individually is to match guidance strategies to the individual child's developmental capabilities and needs—never to label or stereotype the child.

If, for example, a toddler is discovered trying to poke an object into an electrical outlet, the adult may look very concerned and say, "Ouch, that could hurt you. Come play with your toys." But the primary discipline strategy would be to change the environment to protect the toddler more effectively. A specially-designed safety guard could be installed to prevent access to the outlet, or the child could be removed to a safer, better-supervised area.

A five-year-old, however, who is discovered exploring and trying to insert an object into an outlet should be handled quite differently. The adult must determine whether the child is curious, misinformed, or feeling rebellious. When the adult has a sense of why the behavior occurred, he might firmly discuss the cause-and-effect dangers of playing with electric outlets, and then redirect the child's curiosity by allowing the child to explore the characteristics of electricity using a safe six-volt battery, wires, and a tiny flashlight bulb. The child's curiosity could be channeled into a whole new area of interest and knowledge by reading books about electricity, by going outside to look at power lines and talk about how workers protect themselves when they repair dangerous electrical wires, and by making pretend wires out of strings to attach to the child's playhouse.

INFANTS (0–12 MONTHS)

Babies are fascinating. Their big eyes and rounded contours are specially designed to turn grown men and women to mush (Alley, 1981). Babies are soft and warm and cuddly, but few parents are prepared for

Figure 3–2 Who can resist the soft, endearing face of a baby?

the powerful emotions that well up inside them when they, for the first time, have their own child. Some parents feel a jumble of emotions—outrageous pride, a protectiveness as passionate as a tiger for her cubs, jealousy of any imagined competition for affection, over-whelming fatigue, fear of failure, even grief over the loss of infancy as the child grows and matures so quickly.

Parenting is one of the most significant and challenging adventures adult human beings undertake (often with little or no preparation). If additional caregivers are involved in infant care, parents may be re-lieved of some stresses and strains, but other complex feelings or ten-sions may emerge. Many a mother has left her baby in a carefully chosen child-care center for the first time only to sit in the parking lot, collapsed in tears on the steering wheel of her car.

Fathers, grandparents, even siblings also fret over the adequacy of anyone helping to care for the new baby. Jenny, a kindergartener in a day-care center, talked her teacher into letting her go to the nursery where her two-month-old brother was newly enrolled. There, she held her baby brother's tiny hand through the bars of his crib for a long time as she carefully watched every move made by the nursery work-ers. The employees smiled as the little girl pointed out to them, "You mustn't touch his head right up there where it's soft." Although Jenny was only five, she felt protective and concerned about her baby brother.

Reacting to Sensations Without Conscious Intention

Usually, the first kind of upsetting behavior adults must cope with is bouts of crying. A typical scenario pictures the adult trying all the usual problem-solving strategies—warming a bottle, changing a diaper, rocking. Soon, the adult has done everything he knows to do, but the infant cries even more frantically. Some adults hear the infant's wails as a personal indictment of their competence, integrity, or authority—"How dare this baby accuse me of being a bad father (or mother, or caregiver)!" A howling baby can quickly fray the nerves of even the most patient and devoted adult.

A temptation for many of us is the tendency to project intentional motives on the baby for her crying. We say things like, "She's just crying because she knows I'm a pushover," "He always cries when I try to cook, because he thinks he should be the center of attention," or, "She's only crying because she's mad at me. She was born with a fiery temper." These rationalizations may make us feel vindicated for angry or resentful feelings that surge through us as we try to deal with the screaming baby, but they are, nevertheless, inaccurate. Infants don't intentionally do much of anything—they just react spontaneously and unconsciously to their environment.

Sadly, some adults with virtually no understanding of the processes of child development see infant crying as such a clear example of intentional, "bad" behavior that they attempt to punish the infant for her crying. Child protective-service workers and other social agents often deal with parents who begin shaking, hitting, and spanking babies in the first year of life—a very dangerous and inappropriate practice—in the mistaken belief that they are helping their babies learn to be "good."

Can Babies Misbehave on Purpose?

Regardless of many common misconceptions, in the first months of life infants have no capacity for consciously intentional behavior. They are not able to think about or plan actions to get desired results. Until they have object permanence (the mental ability to envision persons, objects, or events that are not in sight) they cannot "think" or "know" that any action will bring about a desired result. They can only react or respond in a very unconscious way to internal feelings such as pain or hunger and to external *stimuli*—sensations the infant sees, feels, hears, tastes, or smells (Piaget, 1968).

Even past six months, some behaviors that may seem intentional are actually unconscious reactions based on the child's having absorbed connections or relationships among day-to-day experiences. Unrelated objects, events, and sensations become connected. If a microwave oven is customarily used to warm a baby's bottle, the sound of the microwave timer dinging becomes connected (or associated) with being given a warm bottle of formula. The baby gets very excited any time she hears it ring. Similarly, we might expect any nine-month-old to show curious interest in a brightly colored, shiny can—but if the child immediately fusses and struggles for the can of soft drink he sees in his mother's hand, it is pretty clear his experience has led him to expect a sip whenever he sees a soft drink can.

Reflex Responses and Unconscious Conditioning

In newborns, almost all actions are simple reflexes over which the child has no control. Infants blink, startle, grasp an object placed in the palm of the hand, and root toward a nipple—but not because they choose to do those things. They do them simply because their brain is designed to make certain behaviors happen automatically. From the moment of birth, however, babies carefully study their environment, at first by staring and eventually by using all their senses. Babies gradually progress beyond reflex behavior. They begin to recognize and associate things they see, feel, hear, taste, and smell with other meaningful sensations or events. A hungry, breast-fed infant will become very agitated when she is held near her mother's breast. The feel, smell, and sight of the breast is closely associated with the memory of the sweet taste of milk.

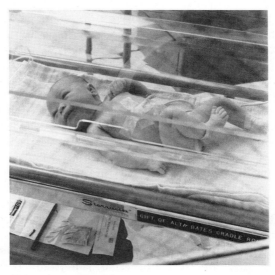

Figure 3–3 The newborn baby comes into the world equipped to learn by looking, listening, feeling, tasting, and smelling.

What Is Classical Conditioning?

To a baby, hearing keys rattle means someone is leaving, being placed in a stroller means going for a walk, and hearing the rustle of plastic wrap means getting a cookie. This kind of learning is generally categorized as *classical conditioning*. Looking at a balloon doesn't normally make babies cry. Seeing a balloon is an unconditioned stimuli. Loud noises, however, certainly do make them cry—crying in response to a loud bang is a naturally occurring stimulus-response connection. If a baby became frightened and cried on several occasions when balloons popped, the baby may begin to cry whenever he even sees a balloon. This is a conditioned stimulus–response connection.

Researchers attempted for decades to document classical conditioning (pairing an unconditioned stimuli with a naturally occurring stimulus–response connection) in newborns. The best yet documented is a rather rough kind of learning now called pseudo-conditioning. Studying early responses is difficult because so little of the newborn's movement can really be classified as voluntary (Rosenblith & Sims-Knight, 1985). However, by the middle of the infant's first year, classical conditioning is clearly a part of the child's learning.

What Is Operant Conditioning?

Operant conditioning is quite different from classical conditioning. It occurs when the child's spontaneous actions (such as crying) are reinforced by pleasurable rewards (such as food). This type of conditioning has been studied and documented in infants from the first days and weeks of life (Sameroff & Cavanagh, 1979). Newborns automatically cry as a response to the discomfort of being hungry. Older babies and toddlers learn to whimper or make a "fake" crying sound to signal that they are hungry. In the classical conditioning example previously described, babies became excited by sensations that unconsciously reminded them of being fed. In operant conditioning, however, hungry babies learn to repeat whatever behaviors in the past resulted in their being fed. For example, if a breast-fed infant is nursed whenever he roots and pulls at his mother's blouse, then that action (rooting and pulling) may become an unconscious but *learned* behavior that he repeats whenever he is hungry.

A baby first turns toward a nipple in response to an unconditioned rooting reflex. Then, over time, the pleasurable reward of warm milk stimulates more active and goal-oriented rooting. Eventually, the sight of the nipple, recognizing the feel of being placed in a nursing position, or other sensory cues (the smell of milk, the sound of a voice) will trigger rooting and sucking. An adult who is unfamiliar with a specific baby may inadvertently cause her to become frustrated and cry simply by holding her, without feeding her, in a position that she associates with nursing.

What Is Metacognition?

Young infants need many repetitions of unfamiliar sensations, actions, and events in order to form associations. By the end of their first year, however, they have learned, through conditioning, to expect many specific responses to accompany certain actions and sensations (Papousek, 1967). This kind of learning is an unconscious process. Although unconscious, conditioned learning continues to take place throughout life, months and years will pass before the child will develop an ability to consciously and intentionally control his own behavior—a process we call *metacognition*.

When a child develops metacognition, she will be able to think about her own thinking processes and to develop strategies to help her manage her own behavior. Children between three and six years old are only beginning to develop metacognition. Schoolage children have a much better-developed ability to plan strategies. For example, one might say, "I'll hide the candy where I can't see it, then I won't be so tempted to eat it before supper." Babies and toddlers possess none of these skills. They just spontaneously react to the positive and negative sensations in their world.

Babies' Control of Their Actions

The first muscles babies can actively control are those around the face and head. (The newborn can move her eyes to follow objects, she can suck effectively, and she can turn her head.) Muscle development proceeds from head to toe and from the trunk to the extremities— *cephalocaudal* (top to bottom) and *proximodistal* (close to far). At first, infants are only able to control a few mouth, eye, and neck muscles. Gradually, the infant expands body control downward into the trunk (she learns to turn over), outward through the arms to the hands (she learns to bat at objects and then to grasp them), and finally down to the legs to the feet (she learns to crawl and then walk). Tiny muscles of the hands and fingers will not be fully developed for years. (Then she will finally be able to use her fingers to button her sweater, tie her shoe laces, and write her name).

Why do babies cry? In the child's first year of life, behaviors result almost exclusively from internal developmental characteristics and gradually increasing conditioned learning. If a baby cries for a prolonged period, that behavior does not stem from manipulativeness, maliciousness, or any other conscious intention, but rather from internal discomfort, stress, or fatigue or from externally-conditioned routines. Babies cannot be held responsible or blamed for their behavior. It is more realistic to think in terms of relieving the cause of a crying infant's unhappiness if the problem is internal, or of gradually changing adult routines to bring about a different kind of conditioned behavior if the problem has been caused externally.

Adults are the ones who establish routines and habits in infants through day-to-day basic care patterns. Infants become *habituated* (accustomed) to those patterns and object loudly when routines are abruptly broken. If an infant is accustomed to being in constant contact with her mother's body, she will cry pitifully when she is left unexpectedly in a playpen. If an infant is accustomed to quiet isolation, he may be terrified by sudden placement in a noisy, bustling daycare center.

Psychologists define stress as the process of recognizing and responding to threat or danger (Fleming, Baum, and Singer, 1984). While working directly with infants over the years in various childcare facilities, I have on several occasions seen babies who seemed especially upset by a separation or by a stark upheaval in their care arrangements. In spite of attentive caregivers, the infants (ranging from three to nine months old) appeared to slip from a long period of anguished, relentless crying into a period of quiet depression with only languid whimpering.

The infants withdrew from social contact, avoided eye contact, lost appetite, refused to play, slept too much or too little, and, apparently as a result, appeared noticeably less healthy after a time. After various lengths of time (ranging from days to months), each of these babies recovered spontaneously eventually and became responsive, robust, and playful. Today, almost a decade later, the most severely affected of these infants gives every appearance of being a bright, healthy, and well-adjusted young girl. Nevertheless, stress should be considered in dealings with children of any age and avoided or modified whenever possible.

Careful planning of basic care and nurturing routines that can be maintained consistently will help protect the child from abrupt and upsetting changes. When changes in routines must occur, careful planning and gradual orientation should take place—especially before drastic upheavals in child-care arrangements occur—in order to avoid subjecting babies to unnecessary stress.

Development of Trust

According to Eric Erikson (1959, 1963, and 1982), trust developed in infancy is a primary foundation for the development of healthy emotional attitudes that must be built upon throughout life. Basic care patterns offer our first opportunity to demonstrate our trustworthiness to an infant. Whenever the infant experiences internal distress, he automatically responds by crying. In time, through operant and classical conditioning, he can come to expect a dependable and pleasurable response from the adult caregivers in his life. This trust in the predictability of his environment and in the responsiveness of his primary caregivers helps the baby develop a sense that he is valued and that he can have impact on his surroundings—the first step toward the development of positive self-esteem.

Learned Helplessness

Babies who are caught in a flow of events that are unpredictable and clearly outside their control may, in contrast, develop an unfortunate style of response termed learned helplessness (Honig, 1986). Heartbreaking but very instructive studies of the Creche, a Lebanese orphanage run by French nuns, helped researchers more fully understand the devastating impact of learned helplessness. Babies in this orphanage were adequately fed, clothed, and kept warm and dry, but the babies stayed in cribs with only uninteresting white crib bumpers and white ceilings to look at. There were few playthings and no structured activities. Caregivers were not aware that talking directly to and interacting with babies was necessary.

Because the babies were fed and changed on a schedule, there was no motivation for caregivers to respond to the babies' cries, so the babies soon learned that there was no use in crying. In effect, the children had no impact on their environment. Nothing that happened to them hinged on either spontaneous or learned actions on their part. They had no incentive to function in any way other than as passive objects in the environment, and, in fact, their behavior was soon not much livelier than that of a potted plant. These babies did not learn to sit up until a year or walk until four or five years. By age six their IQs were about 50, which is half the normal IQ and well into the range of serious mental retardation (Dennis, 1960, 1973).

Sometimes caregivers are tempted to leave babies in cribs or playpens for the sake of convenience, or to put them on a predetermined schedule for feeding, changing, and sleeping regardless of the child's day-to-day rhythms or preferences. A long-standing folk belief in many modern cultures is that responding quickly to babies and holding or playing with them will result in "spoiling" and will make the child excessively demanding and dependent.

Obviously, the fundamental needs of an infant for the kind of care that will foster development of social, emotional, intellectual, and physical growth must take priority over questions of convenience for adults. Quality child care, like most other quality endeavors, involves

Figure 3–4 In order to learn, babies need the freedom to explore a safe, interesting environment. *(Photo courtesy of Lynne Aiken)*

a great deal of effort and hard work. Although overindulgence and overprotection do indeed undermine child guidance, lazy or haphazard caregiving is never in the best interest of children.

Adults who care for babies should be down on the floor laughing, talking, singing, playing, and interacting with the babies—not sitting in rocking chairs watching television programs while babies are isolated and bored in cribs or playpens. Sadly, adults often rationalize this inappropriate behavior by saying, "You shouldn't hold babies and play with them all the time. They'll turn into spoiled brats! It's better for them to learn to entertain themselves."

Flexibility versus Predictable Routines

Two opposing priorities for infants were described so far in this chapter. The reader might well ask at this point, "Should I provide consistent, reliable routines or respond flexibly and spontaneously to cues from the baby?" The relationship of these two opposite needs is something like that of the contrasting philosophies described in an earlier chapter. On one hand, the external environment (the infant's physical surroundings, daily routines, and patterns of interacting with others) are important because they tend to shape future expectations through conditioned learning. On the other hand, the infant's internal sensations and needs are important as a basis for adult responses because that process stimulates the child to initiate self-directed behaviors and to assume responsibility for making things happen.

As was pointed out in the section on philosophical perspectives, there is a third alternative. The developmental–interactionist perspective described an interweaving between external forces and internal processes. In terms of guiding young children, this process is called positive child guidance, the assertive but reasonable nudge method. A caregiver can be very responsive to and respectful of cues (indications of interest or need) from a baby while at the same time gradually nudging the child toward routines that are appropriate and convenient for the adult.

A six-month-old may be allowed to follow her inner drives to explore the sensory qualities of her environment by feeling, squishing, pounding, and smelling her food as she tastes it. However, she can also be gently but persistently nudged over time to handle food in a more traditional manner, gradually to use eating utensils, and eventually, years later, to exhibit polite table manners.

In a domineering (autocratic) setting the baby would be forced to eat neatly with a spoon or not touch the food at all. In a setting where adults abdicate responsibility (anarchy) they would shrug and passively accept the belief that children are hopelessly slovenly in their eating habits and nothing can be done about it. In a respectful (democratic) setting, adults set very reasonable but slightly challenging expectations for the child based on his needs, interests, and abilities. They would assist the interaction between the child and his environment by allowing him freedom to explore, modeling appropriate behaviors for him, and encouraging his first clumsy attempts to master skills.

Secure Attachment to Caregivers

The attachment of babies to their adult caregivers is a critical part of their healthy social and emotional development. Early studies looked only at mother/infant relationships, because that was the only interaction that was considered to be of any importance. Freud focused on the attachment of infants to the mother and theorized that the baby considered her a "love object" simply because she provided pleasurable sucking and warm milk. He believed that the process of weaning, whether it was too rigid or too lenient, set the emotional tone for all of the child's future relationships with people and institutions.

Erikson (1963) extended, revised, and updated Freud's theory. He believed that experiences in the first year of life established in infants a general point of view for perceiving the world—either the positive and accepting reaction of trust or the negative and rejecting reaction of mistrust. He theorized that not only interpersonal relations but also competence in learning to use objects was affected by the baby's relationship to the mother. Exploration is essential for skill development, but babies only have the confidence to function competently in exploring the environment when they have an adult who serves as a "secure base" from which to explore.

Konrad Lorenz discovered a kind of attachment in certain birds (ducks, chickens, etc.) that he called imprinting. The ducks he studied became attached to whatever, or whomever, they saw moving near them when they hatched. Baby ducks that attached to "Papa" Lorenz not only followed him around as they grew but also tried to mate with his leg when they reached maturity. The *ethologists* (scientists who study behaviors in naturalistic surroundings) do not pretend that human beings behave simplistically and instinctively as ducks do, but they do theorize that some early experiences or attachments have long-term impact on human behavior.

Bowlby (1958) and Ainsworth (1973) studied the processes of human attachment as researchers experienced a dawning awareness that biological mothers were not the only people who could develop important emotional relationships with infants. Writers began to use the word parent instead of mother when discussing attachment, to reflect awareness of the impact of father/child relationships. Gradually, the term caregiver came into use to indicate awareness that babies could develop multiple, loving attachments to grandparents, older siblings, and other consistent child-care providers outside the family as well as to adoptive and biological parents.

Why do babies cling? It is essential that the process of early attachment be recognized by adults as a valuable occurrence in babies' early development rather than as an inconvenience to be avoided. Elise, a highly-successful career mother picked up her eleven-month-old son from his day-care center one afternoon. The little boy eagerly crawled to his mother and pulled himself up. As he clutched at her skirt, clung to her legs, and whined to be picked up, Elise breathed a dismayed sigh, looked helplessly at the infant-room teacher, and said, "Look at him. He just clings to me. What am I doing wrong?"

Elise was not aware that her son was only showing the normal indications of healthy emotional ties to his mother, which Ainsworth called "secure attachment." When babies brighten at the sight of a caregiver, visually follow that caregiver's movements, smile or vocalize to get attention, hold out their arms to be picked up, or cling to the caregiver, they are showing the typical signs of healthy attachment. Babies who turn or crawl away when a caregiver returns after an absence may be expressing the angry, rejected feelings that accompany a disrupted or poorly formed attachment. Babies who alternately cling and reject or show a push/pull relationship with the caregiver may not have built a really secure attachment to the caregiver. Developing secure attachments is an essential step in the growth of normal social and emotional skills.

The positive child guidance concept (assertive but reasonable nudging) applies well in the area of attachment. Caregivers can best assist infants' healthy social and emotional development by allowing and supporting closeness but also by gradually, as the child seems ready, nudging the child to move out on her own in exploring the environment. A newborn (or a baby in a new child-care setting) may need to be held a great deal of the time at first, but she can gradually be enticed to spend increasing amounts of time occupying herself looking at or playing with interesting mobiles, toys, and other surroundings. By getting down on the floor to play with the baby, a caregiver can be readily available to serve as a "secure base" to facilitate the baby's moving out into more and more independent explorations of the surrounding environment.

Separation and Stranger Anxieties

Attachment to caregivers serves as a survival mechanism for the species because an infant's safety depends on maintaining proximity with a caretaker. Therefore, it follows logically that an infant would quite naturally resist being separated from the parent figure who provides comfort and security. Sometime between six months and a year, separation and stranger anxieties begin to appear in many children because of their newly developed cognitive adeptness in visually distinguishing between familiar and unfamiliar faces. Coincidentally, many parents first begin to rely on occasional or regular child care at about this same time. We adults are able to think and talk about child-care arrangements. We may have studied a substitute caregiver's references or investigated carefully a center's license to provide care, but a baby has no way of comprehending all this.

When a baby looks up and sees that her daddy is not in sight, she feels the same way she would feel if she suddenly realized she was alone in the middle of a big department store. The swarms of strangers hovering around trying to be helpful would, at first, only be more frightening. Amazingly, it is not uncommon for parents or child-care workers to be heard chiding a crying baby, "Hush! There is no reason for you to cry." If I were riding in an airplane that made an unexpected landing and I were pushed out kicking and screaming and left in a strange land among strangers who didn't speak my language as I watched the plane carrying my family fly away, I might cry too.

The more positive experiences a baby has with meeting new people, the less uncomfortable he will feel when he separates from parents or encounters strangers. In time, the baby develops a concrete understanding that strangers can be relied on to provide care and that after a while parents reappear. Pushing the baby into frightening situations is not helpful, but avoiding encounters with strangers altogether is also counterproductive. Gently nudging the baby into pleasurable and trusting relationships with adults other than parents will assist her in developing confidence and an open, positive attitude toward the world.

Shared Identity with Caregivers

In the first months of life, babies have not yet gained a mental conception of themselves as separate individuals. Their perception of their own existence is limited to that which they see, feel, taste, smell, and hear. They unconsciously perceive their surroundings as if they were the center of the universe and the people and objects around them were extensions of their own existence. They make no distinction between their own physical being and the surroundings they perceive through their senses.

Caregivers take on a very important role in this context. Caring for a baby means that you are, in fact, a part of that baby's life. Adults facilitate and guide older children, whose interests are focused on each other and on their own activities as much, or more, than on adults. In the first year of life, however, infants focus an enormous quantity of their interest and energy on interacting with adult caregivers. They depend on adults for every aspect of physical care and safety as well as for entertainment and affection. Their interest in peers is purely egocentric. A seven-month-old will crawl onto a younger baby and casually grasp a handful of hair to feel and taste, then look quite puzzled by the sudden loud, piercing noises emitted by the little friend.

If the caregiver rushes to rescue the younger baby and graphically exaggerates appropriate behavior—softly stroking the offended baby's head while saying to the offender, "Gentle, gentle. Be gentle"—babies can eventually internalize or adopt more appropriate ways of behaving. Because the baby identifies so closely with the adult caregiver, she will automatically mimic behaviors of that adult. Caregivers who respond harshly or aggressively reinforce inappropriate behaviors in babies by modeling loud or rough interactions.

TODDLERS (12 MONTHS–3 YEARS)

Reacting to Feelings and Needs Without Planning

Burton White has termed toddlers "a force to be reckoned with." Any parent or caregiver/teacher who deals with one or more toddlers probably knows exactly what he means. Young toddlers, the one-year-olds, are phenomenal human beings. For the first time in their lives, they have become upright bipeds like the rest of us. Also, for the first time, they don't depend on us to bring rattles or tacky squeak toys to them for entertainment. They can walk through, wriggle under, or climb over any obstacle a grownup can devise in order to get to the really interesting things that attract their curiosity. The young toddler can be an adorable, timid rabbit one moment, sucking a thumb while peeking from behind a well-worn but snuggly piece of blanket, and in an instant raise the rafters, crumpled on the floor in a full-fledged tantrum.

Young toddlers are totally transparent in their feelings. They are openly affectionate, easily delighted by attention, and full of wonder about their surroundings. They also become confused, frustrated, and overwhelmed by their newfound freedom. One moment they are amazingly grownup and ready to take on the world, the next they regress into helpless, clingy babies again. Their needs are simple—they want food, comfort, affection, approval, and to learn about the huge, booming, wide world around them. As babies, they still respond to their sensations of need by crying for caregivers, but, as growing children, they also begin responding to their own desires by literally moving out into the environment to get what they want.

They use senses (touch, sight, smell, taste, and hearing) to explore the physical attributes of their environment and both small and large

Figure 3–5 The toddler eagerly explores her environment.

muscles (fine and gross) to practice physical skills. They still don't consciously plan or think much about their actions. They just act. If the toddler feels hungry and the box of cereal in the grocery cart with him looks delicious, he may just rip it open and have a snack, then look hurt when his parents seemed shocked by his behavior.

Dawning Awareness of Cause and Effect

Toddlers have made a huge cognitive leap since infancy in their ability to remember things and in their first, crude ability to manipulate ideas mentally. Cause-and-effect relationships become a focal point for their learning. They are fascinated by light switches and will flip the light on and off many times, if allowed, alternately watching the switch and the light fixture and mentally connecting the cause-and-effect relationship between the two.

They also tirelessly explore cause-and-effect relationships in social interactions. The toddler will stick her little pointed index finger out to touch the electrical outlet (covered, of course, with a plastic safety cap) and look up at her caregiver/teacher expectantly as he patiently repeats for the hundredth time, "No, no. That's not for touching." Finally, the little girl will touch the outlet, shaking her head and

repeating soberly, "No, no. No touch." She is preoccupied with connecting the cause-and-effect relationship between her action and the
adult's words and has totally missed the point that he would rather
she didn't touch the outlet. With just a bit more time and patience, she
will be satiated in her curiosity about the cause-and-effect connection,
will be able to remember the connection each time she sees an electrical outlet, and will probably be quite willing to respect her caregiver/
teacher's rule.

Exploration Needs

Healthy, well-developing toddlers have a curiosity that is boundless.
Their desire to explore at times overshadows all other needs. A toddler
who is totally immersed in the miseries of teething will stop crying
when his mother carries him to the refrigerator and opens the freezer
to get his frozen teething ring. For the moment, his pain is forgotten
as he watches the frosty air roll out of the freezer and feels the brisk
difference in temperature from this strange part of his environment he
has never explored before.

Toddlers learn to walk because their fascination with this form of
locomotion outweighs their fear of falling or being hurt. They move
out into the environment, away from the security of caregivers, because the exhilaration of discovery causes them to throw caution to
the wind. Babies might stay in the comfort of their mother's arms
forever if it were not for the powerfully motivating activator we call
curiosity that drives toddlers out into the scary but exciting world.
Baby birds are comfortable, secure, safe, and well-fed in the nest, but
at some point nature intends them to leap precariously into the air.
They flap their little wings until they figure out how to fly, a frightening and exhilarating experience for babies, of course, but also a frightening and exhilarating experience for grownup birds to watch.

Safety Concerns

During toddlerhood, a child's motor development far outstrips her capacity to understand, remember, or abide by rules. Since she has not
yet developed metacognition, she cannot look at a situation and then
think about and plan for the potential consequences of her own behavior in that situation. Toddlers are still a bit unsteady in their walking,
running and climbing, and they are compelled to taste, feel, smell, and
manipulate every interesting object or phenomenon they encounter.
All this adds up to toddlers being in the most vulnerable period of
their lives for accidents.

Unless toddlers are constantly and diligently supervised, they can

Figure 3–6 Safety is a major concern in the care of toddlers. *(Photo courtesy of Cynde Miller, Montessori Country Day School)*

inadvertently swallow objects and poisonous substances. They often fall off or bump into things, and they touch things they shouldn't despite warnings. If crying is the first major area of potential confrontation between infants and adults, then keeping toddlers from harming themselves or the environment is surely the second big area of stress and difficulty for parents and caregivers.

In past years, parents often bragged that their toddler was so well behaved that they could leave the most expensive, fragile, or even dangerous bric-a-brac out on their coffee table and the baby would never so much as touch it. They sometimes accomplished that feat by slapping the baby's hand or saying "no" sharply whenever the child attempted to touch the forbidden items. These adults believed that by teaching the baby to be still and not touch anything, they were helping her become well disciplined and polite.

Information about the processes of cognitive development, generated by research over the past two decades, is changing this popular perception. A commercially-produced poster that has gained some popularity among child-care workers pictures a young toddler standing forlornly in a play pen. The caption reads, "What do you mean, 'Don't touch'? Touching is how I learn." In order to create a richly stimulating environment that is conducive to optimum development while at the same time protecting toddlers from an unreasonable risk of harm, adults must set about "baby-proofing" all accessible areas of children's envi-

Figure 3–7 "Touching is how I learn!"

Figure 3–8 Even the tiniest object arouses a toddler's curiosity. *(Photo courtesy of Margaret Fowler, Montessori Country Day School)*

ronments as soon as they develop the motor skills to move about.

White (1975) theorized that the period from ten months to three years was a critical period in the child's life for social, intellectual, and motor skill development. He also theorized that direct sensory exploration of the physical environment served as a key requirement for optimum development. In his view, toddlers in playpens or restricted in environments that were "hands off," excessively tidy, not baby-proofed, or downright boring were losing a valuable opportunity for early learning.

Toddlers thrive in settings that are made appropriate to their needs and abilities, so that they can move about freely and safely exploring and testing every aspect of their surroundings. Of course, they still need careful supervision, even in the most carefully-planned environment, but they are provided a much more stimulating range for their play when swallowable objects, toxic plants and substances, sharp corners, and electrical cords are simply put out of the child's reach.

Rather than struggling to force toddlers to behave safely and appropriately, adults should simply change the child's environment to make interaction in it safe and appropriate. As toddlers become older and more compliant, sometime around their third birthday, toys with parts small enough to be swallowed, blunt scissors, water-based marking pens, and other materials requiring special care can be introduced.

Gradually, as children are developmentally ready, they can then be gently but firmly guided to understand and follow appropriate safety rules.

Sensitivity to Nonverbal Communication

From birth children respond to facial expression, tone of voice, and body movement. Long before a child understands language, he will react to cues such as the nonverbal body language, inflection, tone, and volume that is a part of an adult's speech.

Betty Jo, the lively young mother of twelve-month-old Jeremy, comes to pick up her son from the registered family-day home where he is cared for. She chats with other parents picking up their children as she zips Jeremy into his snow suit. Jeremy makes a funny sound and his cheeks turn red as it dawns on Betty Jo that she will have to change his diaper.

Everyone downwind of Jeremy is, by this point, quite aware that the diaper is definitely more than just wet. As other parents chuckle, Betty Jo jokingly but energetically scolds Jeremy for being so rude after she has gone to all the trouble of bundling him up to go home. While the little boy clearly does not understand all her words, he unmistakably interprets her fake scowl and sharp tone to mean that she is angry with him. He turns his face away from her and sobs.

Betty Jo is quite startled by his reaction. Because he didn't know how to talk, she assumed he wouldn't have any idea what she was saying. The ability of very young children to make some sense of our feelings from our body language and tone of voice gives us an opportunity to communicate with them nonverbally. Before children master *expressive language* (the ability to speak) they begin to develop *receptive language* (the ability to understand language). Therefore, if we are honest and sincere in the words we speak to babies and toddlers, our body language and tone of voice will quite naturally convey some of our meaning to the child. If we speak to the child for the benefit of other adults, as if the child were not really present or listening, we may miss an important opportunity to build communication with the child.

Adults can begin from the very beginning speaking to babies as if they were (because they definitely are) worthwhile human beings. This has two important benefits for long-term child guidance. First, the child will learn early in life to pay attention to adults, because they seem to say what they mean and mean what they say. Secondly, adults have plenty of time to practice appropriate communication skills so that they will be prepared when the child really does have a command of language.

Using a kind facial expression and a caring tone of voice, an adult can speak reassuringly to a young toddler who resists going to sleep, "I know you would rather play with your toys, but it's time for nap now. Would you like me to rock you for a minute before you lie down?" Even though the child will not understand all the words, she will sense the adult's caring attitude. She will also have an opportunity to hear language and associate it with objects and events in day-to-day living.

Beginnings of Verbal Communication

Toddlers seem to explode into language. At a child's first birthday, he may only know words like "mama," "dada," and "baba" for bottle. Within a few months, the child may know many more single-word labels and a number of holophrases (phrases made of words that are joined like Siamese twins and used as if they were inseparable single words). "Go-fieys" may mean, "Go to McDonalds and get French fries." "Sousite" may mean, "Let's go outside to play." The child soon learns to mix and match words or holophrases to create two-word sentences. Soon the child's speech begins to sound like abbreviated telegrams, including key words but leaving less critical words out: "Paw Paw doggy big!" "No touch daddy gwas [glasses]." By age three, the child's speech begins to sound surprisingly like our own (with a few quirks here and there): "My daddy goed to work an he gots a big office."

The child's language changes each day as he adds new vocabulary and new levels of expression and understanding. At birth the child had no muscular control of his lips and tongue and no comprehension that language existed or had significance. In only three short years, he has learned how to create many different sounds with his lips, tongue, and vocal cords; amassed hundreds of words in his vocabulary; and has grasped the basic syntax (structure) of his native language. His language comprehension is complex but not at a conscious level. For example, he has simply absorbed an intuitive sense that the "s" sound on the end of a naming word means more than one, and that the "d" sound at the end of an action word means that the action has already happened.

Infants and children of all ages need to hear the rich, lyrical words of adult conversational speech as well as the musical word patterns in rhymes, songs, and jingles. These kinds of language experiences especially enrich and stimulate language learning in toddlers. However, for maximum comprehension, the child must hear language that is very close to her own level of development. This language should be at or very slightly ahead of the child's own level. For example, in developing music appreciation, young children are allowed to hear a wide range of classical, folk, and pop music for enrichment, but for learning actual singing they are introduced to extremely simple songs like "Here We Go 'Round the Mulberry Bush."

If a baby's language development is still limited to the cooing and babbling stage, the adult is limited to communicating through facial expression, tone of voice, and body language, and (toward the end of the child's first year) a few single words such as cracker, bye bye, and bottle. If the child is using single words, the adult can best achieve communication through holophrases ("All-gone") or two-word sentences ("More milk?").

Toddlers may hear and comprehend only key words in sentences that are above their comprehension. Often they catch a few accentuated or familiar words from the beginning or from the end of the adult's speech. The toddler may innocently respond to the words, "You . . . candy . . . mouth," from the adult's complicated sentence, "You need to make very sure you don't put that whole big piece of candy that belongs to Jack right in your greedy little mouth." To maximize the toddler's comprehension of important communication, choose key words, speak slowly and clearly, and use facial expression and body gestures to emphasize your meaning.

We might use more elaborate "enrichment" language to say to a toddler, "I believe you need to have your shoelace tied. It could make you trip and fall down." When an immediate response is needed from the child, however, bend down, take the child's hand, and deliberately establish eye contact, then pat the floor expectantly as you articulate carefully, "Sit, please." We can then reinforce the child's cooperativeness the instant he looks as if he will comply by smiling warmly and saying, "Thank you!"

Separation and Stranger Anxieties

Toddlers show a wide range of reactions to strangers, depending on their own experiences and temperament. Some children go through a distinct phase in which they are terrified of strangers and have great difficulty separating from a parent or familiar caregiver. When confronted by a stranger (or even a less-familiar caregiver), they cling to their parent's or caregiver's clothing, hide their faces, and cry if the parent or caregiver attempts to leave them. Other children, those who have had broad exposure to many friendly adults since infancy, may show curiosity about new adults, attempt to make friends, and never give any indication of separation or stranger anxiety.

Making Friends with a Shy Toddler

In order to establish a relationship with a "shy" toddler, it is essential to understand and respect that child's discomfort in interacting with a new adult. Rather than approaching the child directly with a big smile and immediately attempting to touch or hold the child, avoid eye contact with the child at first. Speak quietly and pleasantly with others around the child while moving a bit closer to the child. If the child is standing or sitting on the floor, squat or sit nearby to be at the eye level of the child. Glance briefly in the child's direction occasionally to see if he is evidencing curiosity or stress at your presence. Smile, but avoid looking directly into the child's eyes until you are confident he feels comfortable with your presence.

After allowing the toddler plenty of time to stare at you, it may be helpful to touch the child's hand casually for a moment while glancing briefly in his direction with a smile. Eventually, he will probably indicate his willingness to make friends and allow eye contact. At this point, a diversion in the form of a game or toy may be a perfect way to cement the budding adult/child relationship.

In a child-care center, the teacher may be able, at this point, to interest the toddler in petting the class bunny rabbit, looking at a book, or watching the teacher make a Cookie Monster puppet tell jokes and eat pretend cookies. If no toys are available, sing a song, make up a rhyme, or talk about the child's clothing—"Look at those blue sneakers. I bet you can run really fast in those." An effective

Figure 3–9 Toddlers may be very shy around strangers. *(Photo courtesy of Lynne Aiken, Heights Montessori School)*

diversion at this point will hold the child's interest but not require a great deal of sustained eye contact or active response from him.

Egocentrism, Possessiveness

Young toddlers callously step on each other to get what they want, take toys from each other, and scramble to grab food. Two-year-olds walk into their day-care center in the morning, look suspiciously at their peers, tighten their grip on Dad's hand, and announce defiantly, "My daddy!" Very young children's behavior is not particularly civilized nor polite, because they do not yet have a well-developed ability to put themselves in the place of others. Some toddlers who have observed and experienced a great deal of kindness (empathy) may show concern for others, but their way of expressing concern is totally egocentric. For example, the toddler may try to give her pacifier or Teddy bear to an adult who is crying.

There is little to say about toddlers and sharing, except that it cannot be expected of them. Instead of attempting to coerce toddlers into behaving in a way that is developmentally incompatible, adults can rearrange the environment, change the routines, or increase their supervision to protect toddlers from inadvertent rough or rude treatment by their peers. In time, children develop the ability to recognize that other people have feelings and rights, and they develop the ability to imagine how others would feel if they were treated a certain way. Then it will be possible to teach them manners. Until then, setting a good example and tactfully but assertively protecting children's (and others') rights are all that adults can do.

Insecurity

Toddlers use many "crutches" to help them cope with being very little and very powerless in a big, fast, scary world. Some adults call toddlers' worn blankets, tattered stuffed animals, pacifiers, or whatever else they hold onto the child's "cuddlies" or "friendlies," some call them objects for "cyclical self-stimulation," others just call them nuisances. Whatever they are called, when they are lost, they can cause the toddler's emotional world to come crashing down around him. As strongly as children are attached to these comfort items, they generally begin to lose interest in them by the time they turn three. Some preschoolers hang onto their cuddlies a while longer, but for many of them, their attachment at this point is more habit than emotional need.

In many primitive cultures, children stay in physical contact with their mothers' bodies much of the time during their first three years of life. In modern, industrialized societies children are separated from their mothers at birth to be placed in a hospital nursery, put to sleep in a separate bed (enclosed with bars) in a separate room at home, and buckled into highchairs and car seats. Some children improvise "mother replacements" to cling to for a while and to help them cope (nipple-shaped objects to suck and soft, warm, fuzzy, or silky objects to hold). The child's need for these objects should be respected, although she can be nudged gently to do without them for gradually increasing periods of time when they become little more than habit.

Children especially need to be helped to cope without a pacifier or thumb "plugged in" too much of their day, because it is very difficult to practice language with one's mouth immobilized. It is equally important, on the other hand, to foster language development early in life by allowing infants plenty of sucking to develop the mouth, lip, and tongue muscles necessary for later speech. Because bottle feeding requires less muscular effort and coordination to produce milk than breastfeeding, many babies benefit emotionally and physically from the availability of nonnutritive sucking. Pacifiers are healthier for teeth and easier for eventual weaning than thumbs.

Although some authorities still encourage mothers to wean babies from breast or bottle at about ten months of age, weaning in the first year of life will almost guarantee that a child will seek some form of replacement sucking or self-stimulation. Grandmothers have been saying for generations, "If you baby a baby when he's a baby, you won't have to baby him all the rest of his life."

Quest for Independence

Erikson (1982) focused on the development of autonomy (self-sufficiency or independence) as the second step in his eight stages of social and emotional (affective) growth. After trust is established in infancy, toddlers become immersed in the conflict between autonomy and shame and doubt. Toddlers are able for the first time to do many things that adults consider naughty or destructive. For the first time, adults hold the child responsible for bodily elimination and controlling impulses. The child is torn between trying to conquer the world with her new capabilities and feeling fearful and ashamed for making mistakes and disappointing the parent or caregiver.

Adults can help toddlers through this period by being very supportive of the child's need to break away from infancy. In order to foster autonomy, never do anything for the toddler that she can be helped to do for herself. Toddlers can learn to peel their own banana for snack, pull up their own sock once the adult gets it started, and choose their own clothing from two appropriate choices. They can be allowed to stand on a chair at the sink to wash unbreakable dishes (even though Mom or Dad will undoubtedly have to rewash them later for sanitary reasons). They can even be given a small bucket with a little water, a squirt of liquid soap, and a small piece of sponge or rag to help wash the car or the windows.

Toddlers are interested in having the freedom and independence to be involved in grownup activities. They are not at all interested in achieving specific end products to those processes and are confused and discouraged by adult concern over end products or results rather than processes. Adults usually do things the most expedient way to get the end result that they want. Toddlers spend long periods of time in the process of dipping, pouring, and splashing dishes in soapy water, but lose interest before the dishes are actually rinsed and dried. Sensitive adults will foster the child's involvement in independent processes but wait until the child is older to expect end results. They will redirect unacceptable behavior rather than make the child feel inadequate or naughty for following his curiosity and desire to attempt things he sees adults doing.

Dawning Self-Awareness

When babies look in a mirror they do not necessarily recognize that the image reflected there is their own. At some point in toddlerhood, they finally discover that the face in the mirror is theirs. If they see an unexpected smudge on the nose in the mirror, they touch their own noses to find out what is there. A younger child will only touch the mirror. Toddlers who are not yet aware of their own separate identity seem to think that they cannot be seen by anyone if their own eyes are closed. A toddler being reprimanded for misbehavior may cover her eyes, assuming (because of her egocentricity) that the adults will not be able to see her since she cannot see them.

Toddlers who begin to get a sense of their separateness tend to be very "full of themselves." If a caregiver gathers two-year-olds around him to read a story book, he will often discover that they are more entertained by each other than by the book. They giggle and poke each other, and inevitably one toddler will begin a gloriously spontaneous action like vigorously shaking her head until her hair stands out all around her head. In an instant this action spreads like a contagion, leaving the poor adult sitting rather foolishly, book in hand, watching a band of toddlers laughing uproariously as they shake their heads (and perhaps wiggle their bodies and stamp their feet for good measure).

As toddlers begin to recognize their existence as a separate persons like the people they see around them, they begin to develop a picture (or concept) of who they are primarily based on feedback from the adults around them. Sometimes adults make casual comments that are very cutting—"You are as fat as a pig." "Why are you always so mean?" "I think you like to make me mad."—things we would probably hesitate to say to another adult. Sometimes these hurtful comments come from siblings or other children.

Toddlers are very naive. They tend to believe what we tell them about themselves through our actions and words. (Of course, our actions usually speak louder than our words.) As an older toddler's self-image begins to take shape, we can help him develop a healthy and confident view of himself by being very careful about what we say to him (and what we allow other children to say to him). "What a big boy you are." "Everybody makes mistakes sometime." "I really like your smile." "I didn't like the hitting, but I like you." The toddler's budding self-esteem will serve as a foundation for his growth as a confident, competent, cooperative, and productive human being.

PRESCHOOLERS (3–5 YEARS)

Beginnings of Conscious Decision-Making, Planning, and Intention

Toddlers were only able to conceive of objects in terms of the way those objects actually felt, looked, tasted, smelled, or sounded. Preschoolers have a new mental ability. They can conceive of objects both in terms of what they are perceptually and what they stand for symbolically. For example, a toddler sees a block only as something to bite, hit, throw, or stack. The preschooler can see the block both as a physical object and as a "pretend" bar of soap to bathe a doll or a "pretend" car to zoom around the floor. The block can stand as a symbol for something else.

Preschoolers also become more consciously aware of their own interests and intentions. They look over the toys available to them and make intentional choices. While toddlers functioned primarily by impulse, playing with whatever toy caught their eye for the moment, preschoolers are more inclined to select an activity very carefully and then stay with it longer, sometimes even coming back to play the same game day after day until they finally become bored with it.

Older preschoolers actually verbalize what and how they want to play. For example, they may say, "Let's play like this is our house and you are the daddy and he is the baby and that box is the baby bed." They can become very frustrated or angry if things don't turn out the way they expect. Preschoolers often squabble over their conflicting

Figure 3–10 Preschoolers begin to think about cause and effect. *(Photo courtesy of Cynde Miller and Montessori Country Day School)*

perceptions of how their play should proceed. "I don't want to be the baby. I want to play Masters of the Universe!"

Adults can help children during this stage by focusing their attention on the probable consequences of their actions. Questions should never be used as verbal battering rams, but adults can gently nudge cause-and-effect thinking by asking, "What might happen if someone ran out into the street without looking?" "Hmmm, I wonder what could happen if you paint without putting a smock on over your clothes?" "How would your friend feel if she never got a turn to be the pretend mommy?" Preschoolers are just beginning to be able to manipulate ideas in their heads and eventually can learn to weigh consequences and make appropriate decisions before acting.

Growing Comprehension of Language

Because preschoolers have an increasing command of their native language, they can benefit from talking about their own actions and events that have taken place or will take place in their lives. Before an event takes place, they can be helped to understand that event by parents or teachers talking about it in advance in very simple, concrete terms. Adults often shield preschoolers by whispering about life events they think children are too young to understand.

A three-year-old, whose parents often affectionately called her "our sweet baby girl," cried hysterically when an aunt said, "I hear there's going to be a new baby at your house." She had overheard her parents saying that they thought it best for her not to know yet that there was going to be a new baby. She, of course, knew that when they got a new car the old car vanished, when they got a new refrigerator the old one was hauled away, and when she got new shoes the old ones were dropped unceremoniously into the trash can. She could only guess what happened to little girls who she imagined were so naughty that their parents decided to get "a new one."

A four-year-old boy developed nightmares and bed wetting after he heard family members crying and talking in somber but hushed tones about how his mother had lost the baby she was carrying. His problem behaviors increased until a psychologist was consulted and discovered that the little boy had been nervously searching in closets and under beds to find the lost baby. He knew that those were places to look when you lost something.

Communicating Successfully with a Preschooler

By talking to preschoolers in honest but simplified terms, we can help them to understand and deal with events. We cannot take for granted that just because something is obvious to us it will be obvious to young children. There are many things about this world that pre-schoolers just don't know yet. A caregiver can use very simple but clear sentences to say, "Marcus, your dad just called on the telephone. He will be late picking you up today. His car won't go so he has to get it fixed. It may be dark when he gets here, but it's okay. I will stay with you. We'll get some cheese and crackers and apple juice and play until he comes." Sometimes adults become so preoccupied with their own problems and plans that they forget to tell children what will happen to them.

A parent can prevent potential problems by anticipating and plan-ning for them. Being especially careful not to communicate negative expectations, the parent could say, "Shelley, your friend Jamie will be here soon. Sometimes when she is here it is hard for you to share your favorite toys. That makes Jamie feel sad. Would you like to choose the toys you want to share and put them in this cardboard box? We can take the toys you choose into the back yard, then Jamie will know which toys you want to share and play with." By helping the child positively think through this potential problem before it happens, the child may be able to consciously behave in such a way as to avoid the conflict before it erupts. After a child has become angry or upset, it is unlikely that she will be able to listen to logic or behave rationally.

Using Words to Express Feelings and Needs

In a democracy, people are supposed to use physical force only as a last resort when other reasonable steps to defend oneself have failed. Children need to know that everyone, children and adults, will use words to express feelings and needs. Force is never used to hurt or humiliate, but only to defend life and limb.

Preschoolers can be guided firmly to use words to get a point across, rather than relying on kicking, scratching, and hair pulling. They can be helped to practice appropriate words and allowed to ex-press strong emotions, even anger, through their words. When a pre-schooler runs to tell parents or teachers about another child's action, instead of being chided for "tattling" the child can be encouraged to talk to the other child. "Did you tell Kirin that it was your turn for the swing? Would you like for me to go with you to talk to her?"

Adults often try to squelch children's feelings. We say things to quiet children like, "Don't cry." "Don't make a fuss." "She didn't really mean to hit you." Maybe the other child really did mean to hit. A child deserves to express her feelings in an honest but respectful way—"I feel angry. I don't like it when you push me off the swing." Preschoolers especially need to be allowed to express their feelings.

They can learn that it is okay to feel angry and it is okay to say so, but it is not okay to lash out in a way that verbally attacks or physically hurts others.

Preschoolers can also be helped to verbalize their feelings by having adults mirror those feelings. Young children may not realize that they are cranky because they are hot and tired or cold and hungry. Adults can put words to those feelings and assist preschoolers in learning to identify and express what they feel inside. "Brrr, I feel cold! Look at the chill bumps on my arm. Are you cold? Let me feel how cold your hands are."

This mirroring of feelings is called *active listening*. The adult refrains from lecturing, instructing, commanding, or telling. Instead, she listens and sincerely reflects back what she thinks the child is feeling at the moment. In active listening (a useful communication tool for any age), the adult says things such as, "It sounds like you are really feeling angry with Tommy." "In other words, what you are saying is that you feel hurt and sad when you don't get to play." "You seem pretty frightened when the other children pretend to be monsters." The point of active listening is not to solve the child's problem for her, but only to let her know that she was heard and to give her a chance to talk about, think about, and confront her own feelings.

Learning How to Be a Friend

Babies and toddlers are very curious about other children, but are most concerned about the adults in their lives. Preschoolers, on the other hand, begin to be interested in their relationships with other children. Throughout the rest of childhood they will rely more and more on their friendships with peers and less and less on their attachment to adults. Between three and five, children need to learn how to be a friend and how to have friends, a very important kind of learning for the child's long-term social and emotional adjustment in life (Corsaro, 1981).

This can be a very trying stage for adults. Children are elated when they feel liked by peers and emotionally crushed when they imagine that no other child in the whole world wants to play with them. While some children quickly find a best friend or group of friends with whom they get along very well, other children experience a daily emotional roller coaster as they struggle to establish friendships and deal with peers who say, "I'll be your best friend if you give me your piece of chocolate cake."

Some preschoolers become very cliquish as they decide who is or is not a friend. They say things like, "You can't be our friend because you don't have a football shirt on." "We don't want you to play because

Figure 3–11 The preschooler must learn how to be a friend and how to have a friend. *(Photo courtesy of Cynde Miller, Montessori Country Day School)*

you're a boy." "You draw scribble-scrabble so you can't color in our color book." Adults can feel very frustrated in knowing when or how to intervene in these troublesome and hurtful interactions. Children have a right to choose their own friends and playmates, but they also have an obligation to avoid being downright cruel in expressing those choices. Adults can gently nudge appropriate behavior by saying, "Can you tell Chris, 'I like you but I don't want to play with you right now.' "

Accepting Responsibility

Erikson (1963) focused on the need of four- and five-year-olds to resolve the emotional conflict of initiative versus guilt. Preschoolers are struggling to become independent of adult caregivers and to find their own limits. They want to please adults and feel very guilty when they disappoint or anger parents and teachers. An excessive amount of guilt causes discomfort that the child may relieve by withdrawing from any situations that involve a risk of failure, or by adopting a rebellious "tough guy" facade and appearing to be immune to guilt.

In order to help children develop initiative, they must be encouraged to achieve independence from adults. Instead of doing things for preschoolers, adults must tactfully make it possible for the children to do things for themselves. Adults can simplify tasks and then teach simple skills like how to refill the gerbil's water bottle, how to cut safely with a blunt knife, how to clip paper to an easel with clothes pins, and how to get a jacket zipper started.

Preschoolers relish the opportunity to be in charge of their own environment. They make lots of mistakes and often forget to carry out tasks they have agreed to perform. Adults can respond best by remembering that the process of learning is much more important for preschoolers than the end products resulting from their efforts. Some adults become perfectionist about tasks and say, "It's easier for me to do it myself than to hassle with the kids trying to do it." It may be easier, but it definitely is not better for children, who need encouragement and success in accepting and carrying out responsibilities.

With a great deal of practice, encouragement, and patient teaching (one bite-sized step at a time), preschoolers can learn to carry out tasks very responsibly and well. They will feel so confident about their accomplishments that they will eagerly show initiative (inner drive) in tackling new tasks or projects without having to be prodded or coerced every step of the way like a child who has fallen prey to feelings of guilt.

Figure 3–12 Helping do real work makes children feel strong and capable. *(Photo courtesy of Rod Smalley)*

Following Rules

Preschoolers are ready for simplistic rules. "Be kind! Wait until it's your turn to go down the slide." "Be safe! Stop at the gate so that a grownup can walk with you across the street." "Be neat! Use a sponge to wipe up the tempera paint that has spilled." Preschoolers are preoperational (in Piaget's terms). They perceive rules in a superficial way. They follow rules more to please adults than because they comprehend the relationship between actions and possible consequences. Preschoolers still must be supervised closely because they are not yet able to follow rules consistently. In their play they make up rules on a whim and then break the rules they have made with total abandon when a rule no longer suits them.

They begin to make sense intuitively of adult expectations and anticipate what will or will not be allowed in various situations. They tell each other, "Oh! You're gonna get in trouble." They begin to enforce rules on each other, "You didn't flush. I'm gonna tell on you." Adults can redirect this sudden enthusiasm for rules by setting a good example in their own respectful enforcement of rules. If adults are punitive and critical and seem eager to "catch" wrongdoers, children will imitate that. If adults remind children of rules in an assertive but polite tone then help them comply, children will imitate that too.

Adults can maintain children's interest in rules by making very few rules but making sure that children know and respect the rules that are given. Barraging preschoolers with picky rules will alienate them and trivialize the whole idea of following rules. Children's perception of the value and importance of rules can be greatly enhanced when they are allowed to be part of the rule-making process. At group or circle time in a group setting, or in a family-council meeting at home, children can be invited to think of new rules to solve simple problems like pushing and shoving or taking other people's things without asking. Also, adults can help children by patiently explaining the reasons for rules rather than just saying, "It's a rule because I say so."

Stating, "No one is allowed to climb on that fence!" and then proceeding to ignore children who climb on the fence will convince children that grownups do not really mean the things they say, and that rules are not really to be followed. It is important to remember that following rules is not only to be "kind, safe, and neat" today but to develop habits that will result in the child obeying laws as an adolescent and as an adult.

Developing a Clear Self-Concept

Self-esteem and *self-concept* are two closely-related concepts. Self-concept is one's idea or image of oneself. Self-esteem means that one's image of oneself includes a sense of being worthwhile and valuable. Although the child's self-esteem (or lack of it) has been developing unconsciously since birth, preschool children begin to develop a clear, conscious idea of who and what they are. Children's ideas about themselves come from others around them, particularly from parents (Coopersmith, 1967 and Cotton, 1984). As preschoolers become more adept at language, they also become more susceptible to the opinions of teachers, peers, and others outside the home.

Preschoolers become increasingly aware of their own identity in terms of larger groupings within society. The child may, for the first time, become aware that she is white or black. Self-esteem can grow from pride in one's ethnic, regional, and religious heritage. Sadly, exposure to prejudice devastates self-esteem and creates a cycle of prejudice and low self-esteem, because low self-esteem is one of the causes of prejudice in the first place (Bagley et al, 1979). Every child deserves to know that he or she is special. But, of course, no more special than anyone else!

Preschoolers also become aware, for the first time, that their gender is fixed for life, girls will grow to be women and boys will grow to be men. Toddlers may distinguish between girls and boys or mommies and daddies, but they think they can turn into the opposite sex simply by wearing different clothing. Preschoolers identify with their own gender and may begin playing only with boys or only with girls.

Parents worry about their physically-active daughters who prefer playing with the boys or their quiet, sensitive sons who prefer playing with the girls. Preschoolers worry about playing with toys that their friends consider to be "girl toys" or "boy toys." Preschool teachers often worry about making sure boys feel okay about playing in the housekeeping center with dolls and dressups and girls feel okay about playing in the block center with trucks and cars so that all the children will have well-rounded educational experiences. Everyone worries, but children generally persist in play that reflects the real world as they know it. If they see daddy having a good time feeding the baby and cooking, little boys will probably play house more comfortably than if they have only seen women doing these things. The same is true for little girls who have seen their mothers repair a leaky pipe or wear a police officer's uniform.

Competitiveness

Another factor that affects preschoolers' development of self-concept and self-esteem is competitiveness. Preschoolers are aware of themselves in comparison with others, so competitiveness reaches a peak during the preschool years (Stott and Ball, 1957). It can be very tempting for adults to exploit that tendency by saying things like, "Whoever can be the quietest at nap time will get a special treat." "The one who puts away toys the fastest will get to be first in line to go outside." "See if you can get dressed faster than your brother."

These challenges may strongly motivate some children to behave as the adult wishes, but the competition also stimulates friction rather than cooperativeness among children. Additionally, whenever there are winners, by definition there will be losers. Winners may feel stressed and compulsive about continuing to win, and losers may feel more and more inadequate.

SCHOOL-AGERS (5–12 YEARS)

Growing Ability to Think Logically

School-age children are very different from younger children, not only because of their gap-toothed smiles and taller bodies. Their thinking and language is different, too. They can sometimes be argumentative. Words hurled angrily by others can wound them deeply, but there is a growing rational logic present in their response. Preschoolers yelled, "You're a pooh pooh head an' I hate you." School-agers are more precise, "Why do you act so bossy. You're not my mother!"

School-age children are no longer gullible. They make observations and judgments about everything around them, even though their judgment is based on a simplistic, good-and-evil, winner-or-loser view of the world. They naturally begin to compare themselves with others. Competition begins to rear its ugly head as children struggle to best each other and fight over who likes whom best. Adults sometimes throw fuel onto this fire by urging children to compete. For example, they say, "Let's see who can be first to get their table clean." "The quietest person will get to go first." "I will put gold stars on the very best papers and put them on the bulletin board for parents night." This tactic is tempting because school-agers will practically kill each other to be first or best at anything. Unfortunately, however, we should be finding ways to help children get along and cooperate more rather than less.

Arguing

As school-agers become concrete operational (at about seven), they spend more time thinking about the things and events in their world. Preschoolers were just able to manage manipulating thoughts about cause and effect and about symbols standing for real objects or events. School-agers become able to manage manipulating thoughts about entire concrete processes (it will be years before they can successfully manipulate totally abstract ideas or symbols). School-age children can mentally replay an event to evaluate it carefully and logically, so they are able to detect inconsistencies and gaps in logic. They are quick to see discrepancies in adult actions. "You said that nobody could eat or drink unless they sat down at the table. You're somebody and you're drinking coffee."

Preschoolers accepted blanket statements from adults such as, "You can't eat candy because it will damage your teeth." School-agers think about that explanation logically and answer back with their own rationale, "Okay, then I'll brush my teeth after I eat the candy." After the school-ager has asked a persistent series of logical why or why-not questions, parents and teachers often find themselves snapping with exasperation, "Because I said so!" Of course, this is the phrase they hated to hear as children and promised they would never say when they grew up.

Becoming a Capable Listener

School-age children can be delightful conversationalists. They can listen attentively and respond appropriately in conversations that hold their attention. Preschoolers and toddlers often talked to themselves absentmindedly as they played, or they chatted enthusiastically at the same time others were talking, not noticing that no one was really listening. School-agers are more conscious of their intention to communicate through speech. They are embarrassed if they are caught talking to themselves, and they know that another person cannot really be listening unless he is quiet and alert. School-agers have become fairly skilled at conversational give-and-take and are not as likely to butt into the conversations of adults and other children without waiting for a reasonably appropriate pause in the flow of speech.

School-age children love to talk and listen to each other. Younger children were more inclined to play together in a physically active way, using language as a supplement to running, jumping, climbing, and playing make-believe games. School-age children still love active play, but will sit under a tree or get on the telephone and talk animatedly for long periods of time about themselves, school events, and authority figures. They have discovered that there really isn't a Santa Claus, and they are beginning to realize that grownups are not omnipotent deities, but really just human beings who can make mistakes. When talking privately with a trusted friend or group their own age, school-agers may give an earful of complaints about their parents, teachers, and siblings.

They can also build new, more mature bonds of affection and loyalty to adults who are willing to listen to them and treat them fairly. School-age children are especially sensitive to being "talked down to" by adults. Being in school much of their time places new pressures on them to be quiet and listen to adults for long periods of time. They will especially appreciate an adult who will get down to their level and really listen to their thoughts and feelings in an open-minded, nonjudgmental manner.

Dealing with Authority Figures

School-agers can be quite intimidating to adults. Younger children who misbehaved could be picked up and carried (kicking and screaming) away from a problem situation. School-agers are becoming too large. They can no longer be controlled by physical restraint. We must begin to rely on the child's inner control. One of the reasons that spanking is such an inappropriate and ineffective method for disciplining children, is that it may seem to work quite well at first but it models aggressive, hurtful behavior and habituates children to being controlled by external brute force. It eventually creates a no-win situation for everyone.

The powerful negative effect of spanking very young children lies in its ability to frighten and intimidate them. After a child is spanked on many occasions, however, he becomes so accustomed to the way it feels that it no longer has the same effect. It may make him furious, but it probably won't scare him. Adults who used spanking to control younger children discover that school-age children may be so emotionally immune to being hit that by this age they only respond with apathy, or they may be so angered by being treated like a "baby" that an attempt to spank them could trigger outright defiance. Teachers and caregivers will probably encounter an occasional school-age child who

Figure 3–13 School-aged children can be lively and expressive or quiet and contemplative. *(Photo courtesy of Rod Smalley)*

has been subjected to a great deal of rough treatment in his life and has become aggressive, toughened, cynical, and very difficult to manage.

Child-care workers can be especially intimidated by school-age children who have not yet developed inner control. Often, the youngest and least experienced workers are assigned to care for school-age children who attend the facility only during the early-morning and late-afternoon hours, summers, and holidays. After school, school-age children can be exhausted from long hours of sitting at hard desks, feeling pressured to meet adult expectations. During summers and holidays they may simply have an overwhelming desire to be somewhere else. They may come into the child-care setting with resentment for having to be in a "day-care for babies." They may especially feel frustration over being expected to play quietly with blocks and puzzles they have outgrown in a room filled with all the trappings of a preschool.

In a typical scenario, the school-age children begin to behave a bit wildly. Perhaps they start to throw pine cones at each other on the playground or stir their Graham crackers into their milk, giggling and making a disgusting mush. Adults often respond in an abrasive and humorless attempt to stop this silly behavior. The children, feeling their oats, will likely become sassy or perhaps stop the behaviors just long enough for the adult to turn her back for a moment. The angrier the adult becomes, the less compliant or cooperative the children will be. This situation can cause the adult to feel frighteningly out of control or helpless (a phenomenon that has an effect on older children not unlike sharks smelling blood).

Breaking the Cycle of Misbehavior

The surest way out of this emotional trap is for the adult to break the cycle by letting each individual child know that he or she is liked and respected by the adult. Then the adult can begin to gain the children's respect and loyalty. External-control methods do not work very reliably for bright, capable, thinking children who feel they are being manipulated into doing things they don't want to do by someone who doesn't really like them.

Inner control depends completely on the child wanting to be a cooperative group member. If school-age children see the adult as someone who is absolutely fair, has a sense of humor, is reasonable, and who really cares about the needs and feelings of the children, they will try very diligently to comply with that adult's wishes.

Analyzing and Creating Rules

School-age children will feel more cooperative about rules that they have helped to create. Family-council or class meetings provide an opportunity for school-age children to think about potential rules and to give their own opinions. If these meetings are run democratically, with real input from the children, the children can begin to see rules not as inconveniences capriciously imposed by adults, but as necessary protection for the rights and safety of all group members.

A Sense of Fairness

As previously noted, school-age children are able to see discrepancies in adult behaviors and do not gullibly accept everything adults say as younger children tend to do. "But that's not fair," seems to be the battle cry of school-age children as they go about their daily business. Even though they sometimes gleefully break rules themselves, they may become furious when it seems to them that a rule is being enforced inconsistently. "But you didn't make Jerrod go back inside when he threw his book."

At this age, children's concrete-operational perspective prohibits them from considering some abstract extenuating circumstances that may be an issue for the adult decision-maker. The school-age child may not see it as fair when a child who is new to a setting is just given an explanation of rules while a child who is expected to know the rules is given a stiff penalty for exactly the same offense. Adults must constantly examine their own biases to determine if there really is any possibility that their treatment of the children is unequal.

Adults should be meticulous not only about their fairness but also about their appearance of fairness. If a situation seems unfair to a child, the adult may assist the child's understanding by giving a concrete explanation for the action taken. "When you were younger, you needed many chances to remember rules. Now that you're nine, you really know that throwing books is not allowed. Jerrod is only five now, but when he is nine, he will have to stop playing too if he forgets the rule about throwing books."

A Need to Belong

School-age children have a powerful urge to belong to a peer group. They sometimes make up their own clubs or cliques with some semblance of rules and rituals or even special taboos or requirements in clothing. Younger children may have been oblivious to clothing—they wore whatever their parents bought for them, or they may have had picky, but individual tastes in clothing. School-age children become very concerned about wearing clothing that their friends approve. Even first and second graders today seem to know the popular (and unpopular) brand names for blue jeans and sneakers as well as for dolls and bicycles.

The fact that mom, dad, or teacher really prefer a certain style of clothing, shoes, or haircut may mean that the children automatically prefer something else. This tendency to dress for peers gradually increases, but does not reach a climactic peak until adolescence. Perhaps some entrepreneur will ease the discomfort this problem causes to mothers and fathers by selling buttons for children to wear that say, "Parents are not responsible for the way I look. I dressed myself!"

Adults should first help children feel secure and accepted in the home or classroom because self-confidence and self-esteem greatly assist children in resisting inappropriate peer pressure. Adults can also help children keep material possessions in a proper perspective by respecting the children's tension about peer approval but also playing down the value of objects and focusing attention on valuing people for

Figure 3–14 School-agers need to become actively involved in their world. *(Photo courtesy of Dr. Sharlene Peters)*

their human characteristics rather than for their expensive clothing or toys.

Because early development hinges on the active physical involvement of children in their environment by climbing, jumping, painting, gluing, etc., parents and teachers can cooperate to encourage (or require) clothing that is comfortable, washable, and not physically or socially restrictive. It is impossible to be "ladylike" in a frilly, short dress while climbing a jungle gym, and it is dangerous to climb the jungle gym in heavy, slick cowboy boots. Whatever steps adults take, it is essential to remember how desperately children want to belong, to fit in, and to be viewed as special by their friends.

Becoming Productive

Erikson (1963) identified the emotional crisis for school-age children as one of industry (being productive) versus inferiority (feeling incapable). One of the enjoyable characteristics of school-age children is their ability to function independently. Younger children needed direction and help to do new things. School-age children have the capacity to think of their own projects, to gather the needed materials, and then to work eagerly. They make miscalculations, messes, and mistakes, but they take great delight in having built their own crooked airplane or art object. Unfortunately, if they receive criticism instead of encouragement for their efforts and accomplishments they may develop feelings of inferiority ("I'm no good." "Everything I try fails." "My ideas are stupid.") and may be discouraged from trying new things.

Adults should not compare children's work to adult standards. The child's cookies may turn out tough and strangely shaped, but who cares? The purpose is for the child to experience the successful completion of real work and to have something to show for his effort that makes him feel proud.

Controlling Impulses

School-age children are becoming more adept at controlling their impulses. Although they may lapse from time to time into less mature behavior, throwing tantrums or pouting, they are finally able to wait for a little while when they are bored, hungry, or need to go to the bathroom. They often verbalize their impulses, "Hey, wouldn't it be funny to pour this paint into the fish tank and then the fish would all turn purple." Then, they laugh uproariously and (we hope) resist the urge to really do it. Preschool children aren't quite as able to weigh consequences and resist temptations. For toddlers, thinking is doing!

Maintaining Self-Esteem

The big, wide world begins to have tremendous impact on the school-age child. Once they can read, whole new avenues of information open up to them. They may see toothpaste ads on television and worry that their teeth have plaque monsters chomping away, or see billboards about fire safety and worry that they will burn up in their beds at night. It is not unusual for school-age children to experience night-mares or develop irrational fears. "I'm not going to eat that chicken-noodle soup because it has mushrooms, and they might be the poison kind that'll make you die."

As children leave early childhood and move toward adolescence, life becomes very complicated and stressful. Their bodies seem to take on a life of their own, growing adult genitalia often far too quickly or far too slowly to suit the confused and disoriented owner of the body. We begin to see little children walking around in very adult looking bodies, and suddenly we expect them to act grownup. Just as in toddlerhood, two-year-olds were torn between the security of infancy and the allure of childhood, preadolescents are likely to waver in their feelings about whether to be a little kid or a teenager. One minute the child is sitting on a curb crying over a skinned knee and the next she is choosing her favorite color of lipstick.

Adults must provide a great deal of support, affection, and patience

Figure 3–15 Behaving in a productive and responsible manner fosters feelings of self-worth. *(Photo courtesy of Gary Peters)*

during these years so that school-agers' self-esteem and confidence stay intact. Babies, toddlers, and preschoolers get lots of hugs because they are little and cute. Adolescents and adults get romantic hugs from the opposite sex. School-agers are at an awkward stage and, especially young boys, may be left out of the hugging and cuddling altogether. Everybody needs an appropriate (nonexploitive) hug now and then to feel valued and special.

SUMMARY

Although typical or average patterns can be identified, real children have individual patterns and rates of development that may be normal but not at all average. Comparing a child's individual behaviors to typical behaviors can help adults gear guidance strategies to the child's developmental capabilities. It also can alert adults to special problems requiring further testing or intervention. Comparisons should never be used to label or stereotype the child.

The first behavior-oriented difficulties adults deal with in caring for infants are usually centered around the infant's crying. Regardless of many common misconceptions, in the first months of life infants have no capacity for consciously intentional behavior. Newborn behaviors result almost exclusively from uncontrolled reflexes. Older babies and toddlers simply respond to physiological urges and impulses to practice motor skills and explore surroundings. Self-control hinges on the development of metacognition. Children are past three before they are able to think consciously about their own behavior and past five before they can routinely plan or evaluate their actions.

According to Erikson, trust developed in infancy is a primary foundation for the development of healthy emotional attitudes that must be built upon throughout life. Learned helplessness develops in children who have no control over events in their environment. Infants need a balance between predictable routines and flexible responses to their own needs and preferences.

Exploration is essential for skill development, but babies only have the confidence to function competently in exploring the environment when they have an adult who serves as a "secure base" from which to explore. Developing secure attachments is an essential step in the growth of normal social and emotional skills.

Attachment to caregivers serves as a survival mechanism for the species because an infant's safety depends on maintaining proximity with a caretaker. Therefore, it follows logically that an infant would quite naturally resist being separated from the parent figure who provides comfort and security.

Toddlers' actions are impulsive and emotions transparent. They explore using all of their senses as they learn to coordinate muscles. Cause-and-effect relationships become a focal point for their learning. Toddlers are not yet able to understand or follow rules.

During toddlerhood, a child's motor development far outstrips her capacity to be responsible for her actions, so safety becomes a critical issue for adult caregivers. White theorized that direct sensory exploration of the physical and social environment serves as a key requirement for optimum development and learning.

From infancy children are responsive to nonverbal body language, facial expression, and tone of voice. Toddlers rely on nonverbal expression to enhance their communication with adults. Toddlers need to hear the rich, lyrical sounds of complicated adult speech simply for language enrichment. Verbal and nonverbal communication, however, should be honest, sincere, concrete, and extremely simple since toddlers generally comprehend only key words and nonverbal components of speech.

Stranger and separation anxiety usually peak in young toddlers but vary widely from child to child depending on his or her life experiences. Adults can reduce stress when meeting a shy toddler by maintaining close proximity to the child but avoiding eye contact until the child becomes adjusted to the new adult's presence.

Toddlers perceive their world in an egocentric manner, so they are not yet able to understand or respect the rights of others. Toddlers cope with daily stress by sucking or holding comfort objects.

Toddlers strive to achieve autonomy. They are interested in having the freedom and independence to explore the processes of grownup activities. Toddlers have just begun to grasp a sense of their separateness from other people and things in the environment. They are very naive. They tend to believe what we tell them about themselves.

Preschoolers for the first time develop the capacity to manipulate symbols, letting one object stand as a representation for another.

Preschoolers gradually become more aware of their own interests and intentions. Adults can help them during this stage by focusing their attention on the probable consequences of their actions. By talking to preschoolers in honest but simplified terms, we can help them to understand and deal with events.

In a democracy, people are supposed to use physical force only as a last resort when other reasonable steps for self-defense have failed. Preschoolers can be helped to practice assertiveness by caregivers encouraging them to use appropriate words to express strong emotions or feelings of anger.

Preschoolers begin to be interested in their relationships with other children. Some preschoolers become very cliquish as they decide who is or is not a friend.

In order for preschoolers to resolve their emotional conflict between initiative and guilt, they need encouragement to do things for themselves. Excessive feelings of guilt can cause withdrawal or rebellion.

Preschoolers are ready for positive exposure to simplistic rules. Adults can maintain children's interest in rules by making very few rules and by making sure that children know and respect the rules that are given.

Self-esteem and self-concept are two closely related concepts. Both are essential to optimum development. Preschoolers' views of themselves are affected by others around them, particularly by parents. Competition spurs temporary compliance, but should not be used because it discourages cooperation and may damage self-esteem.

School-age children develop an ability to replay events mentally and, thus, are better able to evaluate components of experience carefully and logically. They are able to detect inconsistencies and gaps in logic. School-agers can be delightful conversationalists. They can also be very trying in their interactions with authority figures.

School-age children's behavior is not easily manipulated externally. Inner control hinges on the school-age child's wanting to be a cooperative group member. In order to overcome ineffective styles of disciplining school-age children, adults must first let each individual child know that he or she is liked and respected and that the adult is fair, reasonable, and caring.

School-age children are passionate about their perception of fairness. They also have a powerful urge to belong to a peer group and to be well-liked by friends. They place great emphasis on dressing in a way that is approved by their peers.

School-age children struggle with the emotional crisis of industry versus inferiority. They make mistakes but they take great delight in their own accomplishments. They are becoming more skilled in controlling impulses.

Adults must provide a great deal of support, affection, and patience during the school years so that children's self-esteem and confidence stay intact.

PRACTICAL APPLICATION/DISCUSSION

"I'm Never Gonna 'Vite You to My Birth'ay!"

Sarah and Lupita claimed a shady spot under a thick magnolia tree on the playground. It is their favorite place to play. They have staunchly defended their little territory against small bands of marauding playmates by insisting, "You can't play. We got here first. This is our house."

Although their teacher does not allow toys from home in the classroom, they were allowed to bring their dolls outside with them for their outdoor play period. Sarah has a well-worn Raggedy Ann doll and Lupita has a new, soft plastic baby doll in a pink blanket that looks just like a newborn baby.

They rocked their dolls to sleep and carefully placed them beside the trunk of the tree while they scurried around gathering leaves and sticks to outline a boundary for their playhouse. Sarah finds a large stick and announces that it is the door. "Nobody can come in unless they open this door. Tick tock. Now it's all locked up."

Robby was watching and listening to the girls as he climbed and jumped off a climbing structure "fort" nearby. He can't resist Sarah's challenge. "I can, too, get in," he taunts as he dances around the line of leaves and sticks that is the pretend wall of the girls' playhouse. He pokes his foot over the line and darts just out of their reach as he sticks his tongue out, laughing and chanting, "Nanny, nanny, boo, boo!"

Sarah chases and yells at Robby while Lupita furiously mends the pretend wall. Robby retreats to the top of the climbing structure insisting, "Uh, huh! I could get in there. It's not really your house."

Lupita plants her feet firmly in the grass and stares viciously at Robby, guarding hearth and home, while Sarah runs to tell on Robby.

Robby, of course, loses all interest in Lupita's mean look. He is perched behind a post at the top of the fort watching carefully to see what his teacher, Miss Gresham, will do next.

Miss Gresham bends down on one knee and listens intently as Sarah rants and raves about Robby's alleged offenses. Quietly, Miss Gresham says, "Did you tell Robby how you felt when he messed up your house? Would you like for me to come with you to talk to Robby?" Sarah takes Miss Gresham's hand and quickly leads the way back to the scene of the crime.

Robby, meanwhile, is huddled on the fort hoping no one can see him. He forgets that Miss Gresham is tall enough to talk eye-to-eye with him at the highest part of the fort.

With a gentle and reassuring voice, Miss Gresham says, "Robby, let's talk with Lupita and Sarah. I think they're feeling very angry." Robby pauses for just a second, but Miss Gresham holds her hands out and says, "It's okay, Robby. Sometimes I make mistakes and people get mad at me too." Robby leans off the fort and Miss Gresham hoists him to the ground.

She looks right into his eyes and pats him as she says, "Thanks, Robby." Then she assumes the role of objective referee as the girls tell Robby, in no uncertain terms, "Don't you break our house no more!"

Robby's lip quivers and a big tear begins to slide down his grimy face as he pulls back his shoulders and announces, "You ain't my best friend and I ain't never gonna 'vite you to my birth'ay party."

Questions for Discussion

1. Guess the ages of Lupita, Sarah, and Robby and explain your rationale for each guess based on the developmental characteristics of children at different ages. Explain how you knew that each child was not much older or younger than the age you guessed.
2. List all of the reasons you can think of for Robby's interference with the girls' play. Why were the girls so angry?
3. Do you agree with Miss Gresham's handling of the problem? Explain. What would you have done differently?
4. What do you think happened next?

Figure 4–1 Sometimes it helps to look at children from a new perspective. *(Photo courtesy of Michell Miller)*

4

Taking a New Look at Children

OBJECTIVES
This chapter will assist you in:

- Identifying personal biases that affect guidance.
- Recognizing the difference between objective and subjective observations.
- Listing effective observation strategies.
- Using observations for prescriptive guidance.
- Identifying components of the observation sequence.

IDENTIFYING PERSONAL BIASES THAT AFFECT GUIDANCE

Gilda is a bright, gregarious ball of energy. When she was in kindergarten, she popped out of bed every morning before the sun was up because she loved going to school each day. Her teacher, Mr. Costa, seemed to really like her. He often invited her to help with classroom chores like feeding the goldfish or passing out napkins for snack. Because she learned concepts very quickly, he encouraged her to help other children, a responsibility she took very seriously. Gilda liked pretending that she was a teacher, and the younger children thrived on her persistent tutoring. Whenever anyone asked her what she wanted to be when she grew up, she always answered quickly, "A schoolteacher just like Mr. Costa!"

During Gilda's first day of first grade, she eagerly tried to get the attention of her new teacher, Mrs. Redwing, and jumped up to help pass out papers. Mrs. Redwing reprimanded Gilda for getting up from her desk without asking and said, "Please stop asking me questions and just sit quietly and listen." Mrs. Redwing thought, "Oh, no, another hyperactive kid. That's all I need."

Over a period of time, Gilda becomes impatient and unhappy. She cries in the morning and tells her father that she doesn't want to go to school anymore. Mrs. Redwing is upset too. She is becoming more and more frustrated with Gilda's behavior, which eventually has become disruptive and, at times, even defiant. Mrs. Redwing has become especially exasperated with Gilda's attempts to help other children do their work whenever they have trouble, an action Mrs. Redwing considers a kind of "cheating."

One day Mr. Costa and Mrs. Redwing are sitting in the teacher's lounge drinking coffee. Mr. Costa says, "How is Gilda doing this year? I really miss her . . . what a terrific little girl she is." Mrs. Redwing chokes on her coffee and sputters, "Gilda? You've got to be kidding! She drives me absolutely up the wall."

How is it possible for two people to see the same child's behavior so differently? We see children differently because we are different. Everything that we actually perceive with our senses (eyes, ears, etc.) is filtered through layers upon layers of our own personal points of view (our bias). Our biases are the sets of beliefs, values, and assumptions that we hold, based on our past experiences and on our own philosophies of life.

Mr. Costa responds favorably to Gilda's energy and spontaneity because she reminds him of himself when he was younger. He values energy and creativity, so he is delighted by Gilda's bright mind. In contrast, because of her very strict upbringing, Mrs. Redwing learned early in life to suppress any fidgety impulses she had, so she finds it particularly annoying to deal with Gilda's chattering and bounciness, behaviors her parents would never have tolerated. These behaviors strike Mrs. Redwing as rude and reckless, even though she can remember resenting her parents' rigidness toward her when she was a child.

Responding Objectively to Individual Children

It is inevitable that some children will be more appealing than others to any given adult. We cannot be perfectly matched to the needs of every child. However, we can at least be fair in our treatment of different children. Within families, parents sometimes admit that one of their own children seems easier to understand and manage while another child's behavior seems totally incomprehensible. In group settings, an adult may concede that he or she is more comfortable with children who are small or large, male or female, black or white, rich or poor.

In order to respond more objectively to children's behaviors, we must focus on our own areas of bias. What preconceived notions do I have about children? Do I expect certain behaviors or motivations from children based on ethnic, gender, or appearance differences?

How can I focus on who an individual child really is rather than on the stereotypes I associate with generalized groups or categories of people?

One way to increase objectivity is to consciously separate facts from opinions. What do I actually perceive (through looking, listening,

Figure 4–2 To be objective, we must focus on the things we actually see and hear. *(Photo courtesy of Montessori Country Day School)*

touching, tasting, and smelling), and what do I interpret intuitively based on my knowledge, experience, and/or bias? By sorting through our own thinking processes to separate facts from opinions, we can more accurately focus on actual child behaviors and scrutinize our interpretations of the meaning of those actions.

Objective Observations

Mr. Costa and Mrs. Redwing both agree that these are accurate facts: Gilda talks frequently, begins tasks quickly, completes work before others in class, is active and quick in physical movements, and expresses interest in the progress of classmates.

Mr. Costa's Interpretations

Gilda is very capable in verbal communications. She is a competent, bright student. She is enthusiastic about her school work. She has leadership potential. She cares intensely about others.

Mrs. Redwing's Interpretations

Gilda ignores the teacher and class rules about talking. She rushes through her work because she doesn't take it seriously enough. She is overactive. She worries about the affairs of other children, when that is none of her business.

When one's opinions are stated separately from observable facts, and those opinions are clearly labeled as "subjective interpretation," it is much easier to recognize and deal with personal bias. If we trick ourselves into believing that our opinions are objective facts, we lose an opportunity to see children as they really are.

We can consciously learn to be more objective in our thinking. For example, the following observation is filled with opinions. "Erik angrily stomped into the kitchen trying to pick a fight with someone. He taunted his sister and hurt her feelings just to see her cry. He hoped she would hit him so he would have an excuse to get her in trouble." These statements are pure fantasy. We cannot see into Erik's head to look at his intentions or hear his thoughts.

What we can actually see and hear is that Erik stomped into the kitchen. He looked around with a frown on his face. He pointed to his sister's sandwich and said, "Yuk, are you going to eat that gooey mess." His sister began to cry and threatened to hit Erik. Erik said, "If you hit me, I'll tell Mom." What we may interpret is that Erik *seemed* irritable. He *appeared* to be unhappy and in a mood to agitate his sister.

The first opinionated description tempts us to punish Erik for his obnoxious behavior because we assume we know why he behaved the way he did. The second, more objective way of reporting Erik's behavior reminds us that we don't know everything that is going on in

Erik's mind and heart. It stimulates us to look for reasons for his actions to better understand his troublesome behavior.

THE OBSERVATION SEQUENCE

In order to be effective in dealing with children, an adult must become a skilled observer. Child guidance is as much an art as a science. There is no clear-cut recipe for handling children that works for all children in all circumstances. But, with careful observation, the adult can gather the information needed to make intelligent decisions and to select appropriate methods to prevent or respond to various problems. Later, the adult can observe to evaluate how effective the chosen guidance technique has been in solving the problem.

Observing

In order for any effort at resolving a behavior problem to be effective, it must be well matched to the child's ability and frame of mind as well as to the circumstances surrounding the behavior. Does the child appear to be feeling angry and destructive or just bored and silly? Is the behavior habitual or a rare event? Is the child capable of benefiting from verbal reminders or is direct physical redirection required? What actually is the problem—when, where, and why does it occur? These are all questions that should be answered through careful observation.

Evaluating Children's Behaviors

There are many excellent checklists, kits, and observational instruments (tests) available commercially to assist early childhood professionals in observing children. For most parents, caregivers, and preschool teachers, however, the most useful record-keeping tool (and definitely the least expensive) is just a pocket-sized spiral notepad and a pencil. If paper and pencil are available whenever something interesting occurs, it will be a great deal easier to get something written down. No record-keeping instrument of any kind is of value if it stays in a desk drawer or a file cabinet.

With a little pocket notepad, an anecdote can be described before the details are forgotten, tidbits can be added regularly to a running account, or some type of sampling checklist can be maintained. It is easy for us to think, "I don't need to write this down. I'm sure I'll remember it." But then, of course, we forget whatever it was that we were so sure we would remember.

Figure 4–3 In order to be effective in dealing with children, we must become skilled observers. *(Photo courtesy of Cynde Miller)*

Interpreting

Interpreting observations is the process of inferring meaning from what one has actually sensed (seen, heard, touched, tasted, or smelled). In order to interpret what was observed, one has to rely on a knowledge of child development in general as well as of the unique development of an individual child. One should, additionally, rely on firsthand experience with children in general as well as with the individual child in question. All of this means that we should take what we sense at the present time and mull over it, using all of our past knowledge and experience to create new ideas about why the child may need to behave as she does.

Looking back over observation notes can be surprisingly enlightening. Children grow and change so quickly that we may be startled to look back at our notes about little Bronwyn and see that only three months ago she cried and clung to us when other children were around. Now she confidently approaches others to initiate play. By seeing a child's progress over time, we can make better sense of the child's immediate behavior, and know what help and guidance the child needs in order to behave more appropriately.

Personal bias must be kept in check while interpreting one's observations. Observation records, particularly objective checklists, may provide convincing evidence that our intuitive assumptions about a particular child were simply wrong. Interpreting observations also gives us an opportunity to see things from the child's point of view. We may be annoyed with a child for interrupting our conversations but, after observing her carefully, realize that she really deserves to be included more in adult interactions and just needs to be taught how to join a conversation politely.

Planning

In a doctor's office, a patient is seen and observation records are written into a chart. The observations of the physician are then carefully interpreted (diagnosed). What is the meaning of the rash? Of the fever? Of the pain in the left foot? Then, most importantly, a plan is formulated (a prescription) to remedy the problem. The doctor prescribes bed rest or an antibiotic. We prescribe such things as an understanding, heart-to-heart talk about hurting people's feelings or a change in our own behaviors toward the child, such as providing more positive attention or more developmentally appropriate activities.

Taking Action

After a plan is formulated, the next step is action. Many adults take a fatalistic attitude toward children's behavior. They think children won't change and, consequently, don't bother doing anything other than complaining about their inappropriate or immature behaviors. Young children are avid learners. They learn new habits much more easily than older children or adults. They just need time, effort, encouragement, and a great deal of practice to master the social skills and control of impulses they need to be responsible, cooperative group members.

Sometimes, even if the action we attempt doesn't really work very well, the simple fact that we are focused on the child's problem (and care enough to try to resolve it) may stimulate the child's own awareness of the problem and commitment to correct it. It will be very therapeutic for the child to see evidence from our actions that "I care about you. I am willing to make a real effort to help you learn to use words rather than fists to express your feelings. I won't give up on you."

As long as the action is positive and respectful of the child, it is far more important for us to formulate a plan and do something than to worry about being right every time. Perfectionists are sometimes so paralyzed by their fear of making mistakes that they never get around to doing anything. Children can learn valuable lessons from our handling of our own mistakes. They can learn that everyone makes mistakes from time to time and that admitting mistakes is nothing to be ashamed of. We could set a good example by saying, "Joshua, I asked you to hold my hand on our walk to help you remember to stay on the sidewalk where it's safe. I made a mistake. I didn't think about how that might make you feel like a baby. Let's think of a different way to help you be safe."

Evaluating

Is what we are doing working? In the evaluation phase, we make a complete circle and come back to observing. The only way we can be sure if we were on target in our first observation, interpretation, plan, and resulting action is to observe again and look for indications that our plan is or is not working. If it is working, we can relax and go on to the next problem. If it is not, we return to square-one again, collect more information through observation, and develop a new and improved plan of action. This cycle repeats until we successfully hit a plan that works (or the child outgrows the behavior, becomes the responsibility of the next teacher, or gets married and moves to another town).

OBSERVATION STRATEGIES

Researchers use carefully orchestrated strategies to collect objective data. Adults who care for young children rarely need such formal methodology. We just need a workable plan for finding out the "what, when, where, and why" of children's problem behaviors so that we can respond effectively and appropriately. The following sections describe some very useful methods for keeping track and making sense of puzzling or upsetting behaviors.

Anecdotal Record

An anecdotal record is an attempt to record in detail a specific episode that is of particular interest or concern. An event takes place that catches the attention of the adult. As soon as possible, the adult sits down and writes a narrative account of every pertinent detail that she can recall. What did she actually see, hear, or otherwise perceive with her senses? She will include verbatim quotes whenever possible to further clarify the interaction. Any personal opinions or interpretations must be set apart and clearly labeled as "observer's comments" or at least preceded by such phrases as, "It appeared to me that . . . " or, "Therefore, it was my impression that . . . ."

Following is an example of an anecdotal record of a toddler biting incident:

Ricky wandered slowly around the room whining and shaking his head. After about five minutes, he abruptly dropped to the floor and began to cry. Periodically he stopped crying to sit up, suck his thumb, and twist a tuft of his hair while he looked around. Then he would close his eyes, drop back on the floor and begin sobbing again.

I picked up a handful of picture books and sat down on the floor beside him. I said, "Ricky, would you like to read a book? Look, it's a book about kitty cats." At first he ignored me, but finally he crawled into my lap and laid his head on my chest as he continued to suck his thumb and make the jerky little sniffing sounds that follow a bout of hard crying. I began to read the story about kittens.

After only a few minutes, Katherine toddled over and plopped into my lap practically on top of Ricky. Before I had even a second to respond, Ricky grabbed Katherine's face and hair and sank his teeth into her cheek.

Comments/Interpretations

Ricky was probably frightened and anxious because he has not been away from his mother very often. He seems to be showing evidence of a great deal of separation anxiety. He may have felt threatened by Katherine's presence because he has no sisters or brothers and may not be accustomed to sharing adult attention with others. I will have to watch Ricky very carefully so that I can help him find ways to cope with his feelings, and I can anticipate and intervene better in situations where he might hurt another child.

Running Account

In a running account, a specific type of behavior is noted each time it occurs. A mother who worries that her child is not eating properly may keep a running account for a period of time, keeping track of when, where, and what her child eats during and between meals each day. After a few days or weeks she could begin to see if specific eating patterns emerge. Does the child pick at meals but consume high-calorie junk food during frequent snacks? Does the child eat a well-balanced lunch and afternoon snack but often refuse supper? Does the child eat whatever is offered at home but get into power struggles over food with a caregiver in the child-care center?

Following is an example of a running account of a four-year-old girl's incidences of nail biting:

Monday, 8:00 a.m. Celia bit her nails while watching cartoons on television. She had a very tense facial expression.

Monday, 3:30 p.m. Celia and her best friend, Joel, had an argument. After he told her he wouldn't play with her anymore, she sat by herself on the steps for a long time, biting her nails. Again, she appeared very tense.

Tuesday, 11:30 a.m. Celia bit her nails while she waited for lunch. She appeared more bored than tense.

Tuesday, 4:30 p.m. Celia bit her nails the whole time she watched a television cartoon. Her whole body appeared to be tense as she sat on the edge of her chair and strained toward the TV.

Comments/Interpretations

Tension (and possibly boredom) seems to be triggering Celia's nail biting. She was not seen biting her nails when she was coloring, playing dolls, or putting together puzzles. It may be helpful to redirect Celia to more active play and to discourage her watching television cartoons on a regular basis.

Time Sampling

The purpose of time sampling is to determine the patterns of occurrence and general frequency of specific behaviors, either in an individual or in the entire group. In time sampling, a particular interval of time is selected—five minutes, thirty minutes, an hour, etc. Then, at the designated time intervals, a checklist is marked to show whether the chosen behavior is or is not occurring at that moment. For example, an individual child could be watched at intervals to determine whether the child is spending more time actively engaged in play or passively watching others. An entire class could be watched to see how often the reading center is used as compared with the block center. This procedure can give factual evidence to back up or refute an adult's intuitive impressions about the occurrence of various patterns of behavior.

Following is a time-sampling checklist used by a preschool teacher to help her study her students' patterns of being "on task" (involved in productive skill development or learning activity) rather than misbehaving, wandering aimlessly, or just watching:

TIME	MISBEHAVING	WANDERING	WATCHING
8:00 a.m.	James, Jill	Suzette, Amy, Tyler	Ben, Ann
8:15 a.m.	James	Amy	Suzette
8:30 a.m.	Amy, Suzette		Ben, Rosa
8:45 a.m.	Tyler		
9:00 a.m.		Suzette	
9:15 a.m.			
9:30 a.m.			Suzette
9:45 a.m.	Amy, Ben	Jill, Tyler	Suzette
10:00 a.m.	Suzette, Ann	Tyler	Jill, Amy
10:15 a.m.	Suzette	Ann, Tyler, Ben	Amy

Comments/Interpretations

This group of children have more difficulty staying on task at the beginning and the end of the morning. Their most productive time is between 8:45 and 9:30. Suzette, Amy, and Tyler may need special attention to help them focus on productive activity. James seemed able to avoid misbehavior after he settled into productive activity.

Event Sampling

The purpose of event sampling is to determine the precise number of times a specific behavior occurs within a set period of time as well as the pattern of occurrence. Individual children can be observed for occurrences of a specific behavior, or an entire group can be watched, and a total number of occurrences of a behavior (such as aggression) can be recorded and tallied. In event sampling, a specific action (or actions) is designated. When the behavior occurs, a checklist is marked so that after a given period of time, the adult can tally the exact number of times the behavior took place.

Following is an event-sampling checklist used by a child-care worker to determine the individual daily progress of several toddlers in their toilet training (each accident has been recorded as an x):

NAMES   TOILETING ACCIDENTS

	Monday	Tuesday	Wednesday	Thursday	Friday
Reily	xxxxxx	xxxx	xxxxx	xx	
Joseph		x			x
Mariette	xxx	xx	xx	xxx	xx
Ella	xxxxxx	xxxxx	xxxxxx	xxxxx	xxxxx
Prichart			x		xx
Bethany	xx	x		x	

Comments/Intrepretations

Ella may not really be ready for toilet training at this time. It may be helpful to observe Mariette more closely to determine if she is having difficulty at a specific time of day or under specific circumstances. Reily had difficulty early in the week but managed to stay dry most of the day Thursday and all day Friday. He should probably be watched further to see what happens the following week.

Checklists versus Narrative Accounts

Checklists and narrative accounts can be used as tools for gathering information in many different kinds of situations. The particular advantage of narrative accounts is that they create word pictures that may provide insight into a child's behavior far beyond that originally anticipated when the decision was first made to record an event.

The adult can look back over several anecdotal records and discover new, previously overlooked relationships or details each time. The biggest drawback to narratives is, of course, that they are very time consuming and so can only be relied on for recording occasional rather than routine occurrences. Narratives collect *qualitative* information while checklists collect *quantitative* information. Qualitative information is focused on the descriptive qualities or characteristics of behaviors. Quantitative information is focused on numerical and statistical calculations that tell how often or to what degree behaviors occur.

Checklists leave out all of the details surrounding behaviors and focus only on the frequencies and distributions of occurrences. They are especially useful for making comparisons—not only of one child's behaviors to that of other children, but to the child's own behaviors at other times of day, in other settings, or at an earlier age. The major advantage of checklists is the ease with which they can be used. The major drawback is that important information about the extenuating background circumstances of a behavior is not recorded.

The checklists above gave more factual information about many more children than the anecdotal record and the running account. However, the reader probably feels that she knows much more about what Ricky and Celia (described in the narrative accounts) are really like than any of the children listed on the checklists.

SUMMARY

We see children differently because we are different. Everything that we actually perceive with our senses (eyes, ears, etc.) is filtered through layers upon layers of our own personal point of view (our bias). One way to increase objectivity is to make a conscious effort to separate facts from opinions.

When one's opinions are stated separately from observable facts, and those opinions are clearly labeled as "subjective interpretation," it is much easier to recognize and deal with personal bias.

There is no clear-cut recipe for handling children that works for all children in all circumstances, but with careful observation the adult can gather the information needed to make intelligent decisions and to select appropriate methods to prevent or respond to various problems. Later, the adult can observe to evaluate how effective the chosen guidance technique was in solving the problem.

Researchers use carefully orchestrated strategies to collect objective data. Adults who care for young children rarely need such formal methodology. We just need a workable plan for finding out the "what, when, where, and why" of children's problem behaviors so that we can respond effectively and appropriately.

An anecdotal record is an attempt to record in detail a specific episode that is of particular interest or concern. In a running account, a specific type of behavior is noted each time it occurs.

The purpose of time sampling is to determine the patterns of occurrence and general frequency of specific behaviors. The purpose of event sampling is to determine the precise number of times a specific behavior occurs within a set period of time as well as the pattern of occurrence.

PRACTICAL APPLICATION/DISCUSSION

The Mysterious Case of the Spinning Peg

Felicia, an afternoon assistant in an infant/toddler child-care center, is sitting on the floor and pulling the string of a "See and Say" toy. Lisa is laughing. Felicia asks, "Where are the fish? Can you see the fish? There they are—seven of them." She laughs and tickles Lisa's tummy. Daniele and Katy push close to Felicia as they laugh and interact with her. They watch every move that Felicia makes.

Lisa wanders away from them toward me as I sit on the vinyl-padded tunnel. Lisa accidentally drops a large, plastic peg she is carrying. When it hits the wooden stair by her, it spins for about five seconds. She stares at it with a look of wonder. She carefully picks it up and with great concentration drops it on the step again, but this time it does not spin. She stares at it, squats beside the stairs, then proceeds to drop it again and again on the carpet.

It does not spin. She stands up and throws it down on the carpet. It does not spin! She bites it hard, throws it two more times, but still it does not spin. She leaves the peg lying on the floor and walks away. Felicia picks it up and puts it away.

Lisa comes over to me, looks at my writing and at my face. She pats my tablet and then pulls at the pages. She looks very seriously at my eyes. She then walks away. I hear her whine as she walks over to the play sink. She stops abruptly, looks at a plastic fruit, then with great interest she watches it as she drops it to the floor. It does not spin.

She sucks her finger and starts to cry. Felicia picks her up and comforts her then walks away saying, "You're getting a little fussy. I wonder if you're hungry. Let me see if you get an afternoon bottle."

QUESTIONS FOR DISCUSSION

1. What are the objective observations you could have actually seen, heard, etc. if you had been observing the above interaction?

2. What are your own personal interpretations of the interaction?
3. Why do you think Lisa started to cry?
4. What can you tell about the relationship between Lisa and her caregiver Felicia?

Section 3

How Can I Prevent Misbehavior?

Figure 5–1 A carefully planned environment sets the stage for appropriate behavior. *(Photo courtesy of Cynde Miller, Montessori Country Day School)*

5

Planning the Prosocial Environment

OBJECTIVES
   This chapter will assist you in:

   • Defining prosocial behavior.
   • Identifying components of the nurturing social environment.

- Recognizing supportive and effective adult behaviors.
- Outlining strategies for initiating positive behavior in children.

PROSOCIAL BEHAVIOR

Prosocial behavior is the opposite of antisocial behavior. Prosocial behavior benefits others and demonstrates the presence of a social conscience, while antisocial behavior harms others and indicates a disregard for the rights and needs of others. The concept of prosocial behavior focuses on three critical elements of a child's beneficial or helping interactions with others:

- Cooperation—The process of working with others unselfishly toward a common goal.
- Empathy—The ability to step into others' shoes, to feel what they feel, to have insight into their thoughts and actions.
- Altruism—Acting in a way that benefits others with no motive of personal gain, generosity.

Because patterns of natural human growth and development teach us that young children always begin life locked into egocentrism (or self-centeredness), we know that prosocial behavior is not an inborn trait, but a slowly learned way of acting that wins approval and affection from others.

Children are not automatically inclined to postpone immediate gratification in order to work cooperatively with others toward a common goal. They don't begin with a capacity to recognize that others have feelings and needs similar to their own. Also, of course, they don't come into the world equipped with the logical, cause-and-effect thinking skills necessary to understand that generously giving a valued object or favor today may bring affection and loyalty from a friend tomorrow (Peterson, 1983). Children adopt prosocial behaviors only after much experience and practice in an environment that demonstrates and nurtures positive social interaction.

SETTING THE STAGE FOR APPROPRIATE BEHAVIOR

We give subtle messages to children about how we expect them to behave by the surroundings we plan for them. We can prevent many behavior problems before they ever begin simply by careful planning, by understanding children's developmental needs, and by creating a perfect match between their needs and the settings around them.

The Physical Environment

Parents need to adapt home environments to make them safe, child-proof, and interesting for children of various ages. Periodically, as children grow, parents must reexamine their children's bedrooms, play-rooms, and play yards to see that the space matches the child's growing skills and interests. Children can gradually deal responsibly with and reliably use and put away more complicated equipment and furnishings.

Adults planning living space for groups of children also face a challenging task. The well-planned early childhood environment is orderly but not rigid, clean but not sterile, and interesting but not overstimulating. In other words, it is carefully balanced. The only way to be sure that it is properly balanced is to watch the children who live, play, and work there, to see if the environment seems overwhelming, boring, frustrating, or just right.

Typical Child-care Environments

Some early childhood settings have an atmosphere that seems halfway between a festival and a flea market. Almost every square inch of the walls is plastered with pictures, posters, signs, crafts, and notices. Things dangle from the ceiling like a swarm of butterflies, and furniture and toys form a wall-to-wall obstacle course on the floor. Walls and furniture are painted colors such as taxicab yellow or iridescent lime green. Special rugs are purchased with bright, busy, dizzying patterns of letters, numbers, and game boards to "stimulate learning."

This environment invites loud, wild, unbridled activity. Children will probably feel comfortable running, leaping off tables, and bellowing across the room. Adults will probably have great difficulty guiding children into quiet concentration on a puzzle or book, or teaching children to walk rather than run and use soft "inside voices" rather than screaming and yelling. Children will initially have great fun in this environment but will likely become bored, tired, and agitated eventually. Because the adults are likely to have difficulty coping with the children's intensity, they may become irritable and restrictive, falling into negative power struggles with the children.

Other early childhood settings have an atmosphere somewhat like a dentist's waiting room. They are stark white or cool, pale pastel colors, and they smell strongly of disinfectant. The sparse furnishings have an eerie appearance as if they have never been touched by human

Figure 5–2 The well-planned environment is warm and homey.

hands. Insipid elevator music may be piped in softly, and any toys or books seem to be on display rather than intended for actual use (they may actually be arranged out of the children's reach). The adults seem most anxious that the children "don't mess anything up." Painting, water play, and messy clay are out of the question. Everything the children do is regimented into rigidly controlled activities that the whole class does together.

Nothing about this environment invites children to explore or interact with the materials provided. They become passive recipients of the experiences adults provide, and they are pressured to "sit still, be quiet, and don't touch anything without permission." The children may at first be subdued, restrained, even intimidated by their surroundings, but they too will eventually become bored, restless, and rebellious.

A Developmentally Appropriate Environment

Developmentally-appropriate early-childhood settings are warm and homey. There are focal points of interest at various places in the environment (displays of children's artwork, holiday decorations, or decorative touches), but they are *not* overwhelming. Ceilings, walls, and floors are muted, neutral tones so that the visual emphasis is on brightly colored toys, learning equipment, and materials.

The environment is well-lighted with plenty of sunny windows. Acoustical-ceiling tiles soften the sound level. Furniture and equipment are arranged to break the floor space into clearly-defined learning centers in order to discourage running, to encourage focused attention on learning materials such as books, puzzles, and blocks, and to allow easy supervision. Messy activities such as food preparation, clay, water play, and painting are regularly available for children past three and structured to be used successfully and independently.

In a preschool classroom, painting may be permanently set up with a day's supply of paper available to be clothes-pinned to a child-sized easel. Just an ounce or two of fairly thick paint in a couple of nontip containers with short, fat paintbrushes makes the activity almost "goof-proof" for a young child wanting to paint "all by herself." A clothes line is ready nearby for hanging wet paintings to dry. There are classroom pets such as hamsters and fish, plants for the children to water and enjoy, and many opportunities for children to be involved in real-life activities, such as preparing food and cleaning up.

Whether an environment is designed for infants, toddlers, preschoolers, or school-age children, the children's actual levels of development and individual interests are considered. Toddlers cannot function properly in environments that are arranged with hazardous and inappropriate furniture and toys, even though that same equipment may be perfectly suited to preschoolers. Infants and toddlers need unstructured toys and materials for sensory exploration and safe motor-skill practice.

School-age children will be bored and offended if they are placed in a room filled with preschool blocks, picture books, and baby dolls. They, too, need a space suited to their special needs and interests. In after-

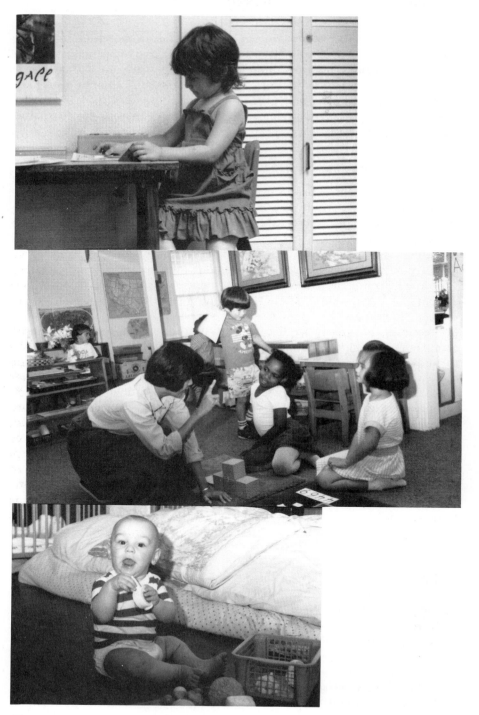

Figure 5–3 The well-planned environment is challenging but not overwhelming. *(Photos courtesy of Lynne Aiken, Heights Montessori School and Rod Smalley, Montessori Country Day School)*

school care settings, children need a "club house" environment with games, music, and quiet places to study. Outdoors they need a soccer field, a basketball goal, and elementary-sized swings and slides.

In developmentally appropriate environments, behavior problems are minimized simply because children are challenged and their needs are met. They are busy and excited about their accomplishments. At the beginning of the year adults often have to simplify an environment to assure that children can manage independently and successfully. Gradually, as the children develop new skills, adults add new materials and increase the complexity of the environment so that it continually challenges the children. Adults are constantly searching for the balance between materials that are so simple that they are boring and materials that are so complex they are overwhelming. They allow the children to carry out their activities individually or in small groups of their own choosing, rather than marching them all lockstep to do the same activities at the same time as a large group. Large group activities for preschoolers are limited to short periods of time for sharing, singing, and hearing stories read. Large group activities are avoided altogether for infants and toddlers.

The adult constantly looks for ways to increase the children's independence and mastery of their environment. She has taught the children how to spread their jackets on the floor, stand with feet near the collar or hood, stick hands in the arm holes, then flip the jackets over their heads. Like magic, they know how to put their own coats on without help. She has used color-coding to help children know where things go. Everything in a yellow container goes in the art center; everything red goes in the science center. She has even taped pictures of toys and games on shelves to remind children where to put things away. Children are allowed to rearrange the playhouse furniture in the housekeeping center, as long as they remember to be good citizens and put it back when they are finished. They feel the environment is *their* space. They feel pride and self-confidence. They know the adult is their ally, not their enemy. The stage is set for positive child guidance.

Scheduling

Another critical concern in planning positive child guidance relates to pacing or scheduling. Young children fiercely resist being hurried, and they can barely tolerate being forced to wait. They have their own pace. Different children have different paces. By scheduling large blocks of time for child-directed (independent) activities, children feel more free to work and play at their own pace. One child may take only three seconds to paint a paper-plate turkey to her satisfaction, while another child may want to spend twenty minutes painting it just the way he wants.

If children are forced into a rigidly-scheduled large group activity, the fast child will be bored and tempted to get into mischief as she waits for others to finish. The slow child will be forced to stop painting before he has fully benefitted from the learning value of the activity. He will also feel frustrated and irritable because he didn't have the opportunity to finish the project he obviously cared about.

Parents also have to pay close attention to scheduling in order to set the stage for positive child guidance. For example, Bill and Irene both work. They hate getting their three children up in the morning. Because evenings are so hectic, the children often don't get to bed until 9:30 or 10. Of course, they are cranky and out-of-sorts when their parents try to wake them at the crack of dawn. Bill and Irene are so rushed in the morning, they wait until the last possible moment to get the kids up. Then there is a mad rush to get them dressed and fed. Almost always there is conflict with one or more of the balky, groggy children.

In order to plan for successful behavior, Bill and Irene will have to reschedule their evenings to make sure they and the children have adequate rest. They will also have to get the children up in the morning as early as possible rather than as late as possible, so that the children have time to wake up and plenty of time to eat and dress without being hassled. Rushing a sleepy child is almost guaranteed to create an unmanageable child.

THE NURTURING SOCIAL ENVIRONMENT

Adults who hope to stimulate prosocial behavior in young children must first establish a nurturing social environment—a setting in which children feel safe enough and comfortable enough to be cooperative, empathetic, and altruistic. Children who worry about being hurt, feel stressed to perform beyond their capability, or feel pushed into competition with playmates will probably have little interest in prosocial behavior. Children who are afraid that their own needs will not be met may not be able to be generous with others. A child may behave in a prosocial manner in one setting but not in another. Her day-to-day behavior depends to a great extent on her surroundings (Hartshorne and May, 1928).

A Relaxed, Playful Atmosphere

Early childhood is a special time in one's life. The young of other mammals (puppies, kittens, colts, etc.) frolic and play as they develop the skills they need to survive in adulthood. Adults of various species go about the serious work of providing food, shelter, and protection

Figure 5–4 The nurturing social environment is relaxed and playful.

while the young chase around, pouncing on bugs, climbing trees, rolling in the grass, and having pretend fights. Their gleeful freedom enables them to coordinate muscles and practice skills.

Young human beings need a protected period of childhood in which to play and explore. If children are forced into somber, little-adult behavior, they may turn sour and critical. Instead of taking pleasure in their friends' playful antics, they may feel compelled to report, or "tattle," to adults about even the most trivial misdeed of another child. Children should feel free to complain to adults when personal rights are violated and to report misbehavior to authorities (adults) when rules are broken or hazardous behavior is taking place. That kind of "telling" is to be respected and should never be labeled tattling. Frivolous or malicious telling, however, is a different matter. The child who obsessively tells, hoping to get peers in trouble, may expect adults to stamp out or punish every silly or childish behavior and to reward him or her for telling, for playing the role of "little Miss Goody Two-Shoes" or "little Mr. Goody Goody."

A child who tattles will seem antisocial to playmates who are tattled on. The child who tattles, however, has probably inferred from adult criticisms of childish behavior that it is not okay to be a child, to be "one of the gang." These children may feel aloof and apart from other children—they may actually view themselves as little adults.

These feelings, unfortunately, hinder the development of friendships that lead to wholesome cooperative play and to optimum social and emotional development.

A relaxed, playful atmosphere for babies and young children helps them develop tolerance and a sense of humor. Exposure to adults who are tolerant of others and do not take themselves too seriously greatly aids children in developing the ability to feel empathy for others. Adults, however, sometimes forget to step into children's shoes to feel what they feel and see things from their perspective.

For example, adults consider sitting back, staring into space, and doing nothing an indulgent luxury. Children consider this sitting and doing nothing an aversive punishment. Adults have a slower, quieter rhythm or pace than children and may feel annoyed by children's squealing, wriggling, wrestling, and running. Intolerant adults force children to function within the adult's comfort zone for noise and movement. In contrast, when young children sense the generosity of adults who kindly tolerate and gently redirect the bustling chaos of active, noisy children, the children in turn learn to demonstrate generosity and tolerance for others.

Instead of expressing exasperation, Allen, a young daddy, sits down and has a good laugh when his toddler walks in wearing underwear on his head rather than on his bottom. Mrs. Farrel, a long-time member of Weight Watchers, grins and takes it as a sincere compliment when little Jennifer says, "I think you're beautiful. You're the prettiest fat lady in the whole world." Even Miss Cindy laughs good-naturedly with her school-agers after the gruesome spider that has startled her turns out to be nothing more than a plastic Halloween party favor.

We might be tempted to take these three events more seriously than necessary or even become angry and punitive with the children described above. In a relaxed, playful atmosphere, however, children can learn discipline, but they can also learn that it is okay to be generous and forgiving (Mussen and Eisenberg-Berg, 1977). It is okay to make mistakes, because parents, teachers, and caregivers are allies, not enemies. It is okay to be playful and silly at times, because others can let down their barriers and share in a good laugh.

Clearly, there is a boundary between silliness and genuine misbehavior, between play and antisocial activity. Playfulness is neither hurtful nor mean-spirited; maliciousness is both. Silly behavior that is not totally appropriate can be dealt with patiently and with a sense of humor even though it may need to be firmly redirected at some point if it begins to interfere with necessary routines or to annoy others.

A Cooperative Rather than Competitive Setting

When adults say things like "See if you can put your lunch box away before anyone else," or "Whoever is quietest can be first in line," children are encouraged to be competitive rather than cooperative. Adults are often tempted to use competitive challenges because they work so much more powerfully and effectively than nagging or threatening, and, relatively speaking, they are less negative. In the long run, however, getting children's coats on quickly or getting trash picked up without a second reminder is not nearly as important as fostering cooperative and caring relationships among children who will someday be adult citizens.

By urging children to win at the expense of others, we may be establishing patterns of greediness and a lack of regard for the feelings of others. It is far more helpful to redirect children's natural competitive urges into competition with their own best records. "I wonder if you can build these blocks even higher than you did yesterday," or, "Deonicia, you are so quiet and still. You must be ready for lunch. Would you like to be our leader today."

Developmentally Appropriate Activities, Materials, and Routines

Bored children become irritable and mischievous. Children who are pushed beyond their limits into irrelevant memorization or tedious busywork may become antagonistic and rebellious. Unhappy children are generally more likely to behave in antisocial ways. When adults hold unrealistic expectations for children, stressful, even angry, relations erupt. This friction becomes contagious and soon interactions among the children themselves are tinged with irritability and annoyance. This is quite obviously not a productive situation for children to learn and to practice prosocial behavior.

The secret to a cooperative, caring, and generous atmosphere among young children lies in our meeting children's basic needs—social, emotional, physical, and intellectual. An overwhelming need of early childhood is the need for engrossing, entertaining, and rewarding activity. John Dewey, Maria Montessori, Jean Piaget, and other experts showed us that children love to learn. These experts made it clear that children learn easily through spontaneous as well as guided play experiences. Children find fulfillment in activities that are:

- Relevant, matched to the child's capabilities and interests.
- Active, involving movement.
- Sensorial, involving the five senses.

Figure 5–5 Children are likely to be happy and cooperative when their needs are met. *(Photo courtesy of Gary Peters)*

Children become deeply involved in their play and are amazingly relaxed and compliant when their need for fulfilling activity is met. This kind of productive, fulfilling activity is defined developmentally appropriate. Developmentally-appropriate activities, materials, and routines are best provided when adults:

- Get to know children personally, respond to their individual capabilities, interests, and preferences.
- Plan room arrangements that minimize frustration, congestion, and confusion for children.
- Prepare and arrange interesting toys and activities that relate to *all* areas of children's development—social, emotional, and physical as well as intellectual.
- Establish routines that allow uninterrupted blocks of time for spontaneous, self-directed play in a carefully planned environment.
- Make arrangements for hands-on exploration of real objects to be a natural and integral part of learning activities.

- Allow children to express their own individuality by making their own choices within clearly defined limits, by saying for example, "Would you rather paint or play with clay?" "Would you rather have orange juice or milk?" "Would you rather wear a skirt or blue jeans?"
- Greatly limit situations in which children are forced to sit still, to wait for something to happen, or to stand in line (toddlers are especially unable to cope with these situations).

Consistency and Predictability

Teachers, parents, and child-care providers quite often are trapped by the idea that if something doesn't work the first time, it will never work. A caregiver who decides that preschoolers should learn to scrape their plates independently after lunch may feel exasperated when the children mistakenly throw their plates and utensils away on their first try. A kindergarten teacher may throw up his hands in frustration after disastrously introducing fingerpainting for the first time to rowdy five-year-olds who leave school looking like splotchy rainbows. Additionally, any adult who has ever dealt with toddlers knows that the point simply doesn't get across the first hundred times one-year-olds are told that sticks and leaves shouldn't go in one's mouth.

Children learn positive ways of interacting with others through exposure to consistency and persistence (not anger and disgust). We can avoid a great deal of irritation simply by recognizing that it takes time for children to absorb new skills and habits. Our task is to structure a consistent and predictable environment for children, where they are allowed adequate periods of time to develop new skills introduced in tiny, bite-sized increments.

We adults are prone to set absurd goals. We focus our attention on children's behavior in fits and spurts. We ignore messiness for months or years then suddenly insist on neatness—this minute! Three-year-old Fernando always traipsed around the house after his bath in a big, soft bath towel. When he was ready to get dressed, he had a habit of dropping the damp towel in a heap on his bedroom floor. Freshly-scrubbed little boys wrapped in towels are so endearing that his parents always quietly tolerated his towel-dropping ritual. One day, however, his poor mom reached the end of her patience and yelled, "Fernando, get this wet towel into the bathroom, and I mean step on it!" After she cooled off a bit, she peeked into the bathroom to check on Fernando. There he stood in the middle of the bathroom, crying pitifully, but standing obediently on the towel!

When we feel a child is old enough to behave in a certain way, we want that behavior instantly. One popular paperback book confidently tells parents that children can be toilet trained in a day. In reality, children can't master toilet training in a day, a week, or even a month. A toddler may go from diapers to dry pants literally overnight. This only happens, however, *after* the child masters hundreds of little prerequisite skills. The toddler must tediously learn how to recognize body sensations, communicate needs, inhibit sudden impulses, consciously manipulate the muscles that control elimination, and even balance on top of a big scary bowl of water. All this just to please grownups!

Consistent, predictable routines help a child ease comfortably into learning new skills. For months, toilet training may consist only of talking about the potty, looking at it, exploring it, and sitting for a second or two on it, just as a playful part of diaper-changing routine. It may be months before the child's consistent, predictable routines expand to include actually using the potty.

Children are quite naturally inclined to resist when they are confronted with a sudden, unexpected demand that they change a long-standing behavior. Likewise, some of us adults put up quite a fuss when we were first told that we ought to wear seat belts in cars. We argued, "But it feels weird. But I'm not accustomed to it. But I don't want to change." A toddler who never had a worry in the world about when or where to relieve himself might well feel those same feelings when we insist that he ought to keep his pants dry by urinating in a toilet.

Consistency and predictability in our expectations for children helps them accept and gradually adapt to our standards. Children don't instantly develop an ability to take turns or to resist greedily grabbing a toy. Slowly and persistently, however, we can nudge children into behaving in a more responsible and prosocial manner.

THE NURTURING ADULT

One might jump to the erroneous conclusion that a nurturing parent, teacher, or caregiver is one who is either a saint or a pushover. The word nurture, however, means to train, to educate, or to nourish. The truly nurturing adult is just an honest, emotionally healthy person who learned how to be assertive and caring at the same time.

Modeling Appropriate Behavior

Teaching children in a way that nourishes them does not mean pointing out every flaw, criticizing every imperfection, and punishing every lapse in judgment. In fact, the first step toward shaping children's behavior positively is simply setting a good example, *modeling* appropriate behavior. Unbeknownst to us, many of children's most upsetting misbehaviors are little more than instant replays of our own behavior, in a context that we don't expect. Take, for example, the classic irony of an adult saying, "If you don't stop hitting people, I'm going to spank you."

When we find that a child's behavior is really annoying to us, we might avoid unfortunate imitation by thinking through the following questions:

1. What specific aspects of the behavior are particularly annoying to me?
2. Is there any way that I may have inadvertently set an example for that behavior?
3. What positive behavior could be modeled and reinforced to replace the undesired behavior?
4. How can I model appropriate behaviors so that the child will be sure to notice and respond?

If a child is overly loud and boisterous, we may focus on being particularly soft-voiced and calm. If a child is angry and unyielding, we could model patience and forgiveness. If a child is aggressive and hurtful, we could demonstrate gentleness and kindness. Being nurturing can't be used as an excuse to avoid dealing with behaviors that must be stopped. Our nurturance (or prosocial behavior) should, however, be apparent to the child as we assertively protect property and personal rights by interrupting and redirecting unacceptable behavior. Additionally, we can make a mental note to find future opportunities, after a conflict situation is resolved, to continue modeling desired behaviors such as calmness, forgiveness, and gentleness.

This focus on assertive but nonaggressive guidance is particularly noteworthy because many adults rely on angry and aggressive methods of discipline. Between eighty-four and ninety-seven percent of all parents use physical punishment at some point as a strategy for disciplining their children (Parke and Slaby, 1983).

Handling Aggression Positively

Mrs. Young cares for one-year-olds in a mothers-day-out program. When a toddler bites, she does whatever she has to—as firmly as necessary, but as gently as possible—to stop the biting, to get the bitten child free from the biter. In a matter-of-fact voice she states firmly to the biter, "No biting, biting hurts." She then takes great pains to model touching the bitten child gently. Mrs. Young delicately strokes the bitten child's arm, saying in a soothing voice, "Gentle. Be gentle." Often the biter will imitate her and touch the other child.

Then she responds, "That was so gentle. Thank you." Slowly, the toddlers begin to absorb the gentleness they see in Mrs. Young's actions every day.

When the children are older, Mrs. Young will begin emphasizing another concept, using words rather than aggression to express anger. Because she uses the word "no" very sparingly and only when she really intends for an action to stop, the children learn through observation that it is a powerful and important word. We will not hear Mrs. Young snapping at a child, "Don't you dare say no to me!" She allows children to express their thoughts and feelings verbally.

By being positive and assertive rather than negative and confrontational with children, Mrs. Young doesn't overuse the word "no" herself. Consequently, she does not hear the word "no" from toddlers very often. When she does, however, she acknowledges the balky child's feelings—even if the child can't reasonably be allowed to have his or her own way. She says, "I know you don't want to wash your hands right now, but you must have clean hands in order to be allowed to eat." Furthermore, she actually coaches her toddlers in the skill of saying "no." She prompts them, "Can you tell Marcus no? Say, 'No, Marcus. My cracker. Mine.' " In time, they learn by direct teaching as well as by imitation to use words rather than aggression to express their feelings of anger.

Imitation

Although babies and toddlers are only able to mimic unrelated bits and pieces of behaviors they observe, even these fragments are critically important to their learning. Preschoolers, on the other hand, imitate entire sequences of behavior. Preschoolers are in a particularly sensitive period of their lives for imitation. As they mime adult actions in their play, we get to see them reenact their world as they perceive it (Mussen and Eisenberg-Berg, 1977). These glimpses into their world range from the delightfully funny to the downright alarming. Children's imitative play discloses their innocent misconceptions of the adult world, as well as the fears and pains they sometimes feel.

School-age children imitate, but they are more selective in choosing role models. Although they are constantly (but unconsciously) absorbing subtle behavioral characteristics from those around them, they are not likely to mimic consciously the behaviors of adults or children they don't like. They will make conscious attempts, however, to talk, dress, and act like those they admire (Bandura, 1977). Adults can enhance positive imitative learning by becoming a respected and admired member of the child's immediate world rather than an aloof and distanced authority figure.

Figure 5–6 Adults should become actively involved in the child's world so they won't be seen as cold, aloof authority figures. *(Photo courtesy of Dr. Glenn Cochran)*

Imitation is such an important and logical tool for teaching prosocial behavior that adults must become particularly aware of their own actions and attitudes as well as those communicated by such cultural media as television (Bandura, 1977; Gerbner and Gross, 1980; Cairns, 1979; Parke and Slaby, 1983; and Lefkowitz and Tesiny, 1980). Can children easily observe cooperation, empathy, and altruism in *our* day-to-day actions? Are our values evidenced clearly in the environment we provide for children? What kinds of books do we read to them? What kinds of toys do we make available? How do the television and movie characters they watch behave? And, most importantly, how do we behave?

Rather than focus all our attention on correcting children's behaviors, we must take a cold, hard look at ourselves in the mirror now and again and correct some of our own flaws. Even if we are unsuccessful in weeding out all of our personal quirks and imperfections, we will certainly become more sensitive to the child's dilemma of truly wanting to stop an undesirable behavior but not being able to. If our goal is to develop children's self-discipline and self-control, then we'd best see how much of those admirable characteristics we are able to muster so we can show children (rather than just tell them) how people should behave.

Showing Attentiveness to Individual Needs

Nurturing adults respond to children's individual needs. Parents generally have no difficulty in seeing their children as individuals. Family intimacy and shared history throughout a child's life make it likely that there is at least awareness of (if not respect for) individual differences. A key problem for parents may be *accepting* individual differences in their children and resisting the temptation to compare them to one another. A parent may say, "I'm sure that Ramona will love taking piano lessons just like her older brother did," while knowing full well that little Ramona would much rather do "wheelies" on a bicycle than learn to play the piano.

In a group setting, however, young children may be seen as tiny cogs in a very large machine. Babies' diapers may be changed not when they become wet or soiled, but at routinely scheduled times. Eating, playing, and sleeping may take place as scheduled for whole groups rather than in response to children's individual feelings of hunger, playfulness, or fatigue. A child may not be hungry for breakfast on a given day or may be really tired before nap time. It is easy for a child to feel very overlooked in a group. While routines are essential to "sanity and survival" for group caregivers, nurturing adults will find ways to be sensitive and to make allowances for children's individual needs.

A nurturing adult will not be callous to children sleeping face-down

Figure 5–7 Nurturing adults care about children's comfort. *(Photo courtesy of Rod Smalley, Montessori Country Day School)*

on uncovered plastic mats in sweaty August heat, or make little ones nap with their shoes on simply because taking shoes off and putting them back on is too much bother. The nurturing adult would not be inclined to toss snack crackers unceremoniously onto a bare table without even the dignity of a napkin or paper plate. A nurturing adult will really care about the comfort and feelings of individual children. Even if every individual need cannot reasonably be met, the nurturing adult will express awareness of and concern for children's individual circumstances. Showing attentiveness to children's individual needs is an excellent way to demonstrate cooperative behavior for them.

Providing Affirmation, Affection, and Acceptance

Affirmation, affection, and acceptance assure a child that she is wanted and appreciated. Unconditional positive regard is the process through which affirmation, affection, and acceptance are conveyed. In contrast, conditional affection is attention given to a child only when he pleases the adult. Conditional affection carries the hidden message, "I will only love you if you are good." Unconditional positive regard lets children know they are liked simply for who they are, not for how they perform at any given time. Children absorb the message, "You are a loved, worthwhile individual even if you sometimes make mistakes."

According to Clarke (1978), in order for children to develop healthy self-esteem, they must absorb the following clear messages from the words and actions of their caregivers :

Affirmations for Being—
"You have a right to be here."
"I'm glad you are who you are."
"It's okay for you to have needs."
Affirmations for Becoming Independent—
"You don't have to do tricks (be cute, sick, sad, mad, or scared) to get attention and approval."
"It's okay to be curious and try new things on your own."
Affirmations for Learning to Think—
"You can stand up for the things you believe even if there is some risk involved."
"You can own the consequences of your own actions; others don't have to rescue you."
"It's okay to make mistakes as long as you accept responsibility for making amends."
Affirmations for Developing an Individual Identity—
"You can express your own thoughts and feelings without fear of rejection."
"It's okay to disagree."
"You can trust your own judgement."

Sometimes the preceding messages of affirmation can be verbally expressed to children. They can also be conveyed to children in day-to-day actions throughout children's lives. Affirmation is communicated to a baby by her caregiver's facial expression during such routines as diaper changing. If she looks up and sees disgust or annoyance in the caregiver's face, she will sense that it is not okay to be a baby and to need a dirty diaper changed. If she sees a relaxed smile, she will know that she is welcome and her needs are okay. If a preschooler accidentally tramples a flower bed while trying to pull weeds like his daddy, he will sense affirmation as his dad patiently acknowledges the child's good intentions and teaches him how to weed the garden without trampling.

Nurturing adults are not afraid to show affection to children (Hoffman, 1979). Smiles, warm hugs, and sincere interest in a child's world let her know that she is the recipient of unconditional positive regard. Appropriate affection should never be intrusive, overwhelming, or one-sided, but rather respectful and reciprocal.

A basic human need is for a sense of belonging. We human beings are essentially social creatures. We cannot really be happy or functional without a secure feeling that we have a place in the social order around us. The most desirable social position is one in which we feel admiration, acceptance, and approval from the important people around us. If that situation can't be found, people (children as well as grown-ups) may opt for negative substitute relationships to find recog-

Figure 5–8 Prosocial behaviors are encouraged by nurturing adults who set a good example. *(Photo courtesy of Cynde Miller and Kyle Heard)*

nition and acceptance. People assume leadership by becoming gang members, achieve recognition by defying rules, and hold others' attention by shocking, frightening, or angering them. The very last thing children (or anyone else) will settle for is being ignored and left out. Only the most emotionally disabled members of society retreat into and accept a life of total social isolation.

In order to stimulate prosocial behavior, the nurturing adult will be generous in making sure children know that they are accepted and approved. Instead of focusing only on children's unacceptable behaviors, the nurturing adult makes a point of noticing and commenting on positive behaviors. She thanks the child for remembering to wipe his feet, comments on the lovely colors in his crayon drawing, and listens with interest to his excited but rambling account of a weekend camping trip. The nurturing adult is careful to separate "bad" actions and "bad" people. "I don't like hitting, but I like you very much. You are a good person. You can learn to use words rather than hitting." In spite of inevitable disciplinary intervention from time to time, the nurtured child *always* knows she is a good and worthwhile human being.

Providing Recognition and Encouragement

On special occasions children want and deserve outright praise, just as we do in our own personal and professional lives. An occasional, sincere pat on the back can trigger a surge of motivation in us (Mussen and Eisenberg-Berg, 1977). Too much praise, however, can be burdensome, causing us to feel pressured to live up to unrealistic standards. We either awkwardly stammer "Thank you" or, worse, become addicted to praise, needing more and more every day to maintain our self-esteem. A suddenly famous guitar player was asked recently what he missed most about the formerly quiet life he led before he found fame. He quickly replied, "I miss just sitting down with people to talk about music. Everyone tells me how much they admire my work and how wonderful they think I am, but how can you answer that?"

Recognition and encouragement are more moderate alternatives to an overabundance of gushy or insincere praise. Often we praise a child by stating a value judgment, "Oh, what a good boy you are!" Unfortunately, by implying that cleaning up makes him "good," we hint that if he doesn't continue the action in the future, he might become "bad." (Young children tend to think in simplistic terms. If you aren't good, then you must be bad.)

Recognizing and encouraging are different from praising. To recognize and encourage a child, we might say, "I noticed that you wiped the table with a sponge. The table is clean and beautiful. Thanks!" The recognition is very specific (tells exactly what the child did) and

Figure 5–9 Adults earn children's respect by respecting children's own motives and interests. *(Photos courtesy of Rod Smalley, Cynde Miller, and Lynne Aiken)*

encourages the child by letting him know that we appreciate the action. He isn't labeled good or bad, just sincerely acknowledged for a job well done. The nurturing adult says "Thank you" very frequently to children.

When children do the right thing, it is not appropriate or helpful to dredge up old problems, saying, for example, "Why didn't you do this yesterday?" or, "Well, now that you have done this, you can do everything else I've been telling you to do." Children who are overwhelmed with criticism become very defeatist. They think, "Why should I even try? Everything I do just gets me into more trouble." The child will feel more encouraged if she is allowed to glow in every little bit of success before tactfully being guided by a nurturing adult to complete other unfinished tasks.

Being Willing to Enforce Appropriate Rules

As stated earlier, the nurturing adult is able to be assertive and caring at the same time. Mr. Leone really enjoys children. He is tender-hearted and kind but has trouble being assertive. When Jenny runs to him complaining, "Anna pulled my hair and broke my new crayons," Mr. Leone shrugs and says, "I'm sure it was just an accident." When children throw food during lunch, Mr. Leone pretends he doesn't notice but tries to distract the ringleaders by talking loudly about the weather, "Listen, I think I hear thunder. Do you hear that?" Mr. Leone is kind, but he is definitely not assertive. Lackadaisical permissiveness actually cultivates antisocial and aggressive behavior in children (Sears et al., 1957).

Children want and need rules. A truly nurturing adult earns children's respect by being firm and fair in a way that reminds children they are surrounded by a safety fence of reasonable limits. Anger is frightening to people generally because it can cause them to lose control of their actions. Children especially feel vulnerable because they have not developed the self-control to stop themselves from doing something they will regret terribly later. Children feel very nurtured and safe when they know they can trust a strong adult to stop them before they behave aggressively or destructively. They also want to know with certainty that their safety and rights will be protected if someone else loses control. The nurturing adult is not hesitant to enforce appropriate rules fairly and firmly.

Being Willing to Protect Individual Rights

Mary Beth is the mother of two young children, a five-year-old boy, Trey, and a three-year-old girl, Betsy. Betsy adores her big brother and attempts to follow every step he takes. Sometimes, when Trey is alone, he seems proud of Betsy's attention and plays with her for hours, but when he has friend his own age to play with, he chases Betsy away and tells her to leave him alone. One day, while Mary Beth is waxing the kitchen floor, she hears a loud altercation in the back yard. Betsy is crying because Trey and his chums won't let her play with them and are taunting her by chanting, "Betsy is a tag-along! Betsy is a tag-along!"

Since Mary Beth's mind is on the "waxy yellow buildup" problem in her kitchen, she is tempted for a moment to *order* Trey to entertain his little sister and stop the silly nonsense with his friends. Luckily, however, she stops to assess the individual rights of everyone involved in the situation. As a parent, she has a right to do her housework without interruption. But, of course, she also has an obligation to care for her children (she thinks children are considerably more important than waxy yellow buildup). Trey has an obligation to treat his sister with kindness and to help out by entertaining her from time to time. But, he also has a right to lead his own life and to play with his own friends. Betsy has a right not to be called names. But, she also has an obligation to respect her brother's privacy and to learn to play alone sometimes.

After Mary Beth patiently listens to complaints from all sides, she says, "Trey, Betsy feels hurt when you call her names. You have a right to play with your friends, but name-calling can't be allowed. Let's make a compromise. Please push Betsy on the swing for a few minutes so that I can finish my work in the kitchen, then I will bring Betsy in the house, and you and your friends can have the back yard to yourselves until your friends go home. Betsy, you may play with Trey for a few minutes, then you and I will go inside, and I will show you how to give your dolls a bath."

Because Mary Beth is a nurturing parent, she is able and willing to make an extra effort to see that everyone's rights are protected and that everyone behaves responsibly. She doesn't do only what seems expedient or convenient at the moment, but tries hard to create an environment of fairness and mutual respect for the rights of others.

SUMMARY

Prosocial behavior benefits others and antisocial behavior harms others. The concept of prosocial behavior focuses on three critical elements of a child's beneficial or helping interactions with others: cooperation, empathy, and altruism. Prosocial behavior is not an inborn trait, but a slowly learned way of acting that wins approval and affection from others.

Figure 5–10 Children should be encouraged to be cooperative—not competitive. *(Photo courtesy of Rod Smalley)*

Adults who hope to stimulate prosocial behavior in young children must first establish a nurturing social environment. Children who are afraid that their own needs will not be met may not be able to be generous with others.

Children need a protected period in early life to play and explore. A relaxed, playful atmosphere for babies and young children helps them grow up tolerant and with a sense of humor.

Encouraging children to compete with each other reduces cooperativeness. By urging children to win at the expense of others, we may be establishing patterns of greediness and a lack of regard for the feelings of others. Children's natural competitive urges should be channeled into improving their own capabilities.

Bored children become irritable and mischievous. Children who are pushed beyond their limits into irrelevant memorization or tedious busywork may become antagonistic and rebellious. Unhappy children are generally more likely to behave in antisocial ways.

The secret to a cooperative, caring, and generous atmosphere among young children lies in the children's having basic needs—social, emotional, physical, and intellectual—met. Children learn easily through spontaneous as well as guided play experiences that are relevant, active, and sensorial. Developmentally-appropriate activities, materials, and routines are essential to effective child guidance.

Children learn positive ways of interacting with others through exposure to consistency and persistence (not anger and disgust). Consistent, predictable routines help a child ease comfortably into learning new skills.

The word nurture means to train, to educate, or to nourish. The nurturing adult is an honest, emotionally healthy person who has learned how to be assertive and caring at the same time.

The first step toward shaping children's behavior positively is simply setting a good example. Begin nurturing can't be used as an excuse to avoid dealing with behaviors that must be stopped.

Babies and toddlers can only mimic unrelated bits and pieces of behaviors they observe. Preschoolers imitate entire sequences of behavior. School-age children imitate, but they are more selective in choosing role models. Imitation is an important and logical tool for teaching prosocial behavior.

Nurturing adults respond to children's individual needs and resist the temptation to compare one to another. In group settings, young children should be seen as individuals. While routines are essential, nurturing adults find ways to be sensitive and to make allowances for children's individual needs.

Affirmation, affection, and acceptance assure a child that she is wanted and appreciated. Unconditional positive regard is the process of conveying affirmation, affection, and acceptance.

Messages of affirmation can be verbally expressed to children as well as nonverbally communicated to them in day-to-day actions from birth (and throughout childhood).

Nurturing adults show affection to children. Appropriate affection, however, should never be intrusive, overwhelming, or one-sided.

A basic human need is for a sense of belonging. If social acceptance can't be found in a positive way, children may attempt to hold others' attention by clinging or by shocking, frightening, or angering them.

In order to stimulate prosocial behavior, the nurturing adult will be generous in making sure children know that they are accepted and approved. The nurtured child knows she is a good and worthwhile human being.

Children want and deserve occasional praise, but too much praise can be burdensome and addictive. Recognition and encouragement are an appropriate alternative to an overabundance of gushy or insincere praise.

Children want and need rules. The nurturing adult is not hesitant to enforce appropriate rules fairly and firmly.

The nurturing adult is able and willing to see that children's rights are protected and that they behave responsibly—to create an environment of fairness and mutual respect for the rights of others.

PRACTICAL APPLICATION/DISCUSSION

William and the Nature Walk

Brenda's three-year-olds were ready to go outside. Several days of heavy autumn rains kept them indoors in the child-care center. Today's clear sky and bright sun were a welcome invitation to break away from usual morning routines and release some pent-up energy.

Brenda and her assistant teacher, Theresa, decided that playing on the playground was out of the question because there were still big puddles in the sandbox and under the swings. "A nature walk," Theresa suggested, "would be perfect. There are lots of pretty fall leaves, and we could walk to the park to collect acorns and leaves for our science center."

The children excitedly prepared for their walk. Each child chose a "buddy" to hold hands with, and the pairs of young children danced and wriggled with anticipation as Brenda and Theresa helped them get into a straight line on the sidewalk.

"Remember," said Brenda, "we need to hold hands with our partners and walk very carefully on the sidewalk until we get to the park." Before they had gone even a few feet, however, William saw a bright yellow leaf and, dropping his partner's hand, bent down to pick it up. Louisa, the little girl directly behind William, immediately tumbled on top of him.

Brenda helped William and Louisa up, then, kneeling at eye level to William, and gently taking his hand said politely but firmly, "Excuse me, William, you must wait until we get to the park, *then* you can look for leaves. Remember—be safe! Hold hands with your partner." She then gave William a little pat on the shoulder and a smile as she announced, "Okay, is this train ready to go again? Let's chug, chug, chug down the railroad track! Whooo, whoo—ding, ding, ding!"

Within minutes, William was again distracted and stooped to pick up an irresistibly bright red leaf, and poor little Louisa was sprawled on top of him just like before. This time, however, she quickly scrambled to her feet, took William's hand and said in a confident voice, "Exsqueeze me, Weeyum! When you do dat, I faw down!" [Excuse me, William! When you do that, I fall down!]

QUESTIONS FOR DISCUSSION

1. Why do you think Louisa was able to use words to express her frustration with William rather than biting or hitting him?

2. How should Brenda respond to the interaction between William and Louisa? Should she do anything further to correct William's behavior? Should she attempt to reinforce Louisa for remembering to use words?

3. What should Brenda and Theresa do if William continues to disrupt the nature walk? Can you think of anything preventive that could be done to stop the problem and avoid difficulty on future walks?

4. Are these children learning prosocial behavior? How?

5. Did Brenda and Theresa seem playful, consistent, assertive, and sensitive to the children's basic needs? Did it appear that developmentally appropriate activities and routines were being carried out?

Figure 6–1 It takes time for children to learn how to adapt their behavior to fit adult expectations. *(Photo courtesy of Margaret Fowler, Montessori Country Day School)*

6

Understanding the Reasons for Problem Behavior

OBJECTIVES

This chapter will assist you in:

• Defining characteristics of inappropriate behavior.
• Articulating subjective perceptions of behavior.

- Recognizing children's behavioral limitations based on normal stages of moral development.
- Listing underlying causes of problem behavior.
- Examining causes of misbehavior.

DEFINING PROBLEM BEHAVIOR

The process by which children learn acceptable behavior is called socialization. Infants have no comprehension of proper or improper behavior. And, they would have no ability to inhibit their impulses, even if they knew what was expected. Gradually over the first few years of life, however, children develop self-control and learn how to get along with others and how to follow the accepted rules of their family and community. During this process, children are very transparent in their feelings and desires. They act like children (of course), making mistakes, acting on impulse, and stubbornly resisting external control—actions we consider to be problem behaviors.

Chapter 1 identified three specific categories of problem behavior and recommended that adults interrupt or redirect any child behavior that:

- Infringes unfairly on the rights of others.
- Presents a clear risk of harm to the child or anyone else.
- Results in the mishandling of objects or living things.

Those three guidelines were used for defining basic ground rules for children. Be kind! Be safe! Be neat! The guidelines, however, do not particularly raise questions about why children might behave in an unkind, unsafe, or careless manner. Although the terms misbehavior, problem behavior, and inappropriate behavior are used interchangeably, the term misbehavior seems to imply mischief. Many inappropriate behaviors, however, are not at all mischievous in intent. A child may not even realize that a specific behavior will be viewed as "naughty" by adults. Positive child guidance requires that adults gauge their reaction to misbehaviors by looking at the child's level of understanding, the severity and intention of the behavior, as well as any likely reasons for it.

A baby who has innocently climbed on top of a coffee table must be dealt with differently than a five-year-old who knowingly uses the couch as if it were a trampoline. Both must be redirected, because the behaviors present a clear risk of harm to the children and involve the mishandling of objects in the environment. To get positive results, adults must hold reasonable expectations for children at various ages and recognize whether they can really be expected to control their actions in particularly difficult or tempting situations.

In many cases, it is far more effective to change the situation than to try to stop a child's behavior. By removing the baby from the coffee table and taking him to a safe piece of play equipment designed for climbing, we can instantly change an inappropriate behavior to an appropriate behavior (even though the child may not yet recognize any difference in the two situations).

If we assume that the five-year-old knows the difference between a living-room sofa and a trampoline, our emphasis should be on giving the child a clear understanding of facts, choices, and consequences. For example, we might say, "The couch is not for jumping. If you want to jump, you may jump outside on the soft grass." If the action continues, we should give the child our close, undivided attention at eye level and add in an assertive but sincere tone, "I know jumping on the couch is fun, but it could break the couch, or you could fall on something hard or sharp in here. If you jump on the couch again, you will not be allowed to play in the living room for the rest of the afternoon." Then, of course, we have to follow-through and see that what we say will happen, actually happens.

Assessing the appropriateness of any individual child's behavior requires us to step into her shoes and see the world from her perspective. It requires accurate insight and wise judgment. We are prone, sometimes quickly and capriciously, to label actions that are inconvenient, annoying, or embarrassing to us at the moment as misbehavior, regardless of any reasons the child might have for behaving in such a manner.

Children are confused when they don't expect a negative reaction from us and when they can't make sense of our logic in requiring different behaviors in different situations. They are bewildered when a behavior is praised in one setting but reprimanded in a situation they don't recognize as being very different. Mr. and Mrs. Perez were horrified when their little son, Albert, who was learning about nutrition in preschool, looked at an overweight diner sitting near them in a quiet restaurant and said in a startlingly loud but sincere voice, "You shouldn't eat that dessert, Mister. It isn't good for you." Young children's inexperience and naivete are just two of the many reasons they behave in ways that adults perceive as naughty.

Three-year-old Allison Jones' mother opened her dishwasher one morning to discover a pile of dirty clothes stuffed where dishes ought to be. Mrs. Jones yelled, "Who put these clothes in the dishwasher?" The look of guilt on Allison's face instantly gave her away as the culprit. Although Mrs. Jones asked repeatedly, "Why did you do this? What would possess you to do such a silly thing?," Allison just hung her head and mumbled, "I dunno."

Figure 6–2 We sometimes fail to see the world from the child's point of view. *(Photo courtesy of Cynde Miller)*

Mrs. Jones never realized that Allison intended to surprise her mother by cleaning the bathroom. Her intentions were good, she was just a little bit confused about which "washing machine" one used to wash dirty clothes. Allison's behavior was inappropriate (clothes shouldn't be put in the dishwasher) but she certainly wasn't misbehaving. Her behavior didn't deserve a reprimand but rather some gentle redirection. An excellent adult response would be for her mother to say, "Thank you so much for wanting to help. Come with me and I'll show you the right place to put dirty clothes."

Functional and Dysfunctional Behaviors

There is no clear-cut definition covering all categories of problem behaviors for every child in every situation, but we can loosely define inappropriate behavior as any behavior that is not reasonably in the best interest of the child, other people, or things in the environment. This broad range of actions includes the numerous little day-to-day behaviors that are not really productive but still cannot be defined as outright disrespectful, dangerous, or damaging. The word inappropriate does not suggest fault or blame, but instead simply implies that a behavior is not seen as a worthwhile or desirable action in a specific situation. In contrast, misbehavior is a term for a kind of inappropriate behavior that suggests direct responsibility on the part of the

Figure 6–3 Being lonely is no fun.

child. It implies that a child has willfully failed to comply with reasonable guidelines.

When children evidence a compulsive and chronic pattern of very inappropriate or self-destructive behavior, the behavior can be termed dysfunctional. Functional behaviors are various appropriate actions that serve some productive or positive function in a child's life. These actions help the child get her needs met. Dysfunctional behaviors, however, often produce a negative reaction that may be opposite to the outcome desired by the child. The child's strategies for coping and for interacting with others simply don't work. This causes the child increasing stress and unhappiness and creating a vicious cycle. A lonely child lacking in social skills may relentlessly tease other children to get their attention, but the teasing is dysfunctional because it doesn't attract friends but, instead, causes the child to be disliked. Consequently, the child becomes more isolated and lonely and even more trapped in the existing cycle of dysfunctional behavior.

Adult-Centered Definition of Misbehavior

Adult-centered definitions of misbehavior focus on the effect of a child's behavior on the adult. Individual actions are evaluated according to the seriousness of their impact on things the adult cares about, as well as the adult's emotional state or mood. If a child spills his juice in the grass during a picnic, the adult may hardly notice, because nothing has to be cleaned up. If the same child spills juice on the kitchen floor, the adult may be annoyed and may reprimand the child. If, however, the spill is grape juice on brand-new, light-colored dining room carpeting, the adult may be very angry and punish or spank the child.

The child learns that her behaviors are not always met with a consistent or predictable adult reaction. Children may learn that they can "get away with" inappropriate behaviors when their caregiver is in a relaxed and playful mood. They may also perceive that nothing they do makes any difference when the adult is in a bad mood. They may believe that they will get in trouble regardless of what they do or don't do.

Since adult-centered definitions of misbehavior focus only on the adult's needs and desires, desirable behaviors are perceived to be actions that are convenient to the adult. Being quiet, staying out of the way, and performing the role of a cute (but undemanding) little kid on cue may be seen as the hallmarks of a "good" child. Crying, squealing with joy, being frightened, or being a chatterbox may be perceived as naughty misbehaviors if they are annoying, embarrassing, or inconvenient for the adult.

Child-Centered Definition of Misbehavior

In contrast, a child-centered definition of misbehavior focuses on the ability level, motives, and long-term well-being of the child. If an action is wrong or inappropriate, it is judged to be wrong because it infringes on the rights of others, is unsafe, or is unnecessarily damaging to the environment—not because the action is a bother or because the adult happens to be in an intolerant mood. Defining behaviors this way brings about consistency and a sense of fairness. Children learn to be responsible for the consequences of their own actions. They learn that there is a direct relationship between their actions and the reaction they receive from authority figures.

By taking into consideration the ages and developmental stages of children, adults can recognize that exploring or "getting into things" is normal and beneficial learning behavior for a baby or toddler, not misbehavior. It is the adult's responsibility to babyproof the environment so that everything that is accessible to the baby is safe and appropriate or to remove the baby to an area that is safe for exploration.

Figure 6–4 Children explore their world because they want to learn—not because they want to be naughty. *(Photo courtesy of Patty Knowlton)*

Children who are allowed to become actively involved in daily processes will undoubtedly make mistakes more often than children who are encouraged to stand by passively while things are done for them. Allowing young children help with food preparation, for example, may be messy and time consuming. It is quicker and easier for the adult to complete such tasks alone, but the confidence and skill development children gain from such experiences are definitely in their best interest. Dropping an egg or inadvertently spilling flour are not seen as mischief from the child-centered perspective, but rather as important opportunities for children to learn responsibility and independence. Instead of being scolded for making a mess, the child is taught how to accomplish daily tasks successfully and how to clean up after himself.

Stages of Moral Development in Young Children

A critical priority for parents, schools, communities, even entire countries, is the moral development of their children and future citizens. *Morality* is the ability to distinguish right from wrong and to act accordingly. *Moral development* is the process by which human beings learn to monitor their own actions and to decide whether a tempting behavior is a "good" or "bad" thing to do and then to inhibit inappropriate impulses. In other words, morally developed people are able to stop themselves from doing things they know are wrong.

Although the guidance children receive early in life is essential to their moral development, moral behavior is not exclusively a concern of early childhood. Adults who are quick to respond harshly to a young child's misbehavior may forget their own difficulty in inhibiting the inappropriate impulses they have in their own daily life. Even adults with well-developed morals experience difficulty resisting the temptation to gossip, smoke cigarettes, indulge in foods that are bad for them, or tell "little white lies" to get out of tight spots. Because one of the key avenues for early childhood learning is imitation, it is essential for adult caregivers consciously to set the best possible example in their day-to-day actions of integrity and strong moral character (Toner, Parke, and Yussen, 1978; Toner and Potts, 1981; and Grusec, Kuczynski, Rushton, and Simutis, 1979).

As children observe adult behaviors and experience the cause-and-effect sequences that are a part of interacting with others, they internalize, or adopt as their own, the character attributes and ethical standards of the important role models in their lives. Attachment, love, and respect for an adult trigger the child's internalization of that adult's values. When a child has internalized, or accepted as his own, the standards of his adult role models, he begins to experience the emotional component of morality, or *moral affect*. When he behaves in a way that he knows to be wrong, he has feelings of guilt and shame.

When he behaves properly, he feels pride. Moral affect (the feelings associated with a guilty or clear conscience) serves as an internal regulator that guides one toward appropriate behavior and away from misbehavior.

Feelings of guilt play a role in regulating moral behavior, but it is not helpful to push guilt on a child by saying such things as, "Aren't you ashamed of yourself, you naughty girl?" Forcing guilt on a young child may actually harden her emotionally and delay her development of moral affect. Guilt that comes from inside us is always more meaningful than guilt imposed on us by someone else.

Two specific child-rearing practices are known to help children internalize values and prosocial moral judgment. These are: nurturing, affectionate caregiver behavior; and consistency in explaining the reasons for rules and commands. Adults help children develop moral behavior by being loving and gentle and by putting into words the rationales for imperatives. Instead of just saying, for example, "Don't touch that!," they say, "Please don't touch that because it belongs to someone else" (Eisenberg-Berg, 1979).

Another important component of moral development is *moral reasoning*, the thinking processes that guide people in deciding what is or is not moral behavior. The way children think about right and wrong changes dramatically as their intellectual capacity matures (Piaget, 1932). Children younger than seven-years-old tend to focus on the concrete consequences of actions rather than on the abstract motivations or intentions behind them. As they become older and their moral capacity increases, they are better able to take into consideration complicated rationales for various actions (Ferguson and Rule, 1983).

If a preschooler is told that Jimmy broke a lot of dishes while trying to help, and Annie broke one dish while trying to steal cookies, the preschooler may insist that Jimmy was naughtier and deserves more punishment than Annie. The child has focused on the idea that breaking a lot of dishes is worse than breaking one dish. The child is not yet able to think about all aspects of the dilemmas presented or to consider such things as motive. Piaget (1932) studied children's sense of right and wrong through a series of interviews in which he confronted children of various ages with moral problems like the one described here. He found that young children's responses contrasted sharply with the responses of older children. The moral reasoning of young children tends to be simplistic and limited to enforcing the letter of the law (or rule) rather than interpreting the spirit or intent of the law.

Kohlberg (1976, 1969) described the stages through which human beings develop moral reasoning. His three levels and six stages are listed as follows:

Level One—Preconventional Morality
Stage One
One obeys rules only to avoid punishment and to gain rewards. For example, a toddler examining an electric outlet may reach for it, then look up at the adult while at the same time saying, "No, no. No touch." The toddler will probably resist the urge to touch the outlet only if the adult appears attentive and ready to enforce the rule.

Stage Two
One bargains to get one's needs met. Prosocial behaviors are intended to bring about favors from others. There is often bargaining. For example, "If you let me ride the tricycle, I'll be your best friend."

Level Two—Conventional Morality
Stage Three
There is an emphasis on gaining approval from others by being nice. The focus is on being a "good girl" or a "good boy" to get praise and approval. For example, while an adult is urging one child to taste just a bite of green beans, another child nearby may hurriedly stuff her mouth full of beans, saying, "See me? I'm eating my vegetables!"

Stage Four
The focus is on "law and order." At this stage, one is concerned that everyone do his duty and follow the letter of the law. It is only okay to break a rule if everyone else is doing it. For example, school-age children become very indignant when rules are broken. They may resent the fact that a child suffering from diabetes is given a candy bar by the teacher. Never mind that the child is ill, it just isn't right.

Level Three—Postconventional Morality
Stage Five
At this stage, correct behavior is defined in terms of individual rights according to widely-held moral beliefs of society. For example, a teacher at this level would recognize that the urgent health need of a diabetic child is more important than usual rules about candy at school, which are normally fair and reasonable. Protecting the health of a child is more valued in this situation than following a rule.

Stage Six
One decides whether a behavior is moral or not based on a personal decision of conscience in accordance with personal ethical principles that are logical, consistent, and universal. For example, a child-care center director might risk the solvency of her business by testifying in accordance with her conscience in a child-abuse case against a powerful and popular community member.

One distinct characteristic of more-advanced levels of moral reasoning is one's eventual ability to consider motivation and intention when

Figure 6–5 It takes time for children to develop a mature understanding of right and wrong. *(Photo courtesy of Cynde Miller)*

evaluating the outcome of a behavior. Young children rarely show this ability, but adult caregivers must, if they wish to be effective disciplinarians.

Adults who enforce rules only when it is convenient or in their best interest to do so are functioning at a very low level of moral behavior. Adults also function at a low level when they blindly enforce rules just because they are rules, regardless of the circumstances, motives, or effects on individual children. Morally mature adults focus on the intents and motives of children, not on the outcomes of their behaviors. If, for example, Alicia tries to knock someone off of the jungle gym but nobody gets hurt, and Albert is being silly and accidentally knocks someone off who is hurt badly, the morally mature adult will recognize that Alicia's behavior was more inappropriate than Albert's.

UNDERLYING CAUSES OF PROBLEM BEHAVIOR

Lying on a couch and watching cartoons for hours is not a desirable use of a child's time. In order to redirect the behavior, an adult may need to think through any potential reasons the child is not involved in healthier, more active play. Is the child reinforced for being quiet and passive? Does the adult respond negatively to active play that is sometimes messy or noisy? Are interesting toys and challenging play equipment accessible to the child? Does the child need someone to play with?

Adults must always take into account possible reasons for undesirable behavior in order to have a chance to change the situation and prevent the behavior. In child guidance, as in health care, the best cure is always prevention!

Inappropriate Expectations

Sometimes children's misbehavior is the direct result of inappropriate expectations on the part of adults. We expect children to be able to do things that they simply are not capable of doing.

Helena and Ray are sitting in the pediatrician's waiting room with their eighteen-month-old son, Billy. The little boy is dressed in his very best clothes with shiny black shoes and a tiny bow tie. He is sitting on his dad's knee looking like a fashion model for baby clothes. Billy sits silently for a while, then looks around at the room and at his mom and dad, who are preoccupied in their discussion of the questions they want to ask Billy's doctor.

After a few more minutes of sitting, Billy points to a large aquarium with huge tropical fish swimming around and says, "Yook!" (his word for look). After a few seconds, he gestures insistently and looks at his mother, repeating, "Yook, Wha' dis?" (What's this?). Helena straightens Billy's tie and says, "Yes, they're fish. Shhh, be still now. You'll get your clothes all messed up."

Billy stared at the aquarium a few seconds longer, then scrambled to get down off his dad's lap. His dad pulled him back in his lap and said firmly, "Those aren't for you to touch. You need to stay here and sit still. If you get down, you'll break something for sure." Billy began to whine and rub his eyes with his fist, periodically struggling to get down from his dad's lap. His mother pulled a bottle from her diaper bag and offered it to Billy, but he threw the bottle on the floor and began kicking and crying loudly.

As the nurse came in to announce that the doctor was ready to see Billy, Helena and Ray seemed to be at their wit's end. With great frustration in her voice, Helena said, "Why does he act like this? What are you supposed to do when they get like this? He's just impossible to deal with sometimes." Practically speaking, by the time Billy was having a tantrum, there was probably very little that could be done to resolve the situation except to remove Billy from the setting and wait for him to wind down.

However, a great deal could have been done to avoid the situation. If Helena and Ray had known more, in advance, about what to expect from a toddler, they might have anticipated that he really couldn't sit still for thirty minutes to an hour. Perhaps they could have brought one of his favorite toys or books with them, or they could have distracted him by playing peek-a-boo or by allowing him to scribble on a notepad from his mother's purse. Or perhaps his dad could have followed up on his interest in the aquarium by supervising him closely and talking with him about the fishes as he looked at and touched the aquarium.

Misunderstanding Expectations

Sometimes children misunderstand what is expected of them. Miss Jean, a preschool teacher, was dismayed to discover that her preschoolers had left the bathroom a mess. Water was all over the floor and paper towels were everywhere except in the trash can. She turned to three-year-old Misha and said, "I'm going to go get a mop. Can you please put all of the paper towels into the trash can, where they belong?"

When Miss Jean returned with her mop, she found poor little Misha struggling to pull clean paper towels out of the dispenser and stuffing them by the handfuls into the trash can. In a pitiful voice, Misha said, "It too much, Teacher. It too much paper towels." Luckily, Miss Jean recognized that although the outcome of Misha's behavior was not the desired one, her intentions were good. Misha simply took her teacher's instructions literally when she said, "Put all the paper towels into the trash can." Miss Jean had not specified "wet paper towels on the floor."

Figure 6–6 Young children may lack the self-control necessary for compliance with adult rules. *(Photo courtesy of Cynde Miller, Montessori Country Day School)*

Miss Jean thanked Misha warmly for trying to help and then proceeded to say matter-of-factly, "Let's put the wet, dirty paper towels in the trash can. The dry ones are good for us to use next time we wash." If Miss Jean had scolded Misha or snapped, "Now look what you've done, you silly thing," Misha might not have been so eager to cooperate the next time someone asked her to help.

Immature Self-Control

Sometimes it seems that children really want to abide by an adult's request, but somehow they just can't seem to manage the self-control needed to accomplish what the adult expects.

Eloise provides child care in her home for six children. She is proud to be a registered family day-home provider and is committed to be an early-childhood educator, not just a babysitter. To help her children learn about science and nature, she bought a furry, baby guinea pig.

The guinea pig caused a flurry of excitement on Monday morning as the children arrived for the day. Eloise sat by the cage with two of the toddlers on her lap and talked with the preschool children about the new pet. The guinea pig ran around in circles making high squealing sounds while the older boys decided that he should be named "Squeaky."

Eloise explained that Squeaky would be frightened if people made too much noise or shook his cage. She also explained that although Squeaky was very gentle, he might be confused if he saw a finger sticking into his cage. He might think it was a carrot or something good to eat and try to nibble on it. The preschool children talked excitedly about Squeaky and managed to keep their hands behind their backs or in their pockets so they didn't forget about shaking the cage or sticking their fingers through the bars.

Eloise left the room to help one of the toddlers use the toilet. Suddenly she heard a commotion with shrieks and squeals from the room with the guinea pig. In her absence, the children forgot about touching the cage, and in their eagerness, pushing and shoving to see Squeaky, the children accidentally tipped the cage off the table, knocking the cage open. Squeaky was running around squealing, the children were running around shrieking, the toddlers were crying, and water and guinea-pig food were spilled everywhere.

Eloise quickly captured the terrified guinea pig and then, gently stroking the shaking Squeaky, said in a calm voice, "Listen boys and girls, can you hear the little sound Squeaky is making. He's very scared. Let's sing a quiet lullaby to Squeaky so that he won't be frightened." Softly, the older children joined Eloise in singing "Rock-a-Bye-Baby" to little Squeaky. The toddlers watched, wide-eyed. When everyone was calm and quiet, Eloise put Squeaky back into his cage and said, "We'll put Squeaky's cage in the storage room for a while so that he can rest. After nap time, we'll get him out and watch him again."

Eloise realized that the children had not maliciously intended to harm or frighten Squeaky, they simply were so excited that they couldn't manage the necessary self-control to deal with the situation successfully. Eloise felt confident that with enough time, patience, and practice, the children could eventually develop the self-control needed to watch the guinea pig properly. She also knew that until that time, she needed to remove Squeaky, except during the times that she was able to supervise the children very closely as they watched him.

Eloise recognized that reprimanding or punishing the children for their lack of self-control was not appropriate or helpful, because the children, at that point, were simply not yet capable of behaving in a more mature or controlled way. Instead, she helped them identify with Squeaky's feelings and needs so that they could understand why they needed to watch without touching. She also knew that it was better to change the environment temporarily rather than trying to force children to behave instantly according to her expectations.

Gleeful Abandon, Group Contagion

Tuesday mornings are always a little strange at the Elm Street Public Library. The sleepy, little library comes to life as neighborhood children troop in for the children's-story hour and other events scheduled especially for youngsters, such as movies and puppet shows.

Mrs. Asaad, the children's librarian, spends hours each week choosing just the right books and practicing reading them, over and over, to make sure her program is interesting and fun for the children. One Tuesday morning, Mrs. Asaad was helping an unusually young group of children get seated on the floor and ready for story time. She positioned a row of the youngest children, a half-dozen particularly enthusiastic two-year-olds, right in front of her as she began singing a song about three little ducks.

One of the toddlers folded his hands under his arm pits (to make duck wings) and helped her with the "quack, quack, quack" part of the song. The other toddlers caught on and began wagging their arms and quacking too, whereupon the first quacking toddler began giggling and falling over on the floor. Of course, all the other toddlers imitated by giggling and falling down and kicking their feet in the air.

Mrs. Asaad finished her song and good naturedly helped Chris, the toddler who appeared to be the leader of the gang to sit up. "Are you ready to hear a story about a little duck named Ping?" she asked. Chris vigorously shook his head "yes." Of course, all of the other toddlers began vigorously shaking their heads too.

Mrs. Asaad, with great suspense in her voice, began the story. "Once upon a time in a faraway land, there was a little duck named Ping." All of the children, even the toddlers, leaned forward to hear every word. But when Mrs. Asaad got to the very exciting part of the story where Ping gets a spank on the bottom for being late, the toddlers were overcome with their enthusiasm. Several began stamping their feet on the floor and Chris let out a squeal. As the other toddlers joined in the squealing, Chris began shaking his head so vigorously that his hair stood out all around his head.

Mrs. Asaad stood watching helplessly as the toddlers, and even some young threes, seemed possessed by this gleeful group contagion of head shaking and foot stamping. Suddenly, it dawned on Mrs. Asaad that the toddlers were more excited about the social presence of the other children than they were about her planned story. She realized that the story was simply not working at that particular time, so she laid down the book and stood up, saying, "Who can stretch high toward the sky? Great! Now, who can stamp your feet? Terrific! Let's sing 'Head and Shoulders, Knees and Toes.' "

After a few rousing choruses of active movement songs, Mrs. Asaad dismissed the group early, with an invitation to anyone who wanted to hear the end of the story about Ping to come sit with her. Some of the older children clustered around her (after the wild toddlers had left) and listened quietly to the end of the story.

Mrs. Asaad was very insightful to recognize that the toddlers' rowdy behavior was not a personal affront to her. Chris and the other twos were not naughty but just immensely happy. They were thrilled to be in a group of children at an exciting event and didn't have a clue about the life of a duck from a faraway land. Singing and moving as a group, not hearing good literature, met their needs at this particular time.

Boredom

Neighborhood Nursery School was closed for the day, but staff members' children hung around, waiting for their parents' staff meeting to end. The nursery school staff took pride in their professionalism and high standards, and in order to reach their goals for quality, met every Thursday afternoon after nursery school to discuss concerns and make plans. This was a pleasurable time for them to talk and laugh and spend time together.

Because most of the staff members were also parents, their own children had no alternative but to wait around while the parents met. Staff members took turns bringing a snack for the "staff kids" and attending to their problems and disagreements during meeting times, but it was clear that the staff kids dreaded the long Thursday afternoons.

In early December, a meeting went on for hours as the staff planned special Christmas events. The staff kids ate their snack, colored pictures, and went through stacks of puzzles and books. Shelley, five, and Jasmine, four-and-a-half, were terribly bored and beginning to get a little silly. They were going through familiar books, making up ridiculous things for the characters to say and then laughing uproariously at themselves.

Next, they decided that they were "Harriet the Spy," so they sneaked around under tables and behind furniture, trying to get a peek at the adults without being seen, then retreating to the restroom to roll on the floor in laughter. The spies decided that the next time they forayed into the enemy territory (the staff meeting room), they would attack the grownups' coffee table. Ever so slowly Shelley crept under the refreshment table, while Jasmine crouched excitedly in the hall, watching with both hands clasped over her mouth to stifle her

Figure 6–7 Bordom and fatigue have a definite effect on children's behavior.   *(Photo courtesy of Lynne Aiken, Heights Montessori School)*

giggles. While the adults talked, a little hand slowly made its way up to the box of sugar cubes by the coffee pot, and a strange sound, a muffled giggly sort of chortle, burst from Jasmine in the hall. The adults droned on, not noticing a thing.

The little hand (now grasping a whole handful of sugar cubes) slowly made its way back down the table. Unfortunately, it snagged the cord to the coffee pot on its way, and abruptly, the whole great adventurous fantasy came crashing down around little Shelley.

While Jasmine watched from the hall in horror, Shelley huddled under the table, her hands full of sugar cubes, surrounded by a dented coffeepot and huge puddles and rivulets of coffee. Her face was flushed with embarrassment as the room full of astonished adults stared at her in disbelief. Her mother looked the most shocked of all because Shelley was the kind of child no one ever expected to misbehave.

Boredom, especially when coupled with lax supervision, is an open invitation to errant behavior (as well as to some extraordinary bursts of creativity).

Fatigue, Discomfort

The Jacobsons spent a wonderful day at the zoo. They left home before sunrise and drove several hours to a large city nearby to expose their four children to the wonders of a first-class zoo. The youngsters, three boys and a girl, ranged in age from fifteen months to eight years.

They enjoyed a nearly perfect day. The weather was great, the orangutan hung upside down and delighted the children with wonderful ape tricks. Allison, the toddler, learned to say "monkey" and "bird" and make lots of new animal sounds. By the end of the day, the car trip home seemed particularly long and tedious. Al drove, and his wife, Regina, and the kids fell asleep shortly before the family reached home.

As they pulled into the driveway and everyone woke up, and it was clear that the children were hungry, crabby, and generally exhausted. Al said, "I think I'll make pancakes for supper. That won't take long at all." Regina got the children bathed and dressed for bed, and everyone sat down to big fluffy pancakes, applesauce, and bacon—usually one of the kids favorite meals.

Regina collapsed into a chair as Al lifted Allison (in her cute little "footy" pajamas and thick overnight diaper) into her highchair. He began to cut her pancake. Suddenly, Allison began to whine, shake her head, and push the highchair tray. Al said, "What's wrong. Didn't you want me to cut up your pancake?" Allison stiffened and struggled, getting louder and louder. Al said, "Here, I'll trade pancakes. Mine isn't cut up." Allison took a swipe at the pancake and it landed on her brother William, causing him to start crying.

Al tried to calm William as Regina lifted Allison out of the high-chair and said, "Honey, I know you're tired. We're all tired, but you may not throw food." Allison stiffened, struggled, and screamed even louder. Over her screams, Al and Regina wracked their brains to figure out what to do. Nothing they tried seemed to help, and every effort just seemed to make matters worse. They finally decided that the only thing to do was just to put Allison in her crib for the night. She sobbed herself to sleep, finally making the little rhythmic gasping sounds children make after they've cried hard.

After the boys were fed and asleep, Al and Regina puzzled over Allison's tantrum. They couldn't decide whether this was a new stage or just the result of her being overstimulated and exhausted from the busy day.

The next morning Regina leaned over Allison's crib to say good morning. Allison was all smiles while her mother unsnapped her damp pajama bottoms and pulled off the plastic pants. Then Regina stopped. She discovered to her dismay that a diaper pin was open. Allison had several bright red scratches and pin pricks on her left side. Regina removed the offending pin and, then, just stood there with tears filling her eyes. "Why," she asked herself, "Why didn't I think to check her diaper pins last night."

Fatigue or anything that causes discomfort can cause children (and adults) to lose control and act aggressively, defy rules, or behave inappropriately. Being hungry, cold, hot, sick, or hurt are all reasons for children to be cranky and uncooperative. Very young children usually don't even realize that the source of their misery is a waistband that is painfully tight, a sock thread twisted around a toe, or scratchy sand in a wet diaper. Even older children sometimes become negative without recognizing that they just don't feel good.

Adults always have to remember that what appears on the surface is not always the whole story.

Desire for Recognition

At three, Kelley was the middle child. His big sister, Kathryn, brought home papers from her elementary schoolteacher saying how smart and good she was. She also had lots of girlfriends who came and knocked on the door almost every day asking to play with her. Whenever Kelley tried to play with Kathryn and her friends, they would tell him to go away, and Kathryn would yell, "Mother, make Kelley go away and leave us alone!"

Kelley's baby brother, Nick, on the other hand, always seemed to be in Mommy's arms—getting fed, or burped, or bathed, or rocked. When Kelley asked his mother to read him a book or push him on the swing, she said, "Kelley, please go play with your toys. The baby's crying and

I can't play with you right now." Kelley thought his mother didn't love him any more, only that stupid baby (and Kathryn with all her important homework and prissy friends).

Kelley wet his pants. His mother said, "Kelley! You're such a big boy. You know how to go to the potty." Kelley sneaked a bottle and climbed into baby Nick's crib. He pretended to be a baby and drank the bottle, even though it tasted pretty nasty. His mother said, "Kelley! What are you doing in there? This crib isn't built for a big boy like you. It's for the baby. Look, your shoes have gotten the sheets all dirty."

Kelley pushed an old lawn chair against a tree and climbed up into the tree. Even though it was very scary, he climbed higher and higher, until he couldn't climb any further. Then he started to cry.

Kelley's mother ran outside when she heard Kelley crying. "Oh, my soul!" she yelled, "Kelley, how in the world did you get up there." She called Kelley's dad and it took two hours and the help of several neighbors to get Kelley safely out of the tree. When his dad got him to the lowest branch, he handed Kelley down to his mother. She hugged him so hard he could hardly breathe, but he didn't mind. He was just glad to be out of that tree.

Kelley's dad sat down on the grass. He was still panting and sweating from all the climbing and worrying. He motioned for Kelley to come sit on his lap. "Son," he said, "your mother and I love you. You're the only Kelley we have. We can't ever get another boy just like you. Kathryn is special and Baby Nick is special, but Kathryn can't ride on my shoulders and Baby Nick can't sing all the words to 'I've Been Working on the Railroad.' You are the only one who can do those things."

He gave Kelley a playful squeeze, and said, "Did you think we could put a penny in a gumball machine and out would roll another Kelley just exactly like you? I could just go down to the grocery store and put a shiny new penny in there and POP, out would come a new Kelley. No siree! We couldn't get a new Kelley that way. You're the only one exactly like you in the whole world."

Kelley sat in his dad's lap, encircled by his dad's strong arms, his face snuggled so close to his dad's chest that he could hear the sound of his dad's big heart thumping, the deep voice, and rumbly laughter. Kelley imagined brightly-colored gumballs with his face on them rolling out of a grocery store gumball machine. He took a deep breath and grinned.

Feeling ignored is far more painful and frightening for young children than being in trouble and having everyone angry or upset. All human beings need to feel a sense of belonging, to feel that they are wanted and needed. If a child feels unwanted or left out, he may not be able to cooperate and follow rules.

Discouragement

Fiona's family moved to a new neighborhood. In her old school, she had already started second grade and really liked the teacher there. She made good marks on her school work, and the teacher often let her help other children when her own work was finished. The teacher especially praised Fiona for her careful block printing and often put Fiona's papers on the bulletin board for all to see.

In her new school, however, Fiona didn't think the new teacher, Miss Crane, was very happy to have her in class. On the first day she attended the new school, Miss Crane acted annoyed. Fiona heard her complain bitterly to another teacher about having to take a student from a different school district in the middle of the year. When Fiona began carefully printing her name in the new workbook Miss Crane gave her, Miss Crane snapped, "Young lady, in this school, second graders do not print! We write in cursive."

Fiona hung her head and stared at her feet, wondering what cursive was. She knew she had heard her mother say many times that she did not like cursing at all. She wondered if her mother would approve of Miss Crane (with her long, blood-red fingernails, bright purple eye-shadow, and high heels).

Miss Crane gave Fiona a little workbook filled with grownup writing and pale-blue straight and dotted lines. She said, "I don't have time to teach you everything I've already gone over with the rest of the class. Just go through this workbook and write the words on each page like the ones in the examples. I don't ever want to see you doing printing in this class again. Do you understand?"

Fiona sat at the back of the room by herself, feeling terribly dejected, but struggling to copy the weirdly shaped letters in the workbook. Finally, it began to make sense to her that some of the words were made of familiar letters. The letters were just hooked together in a long string, like beads on a necklace. She carefully printed the letters she knew and then tediously connected them to make them look like the examples.

Miss Crane did not like Fiona's work at all. She yelled and told Fiona, "This is not how you write in cursive! You will not be allowed to do another thing until you apply yourself and do this work right. Can't you see how the other children are writing." Fiona was too embarrassed to look around. She hoped none of the other children were staring at her.

Fiona became very quiet at home. She didn't bubble with stories about her day. She stopped looking forward to school and began to have stomach aches almost every morning. She begged her mother to let her stay home. She also seemed unusually irritable and often had angry fights with her sisters and brothers. Her mother wondered if Fiona was ill.

At school, Fiona went to the pencil sharpener every time she thought Miss Crane was looking or walking in her direction. With so much sharpening, the pencil lead was always too pointed so it snapped every time she nervously pressed down on the paper. She erased until she finally wore holes in the sheets of paper in her workbook, which began to look like Swiss cheese and made her work look even more awful. Miss Crane became exasperated with Fiona and began to wonder if Fiona was a slow learner or just a difficult, uncooperative little girl.

Actually, Fiona was not sick, slow, or difficult—just very, very discouraged. Her self-esteem had slipped, leaving her vulnerable and disorganized and not at all able to do competent school work, make friends, or live up to teacher expectations. Being harshly criticized and "put down" makes it harder, not easier, for a child to accomplish difficult tasks.

Frustration

Benny was two years old. Hardly a day went by without his mother, Virginia, pointing out to someone that he was a "typical terrible two." He vacillated between acting like a baby and trying to act like a grownup. He whined, "Me do it," whenever his mother tried to tie his shoes. When Virginia became exasperated with him over the shoelaces, she said, "Okay, you tie them." Benny didn't know how to tie them, but he stubbornly worked for fifteen minutes, twisting the laces into a scrambled mass of knots.

Virginia said, "Now look what you've done. I told you that you didn't know how to tie them. Be still so I can get these knots out and tie them right." Benny kicked and fought hard to keep his mother from touching his shoes. She finally spanked him to make him let go of his shoes, so that she could tie them.

Even though Virginia was a single mother with a demanding job and classes two nights a week, she kept her apartment perfectly clean and went to garage sales and resale shops on weekends to see to it that Benny had all the toys and clothes a toddler could need. Every day he was dropped at his child-care center looking freshly scrubbed and starched, with every hair in place.

When Virginia got Benny home on the weekday evenings that she didn't have to go to class, she always had a lot of work facing her. She usually put Benny on the floor and told him to play with his basket of toys while she cooked, cleaned, and studied. Most often, Benny abandoned the toys and followed his mother around getting into her schoolbooks or the kitchen cabinets and making messes. When her patience with him wore thin, she would smack his hand saying "no" or give him a firm swat on the bottom.

Tension built in their little household between the busy, frazzled mother and the clingy, insistent toddler. At his child-care center, Benny began biting other children when they refused to give him a toy or let him have a turn on the tricycle. Even being made to sit on the "thinking chair" for a "time-out" by his teachers seemed to have absolutely no effect on his biting. In fact, it actually seemed to make him more stubborn and agitated.

One day Benny had been in trouble several times and he was sitting by himself playing with a Jack-in-the-Box. He cranked the tiny handle and listened to the tune as it played "Around and around the cobbler's bench the monkey chased the weasel . . . " until out popped the little clown.

Benny watched attentively, then tried to push the little clown back into the box to close the lid so that he could do it again. He pushed the little clown's head down into the box and mashed hard on the lid, but the toy clown's two little flat, plastic hands were sticking out and the lid would not close. Benny pushed on the lid as hard as he could, but his hand slipped and the little clown popped back out. Benny glared at the uncooperative toy clown and then bent down and bit the little clown's hand. Benny bit so long and hard that his whole body shook with the effort and he left a clear imprint of his teeth on the plastic hand.

Much of Benny's aggression probably stemmed from the stress and pressure he encountered in his daily life. His mother, Virginia, had a lot of frustration building up in her as she tried to survive financially and emotionally as a single parent, a working mother of a toddler, and a student. She felt frustrated in her efforts to be a perfect mother while also trying to deal with her own personal and social needs. Benny "caught" some of her stress like a contagious illness. He didn't know why he felt so tense and stubborn all the time, and he didn't know how to make the feelings go away.

Modern-day stress is a very real source of difficulty for many children and families. Children can absorb stress unknowingly from their parents and caregivers, or develop stress symptoms directly from their own life styles. Today, there are children who, from earliest childhood, spend their days going from classroom to tutoring to individual lessons to social events, virtually every day from dawn to dusk. Whatever the cause of stress, its symptoms often include inappropriate behavior (along with health, appetite, and concentration problems).

Rebellion

Coach Sam, a tall, muscular nineteen-year-old, was hired as the gymnastics instructor in a large, inner-city community center that provided after-school care for six- through twelve-year-olds. His childhood dreams of reaching the Olympics were dashed by a troublesome back injury, and he found himself teaching gymnastics to small children— something he never particularly wanted to do.

He decided that in order to create discipline, he would start from the very beginning with his class by being very tough and demanding. He assembled his group of first-, second-, and third-graders on the floor, and, towering in front of them with his hands on his hips, announced in a booming voice, "If you talk without my permission, you're out of here. If you don't pay attention and follow my instructions, you're out of here. And, if you even think about being lazy or careless, you're history. Is that understood?" The children chorused back in unison, "Yes, Coach."

At first the children seemed very intimidated by Coach Sam and did everything he said. They were serious and attentive and jumped when he said jump. Gradually, their obedience became more and more strained. Coach Sam never praised the children's accomplishments other than to make a curt comment such as, "Well, finally you're paying attention." He was, however, very quick to mete out caustic criticism such as, "If that's the best you can do, just go sit by the wall. You're not worth me wasting my time." These comments hurt, and the children grew to dislike Coach Sam intensely.

They began to do little things when Coach Sam's back was turned. It became a game for them to see if they could break rules without getting caught. They smuggled candy and gum into the gym. They giggled and whispered whenever Coach Sam tried to give individual attention to a child. Coach Sam yelled and threatened and punished, but the children continued to become even more open in their unruliness.

The children wondered why Coach Sam so frequently threatened to kick them out of class but never followed through on the threat. They didn't know that he lacked the authority to expel students from class. They did, however, begin to recognize that most of his threats were empty gestures.

In his annoyance and frustration, Coach Sam became colder and more demanding with the children. They became more callous and uncooperative with him. Coach Sam regularly punished children by making them sit by a wall for long periods. Some of the children were sent to sit by the wall so often that they almost never were allowed to participate. They found ways to use their "sitting" time to create more mischief and disruption for Coach Sam. They expressed their dislike of him and his tactics by causing him endless frustration and interruption. Several children even talked their parents into letting them walk home after school and stay alone rather than go to the community-center program at all.

One day, the children in the gymnastics class staged an outright mutiny. They were totally out of control in spite of Coach Sam's yelling and threatening. He ordered a little girl who seemed to be a ring leader to "go sit by the wall for the rest of class." She yelled back, "You can't make me! You're not my Mother!" Several other children joined in the confrontation, shouting, "That's right, you can't make me either!"

Coach Sam was filled with feelings of rage and helplessness. He knew he would be fired instantly if he struck any of the children, but he was overwhelmed with the urge to show them he had control over them. If he couldn't use physical force to control them, then he simply didn't know how to maintain discipline and order. Coach Sam didn't know that positive discipline can best be achieved by establishing an atmosphere of fairness, trust, honesty, and mutual respect—not by trying to create fear and submission.

Figure 6–8 Feelings of discouragement cause children to be less, rather than more, cooperative. *(Photo courtesy of Cynde Miller, Montessori Country Day School)*

The stage is set for rebellion when:

- Children feel anger and contempt, rather than affection and respect, for the authority figures in their lives who set and enforce rules.
- A situation exists in which it is overly difficult for children to abide by specific rules or live up to expectations.
- Children realize that rules are just hollow threats that will not be consistently or fairly enforced.
- Children reach such a point of discouragement that they feel they are in so much trouble that nothing else they do can make things any worse for them.

These conditions not only trigger rebellion in young children, but, in a more general way, are the same kinds of conditions that trigger rebellion and defiance of law and order in segments of adult populations in society. Alienation, discouragement, and outrage at inequity are not feelings limited to adults, but on a much smaller scale, also tempt children to defy authority in spite of the risk of punishment.

SUMMARY

The process by which children learn acceptable behavior is called socialization. Over the first few years of life, children gradually develop self-control and learn how to get along with others and how to follow the accepted rules of their family and community.

Positive child guidance requires that adults gauge their reaction to a child's inappropriate behavior by looking at the child's ability level, the severity and intent of the behavior, as well as possible reasons for the behavior.

We can loosely define inappropriate behavior as any behavior that is not reasonably in the best interest of the child, other people, or things in the environment. The word inappropriate does not suggest fault or blame, but instead simply implies that a behavior is not seen as a worthwhile or desirable action in a specific situation.

When children demonstrate a compulsive and chronic pattern of very inappropriate or self-destructive behavior, the behavior can be termed *dysfunctional*.

Adult-centered definitions of misbehavior focus on the effect a child's behavior has on the adult. In contrast, a child-centered definition of misbehavior focuses on the ability level, motives, and long-term well-being of the child in evaluating the appropriateness or inappropriateness of actions.

A critical priority for parents, schools, communities, even entire countries, is the moral development of their children and future citizens. Morality is the ability to distinguish right from wrong and to act accordingly. Moral development is the process by which human beings learn to monitor their own actions and to decide whether a tempting behavior is a "good" or "bad" thing to do and, then, to inhibit inappropriate impulses.

As children observe adult behaviors and experience the cause-and-effect sequences that are a part of interacting with others, they internalize or adopt the character attributes and ethical standards of the important role models in their lives. Attachment, love, and respect for an adult trigger the child's internalization of that adult's values. When a child internalized, or accepts as his own, the standards of his adult role models, he begins to experience the emotional component of morality, moral affect.

Two specific child-rearing practices are known to help children internalize values and prosocial moral judgment. These are: nurturing and affectionate caregiver behavior, and consistency in explaining the reasons for rules and commands.

Another important component of moral development is moral reasoning, the thinking processes that guide people in deciding what is or is not moral behavior.

Kohlberg's three levels of moral development are:

• Preconventional morality
• Conventional morality
• Postconventional morality

One distinct characteristic of more advanced levels of moral reasoning is one's eventual ability to consider motivation and intention when evaluating the outcome of a behavior. Adults must always take into account the motivations and intentions behind children's undesirable behaviors. We must look at the many causes of misbehavior, in order to have a chance to prevent inappropriate behavior.

Sometimes children's misbehavior is the direct result of inappropriate expectations on the part of adults. Sometimes children misunderstand what is expected of them. Sometimes it seems that children really want to abide by an adult's request, but just can't manage the self-control needed to accomplish what the adult expects. The excitement of being in a group setting may make it particularly difficult for a child to pay attention to an adult.

Boredom, especially when coupled with lax supervision, is an open invitation to inappropriate behavior. Fatigue or anything that causes discomfort can cause children to lose control and act aggressively, defy rules, or behave inappropriately. Being hungry, cold, hot, sick, or hurt are all reasons for children to be cranky and uncooperative.

Feeling ignored is far more painful and frightening for young children than being in trouble and having everyone angry or upset. All human beings need to feel a sense of belonging, to feel that they are wanted and needed. If a child feels unwanted or left out, she may not be able to cooperate and follow rules.

When a child's self-esteem is eroded by overwhelming discouragement, he cannot work productively, make friends, or live up to adult expectations. Being harshly criticized and "put down" makes it harder, not easier, for a child to accomplish difficult tasks.

Stress is a very real source of difficulty for many children and families. Children can develop stress symptoms from their own life styles or just absorb the stress unknowingly from their parents and caregivers. The symptoms of stress can include unhappiness, poor health, and inappropriate behavior.

The stage is set for rebellion when: first, a situation exists in which it is very difficult for a child to abide by an adult's expectations, and, second, the child reaches a point where he feels that he is already in so much trouble that nothing else he does can make things any worse than they already are.

Children need to know that adults will never give up caring about them and seeing that they do the right things.

PRACTICAL APPLICATION/DISCUSSION

Is a "Really Good Spanking" Really Good?

Edna and Wilbert stopped at a neighborhood fast-food restaurant for a quick hamburger on Saturday afternoon. The place was buzzing with activity, and children of all ages were everywhere. Edna and Wilbert had no children of their own, but they watched in amazement as many different types of adults talked to, played with, and reprimanded children.

Wilbert was especially curious about one harried woman who seemed to be in charge of a half-dozen youngsters. One of the little girls shook salt into her hand, licked it, then laughed as she brushed her salty hands over the children near her. They shrieked with laughter as they dodged the salt, throwing napkins to defend themselves. The woman looked sternly at them and threatened to make them sit in the car if they didn't settle down.

Wilbert leaned over and whispered to Edna, "What those children need is a really good spanking!"

QUESTIONS FOR DISCUSSION

1. What could be some possible reasons the children Wilbert was watching were behaving the way they were?
2. Why do you suppose Wilbert believed spanking would be helpful?
3. What do you think would be the most effective and appropriate thing for the woman to do in the situation described above?

Section 4

How Can I Resolve Problems?

Figure 7–1 Effective guidance depends on positive communication. (*Photo courtesy of Cynde Miller, Montessori Country Day School*)

7
Positive Communication

OBJECTIVES
This chapter will assist you in:

- Identifying effective listening strategies.
- Addressing feelings and emotions underlying communication.
- Recognizing the rationale for positive statements of instruction.
- Listing the characteristics of assertive communication.

- Listing the characteristics of nonproductive communication.
- Discussing strategies for positive confrontation.

TYPES OF COMMUNICATION

Positive communication is like a dance filled with expressive and responsive give and take. Children begin this interactive dance early in life, but effective communication skills are acquired gradually over many years. Children can best learn to communicate effectively by imitating and interacting with adults who model well. They set an example for and participate with children in both conversational roles, speaking and listening—leading and following.

When does communication begin? The first semblance of communication begins before birth when the fetus hears the muffled tones of his or her mother's voice. At birth, the auditory physiology of infants is relatively well developed and they may turn toward or startle at sounds and may even be able to distinguish their mother's voice from that of another female (DeCasper & Fifer, 1980). Although newborns have not yet developed any concept of words or grammatical meanings, they respond attentively to the sounds of speech (Eisenberg, 1976; Kuhl, 1981).

One-day-old infants move their bodies in rhythm to the sounds of a caregiver's speech (Condon & Sander, 1974). One-month-olds are able to discriminate between certain vowel sounds (Trehub, 1973). In time babies learn to mimic components of adult communication—inflection, intonation, facial expression, and timing as well as the give-and-take of dialogue.

Adult Assistance of Early Communication Skills

From the time children are infants, adults should both lead and follow in communication with them. An adult may lead by talking to an infant in a way that is sensitive to the baby's mood and attention span. An infant will participate in this interaction by watching and responding as the adult speaks and then, when the interaction becomes too intense and tiring, by looking away, grimacing, or yawning to signal fatigue and the need for a time out (Brazelton, Koslowski, and Main, 1974; Stern, 1974; and Field, 1982).

A sensitive adult will follow the baby's lead by being quiet until after the baby rests for a few seconds and then looks back indicating that he or she is ready to interact again. The adult may also follow the infant by waiting for the infant to make some sound and, then,

Figure 7–2 The beginnings of communication take place in infancy.

repeating the baby's gurgling, cooing, or babbling. This form of baby-talk, in which the baby leads, is very useful for helping babies get a sense of conversational give and take long before they are able to say or understand any words (Bruner, 1978a, 1978b).

When adults pace their interactions with infants so that a specific infant behavior elicits a predictable adult response, infants begin to learn that their environment is controllable and predictable, which increases their motivation for involvement in surroundings and stimulates learning. Infants who sense that they are powerless over interactions may become distressed, irritable, or passive and withdrawn (Watson, 1973)—emotional states that are not productive for learning.

Older babies learn to look back and forth between an object and a caregiver; grunting, pointing, or reaching to indicate desire for the object (Harding and Golinkoff, 1979). This intentional communication reflects the child's growing awareness that he or she can successfully bring about a desired action by communicating with adults. Well-developing toddlers have the rudiments of conversation—meaningful words, intonation, inflection, facial expression, and gesture—but sometimes the child's speech may be very difficult to understand. An adult who is tactful will find ways to avoid undue insistence that toddlers repeat themselves. A positive and supportive response to children's early attempts at speech will encourage continued effort (Hess and Shipman, 1967). Excessive correcting or prodding discourages further practice. Even after two-year-olds master many of the words and phrases of the language, they will need a bit of gentle prompting to carry on a dialogue. Adults can help by asking simple questions (for example, "Is this your big Teddy bear? What is your Teddy bear's name?") to maintain the child's active participation in a conversation (Kaye, 1982).

Often, toddlers seem oblivious to the notion that one should speak only when a listener is present. One- and two-year-olds sometimes carry on animated self-talk while engaging in solitary play (Weiss and Lillywhite, 1976). In fact, toddlers may stare blankly and silently when urged to talk, and jabber freely later when alone or with a very trusted caregiver. Toddlers who are new to a group-care setting may attend for weeks or months before trying to communicate verbally with a nursery-school teacher, even though parents report that they talk a great deal at home with family members.

Three- and four-year-olds gain the vocabulary needed to understand and express many ideas and feelings, and they become more concerned that there is an audience present for conversations. A preschooler who thinks an adult is not listening may move directly into the adult's line of vision or may even try to hold the adult's face to keep the adult from looking away. However, it is not uncommon for two preschoolers to be looking straight at each other, chatting excitedly at the same time without either of them seeming to notice that neither is listening. Preschoolers also talk to inanimate objects such as stuffed animals and television characters without seeming to be bothered that these objects are not very responsive listeners.

School-aged children become more refined in their communication. They finally recognize that communicators must take turns listening and speaking, in order for anyone to be heard. Their growing vocabulary and maturity increase their capacity. Toddlers and younger preschoolers tend to be physical in their expression of feelings. Anger may be expressed by biting or hitting, and affection by bear hugs and moist kisses. School-agers use words more expertly to express affection or to lash out when they feel angry. They tend to use insults, threats, or name calling to express anger and verbal promises of friendship to show affection. Although school-agers are no longer as sensitive to imitation as younger children, who seem to absorb everything they see, school-agers are still likely to emulate, and, thus, be influenced by, adults and children they admire (Bandura, 1977).

Why is positive, mutual communication important for child guidance? As children develop and their communication style changes from stage to stage, adults must recognize and adapt to the various limitations of children in order to guide them toward effective communication. The achievement of effective child guidance really hinges on the achievement of mutual communication. The ultimate goal of positive discipline is not just to control or manipulate children *externally* but rather to stimulate *inner* control based on responsibility and respect for the rights of others. This inner control depends on an understanding of the needs and expectations of oneself and others, gained through open, honest dialogue.

Preparing children to function as adults in a democratic political system requires that children become competent communicators. In an autocracy, citizens can blindly and ignorantly follow leaders without ever discussing or questioning commands. For a democracy to work, citizens must accept responsibility to grasp, understand, and take a stand on various issues. These goals are achieved by communication—listening, reading, discussing, and so forth.

The most effective tools for children to learn communication skills are modeling and practicing. Children learn effective skills as they watch, listen to, and interact with consistent adults who set a good example. Children are able to make those skills a part of their repertoire by practicing again and again the words and interactions they have observed. Therefore, adults who care for and teach children need well-developed communication skills. These skills help them to:

- Understand and interpret children's needs accurately.
- Clearly express expectations to children.
- Teach effective communication to children by modeling.

Adults often complain that children don't listen. The view presented here proposes that children be taught effective communication skills

Figure 7–3 Children learn to listen and to express their feelings and ideas when they are helped by patient, nurturing adults.

through exposure to capable models and by participation in appropriate interactions.

EFFECTIVE LISTENING

Randall pulls his chair up to the table close to his teacher and spreads out a large sheet of drawing paper and an assortment of crayons. He says, "Hi, Miss Katie. I'm gonna color me a big picture."

Miss Katie glances at him and smiles briefly, saying, "Umm humm, that's nice." Miss Katie's attention is focused on a group of children playing across the room. She doesn't seem to notice Randall as he repeats, "Look, Miss Katie, look here!"

Finally, Randall tugs at her sleeve and says, "Look at this. I'm drawing great big mountains. My daddy took me camping and I found lots of rocks. Wanna see my real mountain rocks?"

Randall jumps up from his chair and begins emptying his pockets onto the drawing paper.

Miss Katie suddenly sees his small pile of rocks and pebbles. She says in a stern voice, "Randall! What is all this? Get these dirty rocks off here. Go throw them in the trash. You can't color with rocks all over your paper."

Randall stammers, "But, but . . ." as tears fill his eyes. Miss Katie insists, "Randall, would you quit making such a fuss and just do what I said."

Randall hangs his head and drags his feet as he slowly shuffles across the room to the trash can. One-by-one he ceremoniously drops his pebbles, his "real mountain rocks," into the trash.

Miss Katie didn't listen.

How can attentive listening nurture the child's developing sense of self? One of the greatest needs children have is the need for attention, recognition, and a sense of belonging. If a child is routinely ignored, he or she may begin to feel invisible. Much that is called misbehavior is simply an attempt by a child to become visible—one way or another. A child who does not feel a sense of belonging may gradually become alienated, rebellious, or withdrawn. The more sure a child is that he or she is an accepted member of a group, the more confident and cooperative that child will be.

Adults can indicate their recognition and acceptance of a child by listening well. Attentive listening includes:

- Maintaining eye contact.
- Giving relevant nonverbal gestures such as nodding, smiling, and appropriate touching.

- Giving relevant verbal responses to draw out and encourage the child to continue.
- Waiting patiently for the child to complete what he or she is saying, without rushing the child or trying to finish the child's sentences.

This polite, attentive listening not only gives children the confident feeling that what they have to say is important enough for the adult to listen, but also teaches children by modeling how they should listen to others. More directly, this careful listening will help the adult to hear, interpret, and respond accurately to children's fundamental needs.

Three Basic Human Needs Underlying Requests for Help

Gazda (et al., 1984) defines three needs that are at the heart of communications indicating a desire for some kind of response, or help. Adults and children have the same basic human urge to get their social, emotional, intellectual, and physical needs met. Young children (and sometimes older children and adults) function at an unconscious level in which they react to a vague feeling of need, but may not recognize or understand that need. There are an infinite number of complicated ways that people of all ages approach others to get help, but at the bottom of all that complexity are three simple human needs. These three needs are expressed as requests for:

Figure 7–4 "Nobody will play with me."

- Action or information—Please do this. Please tell me this.
- Understanding and attention—Please listen and show concern for me.
- Inappropriate interaction—Please let me cling, whine, complain, undermine, etc.

Time, effort, and practice are required if one is to become skilled at recognizing the underlying needs hidden in everyday communications. A question such as, "Where is my Mommy?," may be a simple request for information, or it may be an emotion-packed request for understanding and attention by a child who knows very well where Mommy is. A major source of miscommunication is the tendency of persons in the helping role to jump to the wrong conclusion and respond in a way that does not meet the real need of the person requesting help.

The following sections will give strategies for identifying and responding to expressed needs. These strategies are not intended as gimmicks or as a bag-of-tricks to manipulate children's behavior, but as a respectful and effective way of communicating with children and adults. As previously stressed, children learn by modeling. Children will quickly recognize an adult who is snide and sarcastic with other adults but artificially sweet or patronizing with children. The adults in homes and early-childhood programs set the emotional tone for personal relationships. The communication method presented here can be most effective only if applied both to adult/adult and adult/child interactions.

The phrase "children are people too" has become such a cliche that the significance of its meaning is lost. Children really are people who deserve the same dignity and human rights as anyone else. Children's perceptions are different, their logic and experience are limited, and their needs, roles, and responsibilities are not the same as those of adults, but they can definitely feel the sting of humiliation and the pain of rejection. Most adults can remember in vivid detail some painful experience that occurred early in their childhoods. And yet, there is a persistent folk belief that children's feelings don't really merit much consideration. Every baby or child is, in fact, the very same person who will someday be a teacher, senator, artist, or carpenter. The events of that person's early childhood will be an integral part of his or her character and personality, whether or not these events are consciously remembered.

Children learn as if by osmosis. They absorb information simply by living day-to-day in an environment. Effective listening is not only a learning objective for children but also a necessary component of children's daily lives, to be used directly with children as well as among the various adults who interact with children. For example, an ancient proverb says:

Figure 7–5 Effective listening is an important part of daily life.

> Tell me and I forget;
> Show me and I remember;
> Let me experience for myself and I understand.

Children learn to listen well by experiencing respectful listening as a regular part of daily life. Simply telling children to listen is not enough.

Appropriate Responses to Requests for Action or Information

Joey, an eighteen-month-old, sits on a small stool, rocking and crying, "Beah, beah, ma beah."

Miss Rosario squats beside him and gently coaxes him to show her what he wants. Joey quickly leads her to the bathroom. He stretches his arm toward a high shelf where diaper bags are kept. Urgently, he opens and closes his hand pleading, "Beah, beah." Miss Rosario takes his diaper bag from the shelf. Immediately she sees that Joey's fuzzy white teddy bear is inside. She says, "Oh, you want your bear. Is that right, Joey, bear?"

Joey nods and says, "Ma beah." He hugs his bear and toddles away dragging it by one leg.

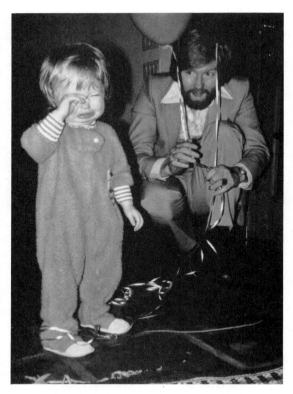

Figure 7–6 Toddlers may not be able to express their feelings in words. *(Photo courtesy of Dr. Sharlene Peters)*

Even though Miss Rosario couldn't understand Joey's words, she recognized that Joey was requesting action from her.

People who work with young children spend a great deal of time responding to requests for action or information. Some requests are straightforward and simple to understand. "Is it time for snack yet?" or, "Tie my shoe, please." Other requests, like Joey's request for his bear, are difficult to interpret. Requests may also be hidden or masked. What sounds like a simple statement may really be intended as a request for action. "I can't sleep," may really mean, "Come sit by me and read me a story." A comment may really mask a request for information. "Latecia's mama is too fat," may really mean, "Latecia told me there is a baby in her mama's tummy, and I am very frightened and confused."

Since children do not have fully developed communication skills, adults must accept additional responsibility for keeping the channels of communication open and clear.

Five-year-old Malika stands on the playground beside her teacher, Mrs. Johnson. She sees a caterpillar crawling toward her and starts to shriek. Mrs. Johnson bends down and gently allows the fuzzy caterpillar to crawl onto a leaf she is holding. Malika screams, "It's gonna kill you! Is it gonna kill you?"

Mrs. Johnson says, "No, Malika. This little caterpillar has a very tiny mouth and no teeth and no poison. He likes to eat leaves. When he gets very fat, he will wrap himself in a cocoon that is like a little blanket. While he is inside, he will change into a beautiful butterfly. Then, after a long time, that beautiful butterfly will come out of the cocoon and fly away."

Mrs. Johnson helps Malika make a suitable home for the caterpillar in a large jar. Later, at circle time, she reads a book called *The Very Hungry Caterpillar*.

Mrs. Johnson redirected Malika's fear of bugs to curiosity about science and nature. Mrs. Johnson recognized that underneath Malika's shrieking and screaming was a need for information. Mrs. Johnson responded to a hidden request for information.

After a birthday party, four-year-old Seth sees that his mother is wrapping leftover cake. He says, "Mommy, I want more cake, please." His mother says, "No, Seth. No more cake." Seth begs, "Please, I'm hungry. I want more cake."

Seth's mother bends down to Seth's eye level and takes his hand gently. In a sympathetic voice, she says, "Seth, I understand that you really want more cake. That cake tasted great, didn't it? But, a lot of cake is not good for you. I love you and I want you to have a healthy body and healthy teeth, so I have to say no. No more cake."

Seth pulls his hand away, bouncing up and down, whining and flapping his arms like an angry old hen (the preschooler's dance of frustration and impending tantrum). Seth's mother doesn't flinch a muscle. In a very calm tone she says, "It's okay to feel angry. Sometimes I feel angry too. Sometimes I get so angry I feel like crying. Sometimes I feel so bad that I just need a hug."

Without looking at her face, Seth climbs into his mother's arms and gets a long hug. Suddenly, he brightens and says, "How 'bout apples. They make you get strong teeth like Superman."

His mom smiles, "You know, Seth, that sounds like a great idea."

Seth's mother clearly understood her son's request for action, but she also knew that providing what he wanted was not in his best interest. Seth's mother loved him enough to say "no" to his request and enough to accept an appropriate compromise. Adults are ultimately responsible for the health, safety, and welfare of children in their care. Complying with potentially harmful or unfair requests hurts children and, eventually, damages adult/child trust and respect. Sometimes adults are tempted to comply with questionable requests in order to avoid conflict or in a misguided attempt to win the child's affection.

Not only did Seth's mother stand firm in making the decision that is in Seth's best interest, but she also taught a very valuable lesson. Her gentle strength showed Seth an example of self-discipline, doing the right thing even though it would be easier to give in and avoid a fuss. Her calm, patient persistence, even when he threatened a tantrum, showed him an appropriate example of coping with a stressful situation. (Some adults reinforce children's tantrums by pitching tantrums of their own.) And, most importantly, her sensitive understanding of his feelings helps him know that he is loved and respected, even while a limit is being enforced.

Appropriate Responses to Requests for Understanding and Attention

Some requests may appear on the surface to be requests for action or information, but they are not. The real need at the core of this type of communication is for someone to listen and show interest.

Mr. Wilke watches as his kindergarteners work and play in various learning centers. Angelica, a shy five-year-old, is alone in the art center. As Mr. Wilke walks past, she calls out, "Mr. Wilke, I need some help." He smiles and perches his tall frame on the little chair beside her. Angelica hands him her paper and plastic scissors and says, "Help me cut. I don't know how to."

Mr. Wilke always makes careful observations and keeps records of his students' levels of skill with learning-center materials. He feels sure that Angelica does know how to use scissors. He looks at the situation and mentally rules out possibilities such as broken scissors or thick paper that is too difficult. He decides that Angelica may not really be seeking action (cutting for her) or information (teaching her how to cut) but, instead, seeking understanding and attention.

Mr. Wilke knows it will not help Angelica to embarrass her by confronting her in a harsh way. He also knows that he doesn't want to reinforce her perception that she can get the attention she needs by feigning incompetence. He says, "Sometimes cutting seems really hard, doesn't it?" He gently pats her shoulder and adds, "Would you like for me to sit beside you while you try cutting this yellow paper?" Angelica eagerly cuts her jagged paper while Mr. Wilke watches attentively. After a few minutes, as he gets up to leave, he says, "Angelica, you must really feel proud that you cut that out all by yourself."

Mr. Wilke was correct in his assumption that Angelica was really requesting understanding and attention. Seeking attention is not a perverse behavior that must always be extinguished in children. Hu-

Figure 7–7 Sometimes all that's needed is a little understanding and attention. *(Photo courtesy of Patty Knowlton)*

man beings are primarily social beings. We all need attention from others in order to thrive. The goal with young children is not to stop attention-getting behaviors, but to teach children how to get an appropriate amount of attention in a socially-acceptable manner.

If Mr. Wilke observed that Angelica continued in a pattern of pretending ineptness to get attention (see requests for dependency and inappropriate interaction), it might be necessary for Mr. Wilke, privately and tactfully, to confront her behavior by saying, "Angelica, you seem to need some attention. It's okay to need attention. Please say, 'Mr. Wilke, I feel lonely. I need some attention.' That will help me know exactly what you need."

In an environment in which needs are respected, children come to know that it is okay to have needs and feelings. Sometimes adults inadvertently give children the impression that their needs or emotions make adults angry. This problem often occurs when the adults have a difficult time getting their own emotional needs met.

A particularly helpful strategy for dealing with feelings and needs honestly and respectfully is through a technique called *active listening* (it is also sometimes referred to as reflective listening, empathetic listening, or responsive listening). In active listening, the listener refrains from lecturing, advising, or informing. She simply listens and reflects back the feelings she perceives from seeing and hearing the other person. This gives the listener plenty of time to really hear the other person, to let the other person know that her feelings and needs are important and respected, and to think of ways to help the person resolve his problem.

Jenny, who directs an infant/toddler child-care program, treats the teaching and caring staff with the same respect and dignity she expects them to extend to the babies. She knows that even infants and toddlers are unconsciously absorbing the behaviors around them. She also knows that caring for little ones can sometimes be incredibly stressful.

Fred, a four-month-old whose mother just returned to work from her maternity leave, is crying. He has attended the child-care program for only a few days and he has cried most of the time. Kate, his primary caregiver, tried everything she knows to calm him. She walked him, patted him, rocked him, and is at the end of her patience.

Kate storms into the director's office and demands, "What is that child's problem? Nothing I do works. What am I supposed to do?" Luckily, Jenny realizes that Kate is not really seeking action or information. What Kate needs most is understanding, so Jenny offers her a chair and closes the door for privacy. Instead of focusing on solving baby Fred's problem, Jenny focuses on hearing and understanding Kate's feelings.

In a caring voice, Jenny says, "Kate, it sounds like you're really frustrated."

"You bet I am," replies Kate, "I don't think I can deal with his crying another minute. I don't even know if I ought to work with children. I am really at my wit's end."

Wisely, Jenny refrains from making judgments, giving information, or taking action. Gazda (et al., 1984, p. 11) notes that rushing to give a helpee a quick solution is "cheap and dirty" advice, because the helper has not had a chance to learn all the facts. If one's problems were so easy to solve that an "off the top of the head" solution were adequate, one would wonder why the person suffering the problem hadn't already thought of it.

Instead of rushing to tell Kate why she has a problem or how to solve it, Jenny simply mirrors to Kate (through active listening) what she hears Kate saying. She responds with nonjudgmental active (or reflective) listening statements that begin with phrases such as:

- What I'm hearing you say is . . .

- In other words, you are saying that . . .
- It sounds as if you feel . . .

Jenny says, "Kate, it sounds like what you're saying is that you're feeling so frustrated that you're afraid you've lost your patience. You seem to be wondering if you're really cut out to work with children."

A calmness settles over Kate as she realizes that she is not being judged or told what to do but that her director is really listening and understanding what she is saying. She thinks for a moment and says, "I guess I'm just having a bad day. I really do love working with babies. It's just that Fred keeps screaming, no matter what I do."

Jenny leans close and touches Kate's arm. "You know, It sounds like you feel inadequate because you can't stop Fred's crying. I think Fred is lucky to have someone like you to care so much and try so hard to comfort him."

Streams of tears spill down Kate's face. She feels enough trust to let go of her feelings and let everything out that has been bottled inside her. Now that her own needs for understanding and attention are met, she can return to her nursery classroom and try again to meet Fred's needs for understanding and attention.

Even though Fred did not see or hear the adult interaction (and would have been too young to make sense of it if he had), he most certainly will feel and benefit from the calmer, more accepting attitude Kate will have when she returns to care for him. Indirectly, by sensing the patience and understanding of his caregiver, Fred will begin learning the coping skills he will need to develop confidence and self-esteem as he grows older.

Response to Requests for Dependency or Inappropriate Interaction

Adults who care for young children often have difficulty knowing where understanding ends and dependency begins. A child begs, "Hold me," "Put my coat on for me," or "Help me finish my puzzle." Many adults struggle to know what is right for the child. Is holding, helping, and nurturing meeting the child's needs or reinforcing a pattern of dependency?

Under usual circumstances, as soon as children are able, they spontaneously break away from various levels of dependence on adults. Toddlers stubbornly resist the hovering care that was necessary to their survival as infants. Adolescents rebel against the close parental attachment that protected them in early childhood.

For most children, achieving independence is the motivating force behind the process of growing up. But this force does not always move

Figure 7–8 "You've skinned your knee—that hurts."

steadily forward. Even highly competent, well-developing children regress from time-to-time and need the security of someone big to depend on. A bit of babying, on infrequent occasions, does little harm to well-developing children. This regression only seems to recharge their energy and desire for independence. But, for chronically dependent children, babying undermines self-esteem and destroys initiative.

In certain situations, children go through a process of actually learning to be helpless (Altenor, Kay, and Richter, 1977; Finkelstein and Ramey, 1977). Some adults have difficulty accepting change and may fail to recognize a child's emerging capabilities. Other adults may inadvertently interfere with children's efforts at learning to function independently because they may simply not understand the process and importance of the development of autonomy.

Children's first efforts to do things by themselves are often messy and fraught with mistakes. Babies learning to feed themselves splatter, smear, and spill food. Toddlers learning to dress themselves put both feet in the same leghole of their training pants. Preschoolers learning to tie their own shoes create inch-long knots in their shoelaces. And, schoolagers learning gardening walk on the seedlings they have just planted. Little mishaps such as these are a necessary part of learning by experience. In a demanding, perfectionist, or punitive atmosphere, where a child begins to fear making mistakes, he or she may learn to avoid risk by becoming passive, by not attempting anything that requires initiative or involves the chance of failure.

Children who have learned to be helpless and dependent need special guidance and support to break away from patterns of dependency. Children sometimes express requests for dependency through such actions as persistent whining, clinging, or *regularly* demanding special favors such as being first in line, sitting in the teacher's lap, or being carried. Indulging these inappropriate requests is not helpful for children.

Solicitation for dependence should be redirected in a way that encourages more appropriate behavior. An infant who whines for help after one half-hearted attempt at reaching a toy needs to be encouraged to try again rather than simply given the toy. A preschooler who whines, feigns exhaustion, and begs for help putting blocks away may respond to a game. "I'll close my eyes. You tell me when to open them, and I'll count how many blocks are on the shelf." Or, a kindergartener who follows the teacher, clinging and asking for help, may need some important responsibility, such as helping a younger child.

In some cases, redirection is not enough. It may be necessary to clearly communicate unwillingness to participate in interactions that indulge or solicit inappropriate dependency, spread gossip, reinforce inordinate complaining, or involve actions that turn adults or children against one another. Gazda (et al., 1984, pp. 38-39) states that, "If you encourage inappropriate behaviors, even by silence, you may lose your opportunity to help and you could unwittingly become a model for negative or hurtful behavior."

Gazda further adds that this rule is easier to preach than to practice, because it is necessary to end the inappropriate interaction without offending the person initiating it. Offending a child or other adult damages trust, closes off communication, and projects an image of haughtiness. The recommended response is a polite but firm refusal to be part of the inappropriateness accompanied by a straightforward, warm, and respectful indication of caring about the person as an individual (Gazda, et al., 1984).

Tactfulness, fairness, and warmth ease the sting of a refusal to participate in an inappropriate interaction. For example, Mr. Hernandez arrives one afternoon and prepares to teach his after-school gymnastics class. Sarah and Cynthia, twin third-graders, eagerly volunteer to help spread mats. As Sarah and Cynthia help, they confide to Mr. Hernandez how much they dislike James, one of the least popular boys in the gymnastics class.

Sarah says, "Ugh! We can't stand James. He's fatter than an elephant." Cynthia chimes in, "Have you ever listened when he laughs. He sort of snorts and makes some weird sound." They giggle uproariously.

Mr. Hernandez values the positive relationship he has with Sarah and Cynthia and does not wish to embarrass them, but he also knows that to smile and say nothing would be tacit approval of their remarks about James. That would be hurtful to James and fails to guide Sarah and Cynthia toward more appropriate behavior.

Mr. Hernandez carefully chooses his words and bends down, touching each girl lightly on the shoulder. He says gently, "I don't feel good talking about James." Then his tone brightens and he deftly changes the subject, "But, you know what, I surely do like all this great help. How about this balance beam, girls? Do you think you both can get at that end and help me move it? Thanks."

Mr. Hernandez has not been judgmental or critical. He simply and politely declined to participate by focusing on his own feelings. The girls probably felt a moment of embarrassment, but they also knew their teacher accepted and cared about them. As a result of this encounter, the girls may become more thoughtful about ridiculing others, not because of an external fear of punishment or chastisement, but from a growing internal sense of right and wrong bolstered by a strong and admired role model in the person of Mr. Hernandez.

Listening and Helping Strategies in the Care of Babies and Toddlers

The complexity of words and sentences must always be adjusted to the level of maturity of one's listener. However, the integrity and content of one's message need not be diluted. Physical actions, facial expression, intonation, and gestures convey a sense of one's message even to an infant.

Mrs. Wang, who cares for infants in her church's Mother's-Day-Out program, hears eleven-month-old Kyle crying. He is banging on a low cabinet door that is locked with a child-guard latch. Mrs. Wang perceives the baby's cry as a request for action. Kyle wants the cabinet door opened. Mrs. Wang tries to distract him with several toys, but he continues to cry and pull at the door.

Mrs. Wang picks Kyle up, kicking and screaming, and carries him to her big rocking chair. She rocks and pats Kyle as she says in a caring voice, "I really understand that you want to explore that cabinet, but the things in there could hurt you. I can't let you play there because I like you and I want to keep you safe."

As Kyle begins to calm down, Mrs. Wang carries him around the nursery, showing him alternative areas to explore and continuing to talk to him. Kyle doesn't understand her words but he definitely can sense her warmth and empathy, and he can sense the firmness of the limit she has set. He may test the limit many more times, but Mrs. Wang's warmth will communicate to him that he is still accepted as a person. Her consistency will communicate to him that limits are sometimes a part of life. She recognizes that babies explore limits because they have a limited capacity to understand or remember rules and because they learn through trial and error. She will refuse Kyle's demands that she open the locked cabinet, but his actions will not change her feelings about him.

Additionally, by talking to Kyle, Mrs. Wang is able to focus her own thoughts and feelings on the situation. She, as well as Kyle, needs to hear the words she has said. By expressing in words the reasons she is doing what she is doing, she feels reassured that she is doing the right thing. Also, by putting her feelings into words, she is able to make sure her facial expression and body language are consistent with the message she wants to convey to Kyle.

Mrs. Wang, knowing that Kyle couldn't really understand her words, might have said instead, "Listen, you little brat, I'm tired of fooling with you. Are you just trying to bug me?" However, it is nearly impossible to say these words in a sincere, warm, and caring way. Mrs. Wang's face and tone would probably have conveyed sarcasm, impatience, and blaming to Kyle. In an unconscious way, he would have absorbed these negative feelings and reflected them in his behavior. Also, words like brat, fooling, and bug are ambiguous cliche words that do not help Kyle learn language. Luckily for Kyle, Mrs. Wang

Figure 7–9 Babies and toddlers pay close attention to an adult's face and tone of voice, even if they don't understand the words that are spoken. *(Photo courtesy of Cynde Miller)*

would not think of behaving rudely to him, any more than she would be rude to anyone else she respected and liked as a person.

ADDRESSING UNDERLYING FEELINGS

Any discussion of communication would be incomplete without a consideration of underlying feelings. Most people who work with children would agree that child care and early-childhood education are emotionally draining occupations. Young children ride an emotional roller coaster. They can go from laughter to tears in the blink of an eye. Responsive adults who are closely involved in the lives of young children are pulled along in the wave of emotions—from the elation of a new discovery to the heart break of a best friend who says, "I hate you."

Children's emotions are real. Before six months, infants are only capable of three undifferentiated emotions: pleasure, wariness (cautiousness), and rage. By nine months the baby has a dramatically increased range of emotional responses. By age three, children have virtually the entire panorama of human emotions (Stroufe, 1979).

An important part of early childhood learning is the child's gradually developing awareness of feelings and the child's growing ability to express those feelings. Very young children react unconsciously. A

Figure 7–10 By nine months of age, babies show a wide range of emotional responses. *(Photo courtesy of Dr. Sharlene Peters)*

toddler may whine and act out in an aggressive way without realizing that he or she is feeling hunger, discomfort, fatigue, etc. Adults play an important role in identifying, labeling, and explaining children's feelings to them. Adults also give children important feedback about certain behaviors by expressing relevant adult feelings.

Discretion must be used in expressing adult feelings. Young children can be overwhelmed if adults unload too much on them, or if the expression is too intense. Simple, clear statements of feeling limited to relevant situations are most helpful. Following is a fill-in-the-blank statement called an "I message" that is very helpful for stating feelings appropriately and in a non-threatening way (Gordon, 1970):

When _____ happens, I feel _____ because _____.

This statement does not contain the word "you." Statements such as, "You make me angry," or "You are hurting my ears with your yelling," may induce an unnecessary feeling of guilt in the child. Positive discipline should bring about responsibility, rather than guilt. It is more helpful to say simply and sincerely, "When there is loud screaming, I feel uncomfortable because the noise hurts my ears. I need for you to use a soft voice." "Biting makes me feel really upset because biting hurts and biting is dangerous. It is okay to bite crackers and apples, but it is never okay to bite people."

Figure 7–11 "When you climb on the fence, I feel worried because I am afraid you could get hurt." *(Photo courtesy of Lynne Aiken)*

If adults consistently use assertive but controlled words to express strong feelings, children will eventually model using words instead of physical attacks to express anger or frustration. A child will also feel more compliant when the adult's anger is focused on the action rather than on the child.

Additionally, adults can clarify and express positive feelings using the same sample sentence. (In positive contexts the word "you" can be included.) For example, "When I see you share a special toy, I feel proud because I know you are growing up." "When the sun is shining, I feel elated because we can go outside and enjoy the grass and trees." "When I discovered that you put every single block away all by yourself, I felt like jumping up and down because I felt so happy and proud."

Positive and negative expressions of feelings can have a powerful impact on a child's behavior, but only when the person expressing those feelings is admired and liked by the child. Neither adults nor children are particularly concerned about the feelings of someone who is not liked or respected. In fact, knowing that a disliked adult's ears hurt with loud noise would stimulate screaming from some children, who may purposely intend to inflict pain or to manipulate attention from the adult.

Helping Children Understand Their Feelings

In the previous section about requests for understanding and attention, nonjudgmental, active (or reflective) listening was described. This kind of listening and responding can assist children in identifying, labeling, and understanding their feelings. A major difference here is that often the child's feelings must be inferred from his or her behavior.

Carolyn is a child-care professional teaching and caring for a group of four-year-olds. As her children come inside for a snack from the playground, she says, "Ummm, I feel hungry. Do you feel hungry, Clay?" Clay agrees and the children expand on Carolyn's expression of hunger. "I am as hungry as a tiger." "I'm so hungry I could eat this whole building." "I'm so hungry I could eat the whole world!"

The children giggle about eating the whole world as they find their seats at the table. Clay rushes to sit by his best friend, Misha, but Ellen has already taken the chair. Clay stamps his foot and complains loudly as he shakes the back of the chair he wants. The child in the chair stubbornly holds on.

Carolyn quickly comes to intervene in the brewing fight. She kneels down at eye level to Clay and says, "You feel angry because someone took the chair you wanted. Can you use words to tell Ellen how you feel?"

Clay shouts, "I want that chair. Gimme it, now!" Ellen grips the chair tighter and ignores him. Carolyn turns to Ellen and says, "Ellen, can you tell Clay how you feel?" Ellen looks at the floor and shakes her head "no." Carolyn asks her, "Would you like me to tell Clay how you feel?" Ellen vigorously nods "yes."

Carolyn says, "Clay, Ellen is feeling very upset because you are shaking her chair and yelling at her. She got here first and she doesn't want you to take her chair away." Clay begins to shake the chair again, so Carolyn firmly removes his hands from the chair. Then, restraining his hands, but with concern and empathy in her voice, Carolyn says, "Clay, I know you feel really frustrated, but you have two choices. You may choose another chair and have a snack, or you may come out in the hall and talk with me until you feel better. What do you choose?"

From experience, Clay knows Carolyn is gentle and caring, but he also knows that she always means what she says. He doesn't relish the idea of throwing a tantrum that will only succeed in delaying his snack.

Carolyn sees a look of indecision on his face and quickly says, "Look, Clay, there is an empty chair right at the end of the table by Joey. Would you like to sit there?" Clay decides that Joey wouldn't be so bad to sit by after all and shuffles along to take a seat.

Carolyn smiles and pats his shoulder.

Confronting Troublesome Feelings

Adlerian psychologists focus on exploring the motives for negative behavior. Dreikurs and Cassel (1972) list four goals of misbehaviors that are based on children's mistaken logic:

- Children who are deprived of opportunities to gain status through useful contributions often seek attention by acting helpless, silly, bratty, artificially charming, lazy, inept, or obnoxious.
- Children who do not feel that they are accepted members of their family or social groups may seek power by acting bossy, rebellious, stubborn, vengeful, or disobedient.
- Children who feel so beaten down that they no longer care about struggling for power retaliate by seeking revenge by hurting others the way they feel hurt. They may injure peers, destroy property, express contempt, distrust others, and defy authority.
- Children who become trapped in passive-destructive forms of attention-getting by being overly criticized may eventually become so discouraged they give up all hope and expect only failure and defeat. They seek only to be left alone. They may be passive, withdrawn, and depressed—paralyzed by feelings of inadequacy and hopelessness.

Dreikurs recommends that older children be confronted in a friendly, noncritical way at a relaxed time rather than during a time of conflict. A caregiver can engage and a child in conversation by exploring the motives for his typical behaviors and tactfully asking the following questions:

• Could it be that you want attention?
• Could it be that you want your own way and hope to be boss?
• Could it be that you want to hurt others as much as you feel hurt by them?
• Could it be that you want to be left alone?

While these questions are not appropriate to ask infants and very young children, adults may find it helpful to run through the list of questions to gain insight into possible unconscious causes of misbehavior in children under three. For children of any age, identifying the underlying feelings that motivate behavior makes it possible to respond to children's emotional well-being, rather than only chasing and eliminating symptomatic misbehaviors.

Once the motive for behavior is diagnosed, adults can better respond to the misbehavior. If attention is the goal of the misbehavior, the caregiver can remove attention as a response for inappropriate

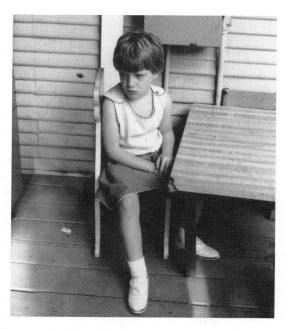

Figure 7–12 Attempting to identify the underlying causes of behavior focuses our attention on the child's emotional well-being.

behaviors and give it bountifully for appropriate or constructive behaviors. If bullying is the goal, adults can extricate themselves from power struggles and allow children to feel respected and responsible. If revenge is the goal, adults can assist children in making friends and experiencing successful accomplishments. If solitude is the goal, adults can offer encouragement, persist in including the child, and find ways to make the child feel worthwhile.

By seeking understanding of behavior rather than blaming for it, adults have an opportunity to open new doors of communication with children. As children mature and develop self-awareness, open lines of communication will help them assume greater responsibility for their own actions and choices. By the time children reach adolescence, it is especially important that they have some conscious awareness of their own motives and goals. It is also essential that open, honest communication is an accepted and routine part of daily life.

POSITIVE INSTRUCTIONS VERSUS NEGATIVE COMMANDS

A key factor in positive communication is the focus on identifying and stating desired behaviors, rather than focusing on inappropriate behaviors. Children and adults tend to respond more cooperatively to positive requests than negative admonitions. For example, a parent would probably feel more responsive to a request from a child-care worker worded, "Please check to see that Kelly has enough diapers for the day," than, "You never bring enough diapers for Kelly." The difference in children's responses to negative and positive commands is stark.

Additionally, toddlers are so limited in their comprehension of language that they tend to hear and respond only to key words in sentences. If an adult tells a toddler, "I do not want you to touch this cake," the toddler may actually hear," Do want touch cake." And of course, because the toddler wants to touch the cake, he or she probably will. The adult could bring about better communication by designating a desired activity to replace touching the cake. The adult could provide paper and crayons at a location away from the cake and say, "Please color on the paper," which the toddler may accurately interpret as, "Color on paper."

Not only do toddlers and young preschoolers have difficulty hearing and interpreting every word of sentences, they also have difficulty thinking about a behavior and then inhibiting that behavior. Thinking and doing are almost inseparable at this stage of development. For example, if an adult says firmly, "No spitting," to a young child who has not yet even thought of spitting, he or she may comprehend both words but, as he or she thinks about not spitting, it is almost inevitable that the child will act out the spitting. The statement, "Don't wet your pants," causes the child to have a mental image of wetting pants, which may trigger urination. The statement, "It is time to use the potty," evokes a mental image of sitting on the toilet, which is desired.

Following is a list of typical negative commands and alternate positive commands:

NEGATIVE COMMANDS	POSITIVE STATEMENTS
Don't run in the hall.	Walk slowly, please.
Don't spill your milk.	Hold your milk with two hands.
Quit poking at Jimmy.	Put your hands in your lap, please.
Shut up.	Please listen quietly.
Stop interrupting me.	It is my turn to talk now.
Don't talk with a full mouth.	Chew and swallow first, then talk.
Quit shoving in line.	Put your arms by your sides.
Stop yelling my name.	Come tap my shoulder, please.

Negative commands are strongly entrenched as habit patterns for many adults. Time, commitment, motivation, and persistence are needed to break any habit pattern, and communication habits are no exception. Many adults find that as they try to improve their communication style, they first begin to hear themselves using ineffective phrases, but can't seem to stop using them. A toddler standing in a puddle with an innocent and surprised look saying, "Go potty," is taking the first tentative step toward changing a habit pattern. An adult who feels guilty about yelling "shut up" to a child may be taking the first step toward consciously controlling and changing an ineffective communication strategy.

CHARACTERISTICS OF ASSERTIVE COMMUNICATION

Communication is always intended to convey a message, just as a radio transmitter is intended to transmit a radio program. In order for the music of a radio program to be heard, the waves sent from the transmitter have to match the receiver equipment in one's radio. The communication transmitted from an adult must match the mental and emotional equipment of the child, or the message will simply not be received.

Children, and adults as well, will close off communication that is incomprehensible, threatening, vague, or rude—like tuning out or turning off a radio with unpleasant static noise. Although one may sometimes feel justified in lecturing or lashing out, there is no value in conveying a message if the message is rejected. The goal here is to have messages accepted and acted on.

Key Factors in Assertive Communication

Simplicity is the first rule for assertive communication. While babies, toddlers, and young children need plenty of opportunities to hear the rhythm and flow of complex adult language, assertive statements should be short and to the point. Decide what needs to be said and say it in as few words as possible. Verbal clutter gets in the way of stating a desired action.

The younger the child, the more essential simplicity becomes. Toddlers need simple two- or three-word sentences such as, "Sit, please," or (if a child has already bitten), "No biting. Biting hurts." Preschoolers need only slightly longer sentences such as, "Apples are for eating, not for throwing," "Please hold your glass with two hands," or, "A chair is for your seat not your feet."

Honesty is essential for assertive communication. Children quickly identify adults who don't really mean what they say. Empty threats are counterproductive. They only teach children that adults cannot be relied on to do what they say, no matter how many times they insist that, "This time I really mean it!" It is never acceptable to lie to children to trick them into compliance. They should be told honestly when a parent is leaving, even if that causes tears. Feeling sad is a natural and healthy response; feeling tricked is not.

Directness helps communicators get right to the point. Rambling, hinting, and insinuating are of little value to adult listeners and are totally lost on children. Instead of saying "The art area is getting pretty sloppy, children," say, "Please pick up all of the scrap paper and put it in the trash can. Thank you. Now get a sponge and wipe the table." Instead of saying, "Let's keep it down now," say, "Please walk softly and speak quietly." Words used with children should be literal words with clearly definable meanings. A phrase such as "You two cut it out now" should mean that scissors and paper are involved.

Tactfulness keeps channels of communication open. Gushing sweetness is usually not any more palatable to young children than it is to adults, but tactfulness and sincerity are greatly appreciated. It is tactful to say, "Your glass may tip off the table. Please push it back away from the edge. Thank you." It is not tactful to say, "Stop being so careless with your glass of milk." It is overly patronizing to say, "Here, sweetheart, let's push our little glass back so we don't spill it, okay honey?" Children can be given affection and kindness without being drowned in cloying sweetness.

Concreteness makes communication clear. Abstractions like goodness and badness can be very confusing to children. The statement that lying is bad, for example, may cause a child to think he or she is a bad person. It is more concrete to say "If you lie, other people may not trust you. They may learn not to believe things you say."

With younger children, concreteness is expressed through actions. It is not concrete to tell a toddler, "Be nice to your friends." A toddler has no real concept of the word nice. It is a vague, value-laden term for which no two adults would have exactly the same definition. A toddler would not know precisely what one does to be nice. It is concrete to repeat, "Touch softly," while demonstrating stroking the friend's arm gently. The toddler can see and comprehend exactly what action is expected.

Respectfulness is an integral part of assertive communication. It is impossible to have open, honest communication with someone for whom one has disgust and disdain. In a democracy, one should have as much respect for the personhood of a garbage collector as for the President, even though each has distinctly different roles and responsibilities. One should have as much respect for the personhood and human rights of a newborn as for any other member of society. Respect for children is expressed by recognizing and protecting their dignity and rights.

A police officer may stop a citizen and issue a penalty that makes the citizen feel very unhappy, but the officer has no right to hurt, humiliate, or threaten the citizen. Respectful adults assertively enforce fair rules without name-calling, teasing, embarrassing, hurting, or bullying. A respectful adult confronts children privately and focuses on improving behaviors rather than on punishing children.

Optimism boosts cooperativeness by sharing hope. A child trying to cope with an assertive adult needs to know that the adult really believes he or she can succeed. Confrontation is softened and made more acceptable by reassurance that problems can indeed be solved. After confronting Jennifer, one might say, "Jennifer, everyone makes mistakes. Our mistakes help us learn. Perhaps tomorrow you can help by reminding the younger children how important it is not to run out of the gate without permission."

Flexibility is necessary to distinguish assertiveness from stubbornness. No matter how firmly one intends to carry out a plan of action, the possibility always exists that additional information could indicate the need for a change in plans. In dealing with young children, consistency is mandatory so that children can make sense of what is expected of them. The need for flexibility, therefore, could be construed as contradictory. Effective, assertive guidance, however, requires that adults provide as much consistency as possible, but also as much flexibility as necessary to make discipline humane and reasonable.

Figure 7–13 Children learn to trust adults who are confident and sincere. *(Photo courtesy of Lynne Aiken)*

Adults must constantly seek a balance between firm, predictable limits and the flexibility to listen, adapt, and compromise appropriately. For example, an adult might firmly refuse to talk about or compromise a stated rule while a child is pitching a tantrum and behaving very inappropriately. Later, however, when the child is calm and able to explain logically her problem with the rule, the adult might decide that justice is best served by bending or eliminating the rule. With a very young child, the adult may rely on direct observations rather than verbal discussions to determine if a rule is fair and reasonable.

Confidence strengthens assertive communication by projecting assurance that what is being said is really meant. Children are especially sensitive to nonverbal signals or cues from facial expression, intonation, body positioning, and the use of hands and feet. Adults who do not really believe children will do what is asked of them project an air of uncertainty and weakness. A clear-eyed look of confidence greatly increases the probability of compliance from children as well as from listeners of any other age. Fidgeting, speaking in a weak or shrill voice, and avoiding eye contact hint to the child that we don't really expect compliance.

When adults say sarcastic things such as "Well, let's see if you can keep from being a little monster, as usual, running around and tearing everything up while we wait for the doctor," children know immediately that they are expected to behave badly. In contrast, a confident adult might say firmly but caringly, "Here is a book to look at quietly while we wait. We must sit very still. People are not allowed to be rowdy and noisy in a doctor's office." This indicates assurance that the adult believes the child can and will behave appropriately.

Persistence makes assertive communication work. Punishing, threatening, and intimidating get quick results on the surface, but undermine discipline in the long run. Assertive communication does not always bring about an immediate solution, but persistence over time makes it an effective and lasting technique for solving problems. Adults are sometimes tempted to surrender to children's demands when first efforts at communication don't bring about an immediate resolution. However, a generous amount of persistence will reap important benefits by letting children know that we really mean what we say. A child may stubbornly reject a rule on a whim, but if we persist in letting her know we expect the rule to be followed, she will almost surely comply eventually. As with the tortoise and the hare in their fabled contest—slow and steady wins the race.

Empathy may seem out of context with assertiveness, but, instead, it is absolutely essential. Sympathy means feeling sorry for others; empathy means walking in their shoes, feeling what they feel. Assertiveness without empathy is hollow and insincere. Assertiveness with empathy is strength and love rolled into one. A little person with grimy hands, a runny nose, and a knack for creating havoc does not always trigger feelings of warmth and empathy in parents and caregivers. Nonetheless, effective communication requires sincere understanding and caring. Empathy is expressed to listeners, from infancy to adulthood, primarily through the eyes and face, but all other verbal and nonverbal cues can also express empathy (or the lack of it).

For example, adults can begin reprimands by making an initial positive statement of some kind to show empathy. An adult might take a child by the hand and say, "I know you're a good kid. I know you would not intentionally hurt the cat, but teasing the cat and pulling at his tail really frightens him. Would you like to feed him to show him you're his friend?"

CHARACTERISTICS OF NONPRODUCTIVE COMMUNICATION

Adults use many different communication styles. Of course, some styles are more effective than others. The least effective styles usually deal only superficially with the content of the communication and fail completely to address the feelings or emotions of the persons sharing in the communication. It is most important that adults avoid the communication pitfalls that inhibit dialogue and alienate children (or others of any age).

Gazda (et al., 1984) lists nine common stereotypes of ineffective communication styles:
· Florist—Avoids issues through flowery euphemisms.
· Detective—Skirts issues by persistently prying with questions.
· Magician—Vaporizes problems with the wave of a wand.
· Drill Sergeant—Avoids conflict by barking orders.
· Foreman—Clouds issues by the use of compulsive busyness.
· Hangman—Induces guilt to avoid confronting problems.
· Guru—Covers over issues by giving a cliche for every occasion.
· Swami—Smoke screens issues by predicting dismal outcomes.
· Sign Painter—Dismisses problems by tacking labels on them.

While two-dimensional stereotypes do not reflect the complex facets of real people, they are helpful for identifying characteristics that real people display from time to time. One stereotype may be the predominant way an individual responds, but others might occasionally recognize a little bit of each stereotype in their behavior. The purpose of these stereotypes is not to label children or adults, but to better recognize and understand ineffective communication styles.

Florists simply don't see any problems. If a child communicates that he or she has been hurt by another child, the florist, ever so sweetly, says, "Why Suzy, I'm sure he didn't mean to hurt you!" If a parent complains bitterly about a teacher, the florist director says, "Now, Bill, I'm sure you don't really mean that. There must just be some kind of misunderstanding here."

If a tearful child sobs, "I hate my mommy," the florist teacher just smiles knowingly and says, "Of, course you don't hate your mommy. Children don't hate their mommies." The florist loses many opportunities for communication by tossing garlands of optimism rather than confronting and exploring problems.

Detectives want answers—"Why did you do that?" "Who did it first?" "Did I tell you not to do that?" "What do you think you're going to do now?" The listener is not only dazed by the battery of questions but also tempted to lie or to give whatever answers the detective seems to want.

Magicians dismiss issues conveniently. If a child says, "Someone pushed me off the swing," the magician says with flourish, "Yes, but playtime is over now so it really doesn't matter does it?" If a father expresses concern that his baby's pacifier is lost, the magician responds, "That's okay. Sarah really doesn't need a pacifier. She'll scream for an hour or two and then forget all about it."

Drill Sergeants don't have time to communicate; they are too busy barking orders. The drill sergeant nursery school teacher hears a heated argument in the block center. Instead of encouraging communication, she says, "Get these blocks picked up off the floor. Kaleb, tuck in your shirt. Samantha, you wouldn't have these problems if you'd pay attention and mind your own business."

Foremen keep everyone too busy to think about problems. A mother confides to her child's kindergarten teacher that her husband left her and she lost her job. She is worried that her son, Joshua, is being affected by her stress and depression. The foreman teacher responds, "You need to get out of the house and stop feeling sorry for yourself. Take an art class. Volunteer at the hospital. Throw a party." The mother leaves feeling even more guilty and overwhelmed.

Hangmen dish out blame. The hangman's favorite phrase is, "Well, I'm not surprised. You know, it's your own fault." When Jamey asks his hangman preschool teacher, Miss Judy, for help printing his name, she says, "If you paid attention last week, you would already know how to do this." When the director asks Miss Judy for help with a new child who is crying for his mother, Miss Judy says, "Of course he's crying. What do you expect? Did you see the way his mother let him manipulate her? She's to blame for this."

Gurus have a mental storehouse of meaningless cliches to scatter like rose petals over problems. A mother asks her toddler's nursery

Figure 7–14 Sometimes, because we forget about feelings, we inadvertently cloud the issues rather than uncover the source of problems for a child.

teacher if she thinks speech therapy is needed for the child. The guru teacher answers brightly, "Well, a stitch in time saves nine!"

A nine-year-old boy asks his guru dad why countries have scary things like nuclear bombs and is told, "An ounce of prevention is worth a pound of cure." A four-year-old cries, "Nobody likes me. I don't have any friends." Her guru teacher responds, "Well, you have to be a friend to have a friend." The guru's pat answers end dialogue rather than stimulate insight and understanding of problems.

Swamis are not exactly a comfort in time of need. He or she is always prepared to predict all the terrible and hopeless things that will probably happen as a result of the listener's actions. When a three-year-old runs into the house crying because she has a splinter in her finger, her swami mother says, "I told you not to play on that seesaw. Now you're going to get an infection and I'm going to be stuck with a big doctor bill. Look at this, your fingernail will probably turn black and fall off."

Of course, there is the classic swami response, "Johnny, when you fall out of that tree and break both your legs, don't come running to me."

Sign painters make quick work of problems by assigning labels. A nursery school teacher complains to her co-worker that she is having difficulty with one of her toddlers having temper tantrums. The sign-painter co-worker shrugs his shoulders and says, "I don't know of anything you can do about terrible twos. They're just that way."

In a parent conference with child-care staff, a single mother asks, "What is happening to my son? He seems to be trying to hurt everyone and everything around him?" A sign-painter teacher pats her on the shoulder and says, "Hey—all hyperactive kids do that." Meaningful communication is hindered by sign painters. There hardly seems any reason to discuss a problem after a label has been stamped on it with such finality.

In each of the above stereotypes, the communicator avoids, dismisses, evades, or thwarts problem issues. An effective, assertive communicator confronts problem issues with kindness and respect, but also with honesty. Often, it seems easiest to do whatever is expedient to stop a child's crying, end a dispute, or make a parent or co-worker feel better. Unfortunately, when problems are pushed under the rug, they can fester into even more unmanageable problems.

MANAGING THE POSITIVE CONFRONTATION

When confronting a problem issue, one should first use active listening to allow the child or adult to identify, explore, and express feelings about the situation. "Cheap and dirty" advice should not be tossed out lightly. Instead, persons being helped can be guided to recognize the choices they have and the possible outcomes of those choices. Only then can a person be assisted in solving his or her problem.

Adults must assume responsibility for solving their own problems before they can give real help. Imposing unwanted help on another adult is usually counterproductive. Helping children is another matter. If a child does not show motivation to solve a problem, parents and caregivers must assume that responsibility for the child. The child should be assisted as firmly as necessary but as gently as possible in confronting and solving problems.

Confrontation

Albert waits excitedly for his dad to pick him up from his child-care center. He and his buddy, Joshua, have planned to ask if they can spend the night together. As they dig in the sand, they giggle and scheme about the fun they will have watching television and eating grape Popsicles.

Finally, Albert sees his dad. Both boys run to the gate and watch as Albert's dad parks his car. Before his dad is even inside the gate, Albert is talking so fast that his dad cannot understand him.

Albert's dad hoists him into the air saying, "How's my big boy?" Albert excitedly says, "Daddy, can Joshua spend the night? Can he? Huh? Can he?"

Albert's dad takes both boys by the hand and as they walk up the sidewalk, he says quietly, "No, son, I have some paperwork I need to do tonight. This is not a good day. I will be happy to call Joshua's parents, though, and arrange for him to stay over one night next week."

Albert pulls his hand away and starts to cry. His dad bends down and says, "You really had your heart set on having Joshua spend the night didn't you?" Albert nods through his tears. His dad continues, "You feel sad and angry because next week seems a long time away." Albert nods again.

His dad hugs him and says, "It's okay to cry. Even grown people cry sometimes. I bet Joshua feels pretty bad too." Albert stops rubbing his eyes and looks at Joshua.

Albert throws his arms around his dad's neck for one last round of begging—"Pleeeeease, Daddy, I promise we won't bother you."

His dad's expression remains calm and empathetic. He says, "Albert, it is okay to ask, and it is okay to cry and feel sad, but the answer won't change. Joshua can't spend the night tonight."

Albert's next tactic' is pouting, but his dad remains calm and firm as he gathers Alberts belongings and prepares to leave.

As his dad buckles him into his seat belt, Albert plants a wet kiss on his cheek and says, "I love you, Daddy." His dad grins and says, "I love you too, son."

Albert's dad successfully avoided the stereotypes described previously. He did not delay confrontation by saying, "We'll talk about it later." He didn't avoid confrontation by giving in to something he knew he would regret. He didn't squelch confrontation by saying, "I don't want to hear another word about this. Hush right now or I won't let Joshua stay with you next week either." He didn't try to force Albert to like the decision by arguing with him, and he didn't try to make Albert agree with him and stop being mad.

He confronted Albert simply, directly, and immediately but with a great deal of empathy and respect. He listened, made what he believed was a fair decision, allowed Albert to express his feelings, and then recognized and reflected those feelings. In the end, Albert probably felt very secure in knowing his dad was a strong authority figure to be relied on rather than a weakling to be manipulated or a tyrant to be dreaded.

Positive and Assertive Confrontations

Anger undermines assertive confrontation. An adult who becomes enraged with a child should do only what is necessary to protect the child's safety and well-being on an immediate basis. He or she could ask for assistance from another adult who is calm, leave the baby screaming in the crib and do deep breathing and relaxation exercises, or say to an older child, "I am angry now. I will talk to you when I feel calm."

Confrontation should be delayed until the adult feels in control and is able to muster some level of empathy. Hurtful confrontations attack children in an angry, punitive way. Effective, assertive confrontations guide, protect, and nurture children.

An angry adult may find it helpful to think about and answer the following questions:

1. "Why do I feel the way I feel?"
2. "What did I feel before I felt anger? Was it frustration? Fear? Embarrassment?"
3. "Am I simply afraid to say no to this child?"
4. "Am I tired, hungry, not feeling well?"
5. "How would I feel right now if I were the child?"
6. "Are my expectations reasonable?"

Adults who lack assertiveness need to add three phrases to their daily speech, "I want . . . ," "I need . . . ," and, "I feel . . . ." Parents and other caregivers often try so hard to keep children happy that they suppress their own wants, needs, and feelings. Then, instead of being

Figure 7–15 "How would I feel right now if I were this child?"

appreciated as long-suffering martyrs, they are taken advantage of, and eventually they explode in anger and resentment. They are rarely appreciated. The more they try to give, the more children and other adults expect of them. As they learn to take an assertive stand, they discover that they are less angry, more appreciated, and a great deal happier.

The stereotypical communication styles previously presented were described as adult characteristics. However, these same evasion tactics are sometimes used by children. Children who have imitated parents and caregivers with poor or manipulative communication styles are especially prone to use those styles to evade issues.

Children evade confrontations by persistently asking questions, by issuing bossy little commands, and by giving cliche responses such as, "Everyone else's mother lets them stay up as long as they want." Children not only learn roles directly by imitating them, but also create roles as mirror-image opposites of those to which they are exposed. The child of a drill sergeant parent may learn to behave as a magician—"Get that trash picked up off the floor!" "What trash? I don't see any trash. Where? That's not trash. That's my cans I'm saving."

The more adept adults become in direct, assertive communication, the more successful they will be in keeping children's attention focused on confronting and resolving problem issues. Children will not need to evade issues when they trust adults to confront issues in a gentle but firm and fair manner. For many children and adults, the thought of a confrontation triggers terror, because their primary experiences with confrontation have been frightening interactions filled with rage— their own rage as well as the rage of powerful, threatening adults.

Confrontation, without anger, is an important and healthy part of social interaction.

Responsibility

Responsibility cannot be taught. It can be shown through example, it can be nurtured and reinforced, and, most importantly, it can be learned firsthand by dealing with the consequences of one's own actions. Adults often feel compelled to prevent children from experiencing consequences—"You have to eat this! You might get hungry

Figure 7–16 Gradually, through first-hand experience, children learn about the natural or logical consequences of their own actions.

later." They rescue children. "You were careless and left your doll in the rain. Now I'll have to buy you another." The child feels only the adult's annoyance. He or she is not allowed to feel the natural consequences of behaviors.

It is better for the child to have support and warmth from adults as he or she feels and owns the sting of unpleasant consequences from poor decisions. Adults must prevent dangerous or damaging consequences. A child cannot learn firsthand the consequences of such things as running out into a busy street, or never brushing teeth. However, exploring and discussing possible consequences should be a part of confrontations.

Rather than lecturing children about consequences, adults should make simple statements ("If you throw food, you will have to leave the table.") and ask simple questions ("What do you think could happen if you stood on the edge of the balcony?") Children can be encouraged on a regular basis to explore potential consequences.

Children who have a habit of considering and weighing consequences are well on their way to becoming responsible and self-directed.

SUMMARY

Communication skills are developed early in life. Adults influence children by setting a good example for them and by encouraging them to practice appropriate communication skills.

Responsive and active listening is an integral part of child guidance, but dependency and inappropriate interaction must be firmly and respectfully redirected.

Feelings and emotions must be considered in order to provide appropriate responses to behaviors. One can help children to understand the motives for their own misbehaviors.

Positive instructions are more likely to elicit cooperative behavior than imperative commands or negative statements. Assertive communication is honest but not brutal. Assertiveness always requires respect and empathy in order to be effective.

Adults often behave in stereotypical ways to avoid, squelch, dismiss, or deny problems. These evasive tactics are ineffective and harmful to open, honest communication.

Positive confrontation is a healthy and natural part of social interaction. Consequences (that are neither dangerous nor unreasonable) provide children feedback about the appropriateness of their behavior. Adults can assist children in developing responsibility by encouraging children to talk about and think about the potential consequences of their behavior.

PRACTICAL APPLICATION/DISCUSSION

"I'll Leave You Here Forever"

Marlene pauses in the shopping mall waiting for her two-year-old to catch up with her. Her four-month-old, who is asleep on her shoulder, is beginning to feel very heavy. "Crystal," she calls to her two-year-old, "Please come on. We need to get home."

Crystal stalls as she climbs on and off benches and stops to look at other shoppers. Her mother loses patience, "Crystal! You come here now or you're going to be sorry." Crystal ignores her.

Marlene walks quickly back to Crystal and, taking her firmly by the wrist, says, "Let's go." Crystal responds with the rubbery-legs strategy toddlers use when they rebel. Her legs go limp as she slumps to the floor, dangling from the wrist her mother is clutching and whining, "Don't want go home."

Marlene realizes that she can't safely carry her baby and Crystal both out of the shopping mall. In exasperation, she snaps, "That's it, I'm leaving. If you won't come then I'll just leave you here forever. Good-bye!"

She turns and begins to walk briskly out of the mall. She hears Crystal howling and running to catch up with her.

QUESTIONS FOR DISCUSSION

1. What would you have done in Marlene's place? Why?
2. What has Crystal really learned from the interaction?
3. Could anything have been done to prevent Marlene's predicament?
4. Role play the scene using positive, assertive communication and confrontation and compare possible outcomes.

Figure 8–1 Adults can take positive action to assure appropriate behavior. *(Photo courtesy of Cynde Miller)*

8
Positive Action

OBJECTIVES
This chapter will assist you in:

• Creating a setting that is supportive to positive child guidance.

- Focusing on the role of nonverbal communication and body language in assisting positive behavior.
- Defining logical and natural consequences and understanding their importance in guidance.
- Identifying reasonable and effective circumstances for the use of external reinforcement.

NONVERBAL CUES, BODY LANGUAGE

Not only does the environment give messages to children about what we expect from them, but also our own physical postures, movements, and gestures communicate a great deal of information to them. We may not even be aware of the body language signals we are sending out that children are receiving and reacting to.

Significance of Nonverbal Cues for Young Children

Before verbal language is well-developed, young children rely heavily on nonverbal communication in their interactions with others. Infants pay attention to the touch, facial expressions, and sounds of their caregivers to interpret the adult's moods and expectations. Even a six-month-old baby can recognize clear differences between the meaning of a frowning parent with his hands firmly on his hips and a smiling parent with his arms stretched toward the baby. Rather than interpreting the meaning of a caregiver's words or sentences, very young children focus all their attention on sense perception. They pay attention to things they can actually see, hear, feel, taste, or smell.

As children reach preschool age, they gradually pay more attention to the actual words in adults' speech, but they are still very sensitive to nonverbal cues or signals. Elena, a preschool teacher in a child-care center, took her youngsters outside to play early one summer morning to avoid the midday heat and humidity. As the children played happily, Elena looked up and noticed swarms of hungry mosquitos circling in clusters near the eaves of the building.

She stood silently, with her arms tightly folded across her chest, staring at the buzzing dive-bombers and wondering what she should do. Should she take the children back inside? Should she spray the children with repellant? She felt a tug at her skirt. Willie, a three-year-old who was riding around Elena on a tricycle and watching her carefully, blurted out in a sad voice, "Miss Elena, how come you're mad at me?" Willie read Elena's body language and sensed tension and frustration. Because he was a normally developing preoperational

Figure 8-2 Children pay close attention to the nonverbal signals adults give as part of their communication.

child, he naturally (and egocentrically) assumed that he was the cause of Elena's unhappiness.

Elena did not realize the effect her nonverbal behavior could have on the children around her. Because the vocabulary and language comprehension skills of young children are so limited, their understanding of their environment hinges on their ability to be very alert to nonverbal cues from those around them.

Consistency of Nonverbal Cues with Verbal Communication

Adults must consider nonverbal expressions whenever they attempt to communicate with children. A typical situation in which children receive conflicting messages between verbal and nonverbal cues occurs when children are brought to an early-childhood setting for the first time. Typically, a parent will say, "You'll have a lot of fun playing with other children, and I will be back later to pick you up. It's okay now, go ahead with your teacher." The words are full of confidence and optimism. The adult, who focuses only on the words, may not notice that she is tense, strained, and fretful in appearance.

The adult's facial expression may be one of uncertainty, her voice may sound uncharacteristically high, and her hands may be wringing and twisting nervously. Instead of leaving quickly, the adult hangs near the child while insisting verbally that the child "act like a big boy and go play." The parent says she is going, but looks as if she is staying.

Of course, the child pays more attention to the nonverbal cues than to the spoken words. He will sense that the parent is frightened and unsure about leaving him, and he will probably feel frightened and unsure about being left. He will probably resist being left—with a great deal of volume and energy. If, on the other hand, he senses that his parent is confident and optimistic, he may feel a bit uncomfortable at first, but he is likely to adjust more quickly and easily to the separation. He absorbs the confidence of his parent as she smiles and says in a relaxed tone of voice, "I know you will have a great time today," then leaves.

Focused Attention at the Child's Eye Level

An adult stands across the room from a child and casually looks over a shoulder, saying, "Letecia, don't touch those scissors. You'll cut yourself." Letecia will probably interpret that the adult is not too concerned about the danger of the scissors, and will probably not enforce the command. It is likely that Letecia will continue to touch the scissors while watching the adult carefully for stronger or more direct cues about the scissors.

Another adult stops what she is doing and bends down to the child's eye level, holding out a hand for the scissors and saying, "Please give me the scissors. These are too sharp. They could cut you. We'll find you a plastic pair." The adult's assertive, nonverbal communication matches her verbal communication. Letecia is likely to perceive that the adult "means business" and is willing to follow through to see that the sharp scissors are removed.

As Letecia decides whether or not to comply with the command she was given, she will read the adult's facial expression (Is there a playful twinke in the eye or a look of concerned resolve?), tone of voice (Is there a weak tone of uncertainty or absolute confidence?), and hand gestures (Are hand motions assertive or physically threatening?). If the adult's nonverbal cues are too playful or casual, Letecia will assume that she really doesn't have to comply. If they are too threatening and intrusive, Letecia will likely bristle and resist the command. If they are assertive, caring, confident, and no-nonsense, Letecia may decide that it is in her own best interest to comply quickly and willingly.

HELPING CHILDREN LEARN TO RESOLVE PROBLEMS INDEPENDENTLY

A primary goal for early childhood development is the growth of personal responsibility and independence in children. Learning how to behave appropriately requires self-control, which is closely related to

Figure 8–3 Children have a right to ask for adult help when their rights are infringed upon.

ponsibility and independence. In order to become socially competent, children need to master active negotiation skills so that they can successfully resolve at least some of their own problems.

Children often come to adults begging to be rescued from various unhappy situations. Sometimes, the child's grievance is legitimate. Children have a right to call on someone bigger, stronger, and with more authority when their rights have been violated, just as I have a right to request legal help if my own rights have been violated.

If I call a police officer for help because my purse was stolen, I will feel very resentful if the officer responds by saying things like:

"Don't tattle!"

"Don't be so stingy, the thief probably needed the money worse than you do anyway."

"You got what you deserved. You shouldn't have been carrying a purse that would tempt people anyway."

"Well, did you tell the purse-snatcher you didn't like that?"

We are a tiny bit embarrassed by some of our most frequently-used expressions when we step back and compare them with what we expect from others.

Nevertheless, there are occasions when the child should not be rescued by an adult. In order to foster independence, children should be *helped* to do as much for themselves as they can reasonably be expected to handle successfully. Common sense will tell us that there are times we need to nudge children firmly into assuming responsibility for resolving problems they encounter.

Facilitating Child-to-Child Communication

Toddlers scream, hit, shove, and bite primarily because they lack the verbal ability to express themselves otherwise. They are transparent and physical in letting another child or adult know they feel angry. We may regret the onset of name-calling in children past three, but we are very likely to see a decrease in physical aggression as verbal communication skills are mastered. Preschoolers discover they can cause a peer to dissolve in tears just by calling her a "weenie baby" or by tauntingly chanting nonsense words such as "Nanny, nanny, boo, boo! Nanny, nanny, boo, boo!"

In positive child guidance, children are taught ways to communicate feelings honestly and assertively without having to resort to verbal aggression. Following is a list of ways to facilitate child-to-child communication:

"Jarrod, please say, 'Excuse me, Christie, I need to get past.' Christie doesn't like to be shoved."

"Alva, use words. Tell Erin you feel very angry when he grabs your crayons without asking. Would you like for me to help you tell him?"

"Erin, Alva feels really mad when you grab her crayons. Can you ask for a crayon? Can you say, 'Please, may I have a crayon?' "

"Jerusha, thank you for saying, 'Excuse me, this chair is mine.' "

"Adam and Beth, you need to sit here on the step and talk until you both feel better."

"Beth, your friend Adam says you scratched his face. Adam, Beth says you wadded up her drawing and threw it in the waste basket."

"Adam, you're upset because your face really hurts."

"Beth, you're sad because you really wanted to take that picture home to your mother."

"Can either of you think of some way to make your friend feel better."

"That's a great idea, Adam, you could get the drawing out of the trash can and try to smooth it out."

"Yes, Beth, I think Adam would really like a wet paper towel to hold on his scratched cheek."

By giving children help in knowing exactly what to say to playmates when trouble breaks out, we encourage them to use appropriate words, rather than inappropriate physical or verbal aggression. It is okay (even desirable) for children to express strong emotions. We never should push children into being so "nice" that they hold their emotions inside. Our goal is to channel their emotional expression into words that *inform* rather than words that *hurt*.

Encouraging Voluntary Apologies

It seems very odd that we tell children, "Be honest. Always tell the truth," and then proceed to order them to "Tell so-and-so you're sorry" (never even wondering if they actually feel sorry). No child should be encouraged to say she feels something that she really doesn't feel. It is more appropriate to point out how the other child feels then wait for some indication of remorse or regret.

If a child appears to be sorry for something she has done, it may be helpful to say, "Would you *like* to tell Ricky that you're sorry about what happened?" "Would you *like* for me to tell him for you?" It is even more important for us to find some way to help the child make amends to Ricky. She will feel good about herself if she has a chance to make things right. We discourage children terribly when we imply to them, "You have made such a mess of things that there is no way you can undo what you've done."

Encouraging Voluntary Sharing

Sharing should also be voluntary. If an adult peer of mine picked up a book I was reading and walked off with it, I would think him very rude. Strangely though, when one child is looking at a book and a peer takes the book without asking, we are tempted to say, "You need to share. Look, there are lots of books. Just choose a different book. Don't be so stingy with the books."

I believe I have a right to my own property and possessions. I can offer someone the use of my scissors, but they really shouldn't barge in and take them, especially if I am using them at the moment. I expect guests in my house to be respectful of my personal possessions, yet parents often allow visiting children to barge into their own child's room and play with any toy they want. If their own child puts up a fuss, we hear them say, "You have to share."

We all want children to be generous and polite, but we can encourage generosity most by protecting a child's property rights, so he feels it is safe to invite others to share. The more vulnerable the child feels about losing his possessions, the more tightly and greedily he will guard them.

LOGICAL AND NATURAL CONSEQUENCES

Children learn skills and information through active involvement in their day-to-day environment. They learn by watching others, by being told things, and (most importantly) by experiencing life. In life, actions are often followed by logical or natural consequences. If I forget to water my potted plant, it will probably die (a natural consequence). If I am regularly late to work, I may lose my job (a logical consequence). No one is trying to hurt or annoy me. These consequences are merely the way the world works. Through them, I learn that I must behave in certain ways if I want to avoid undesired results and achieve desired goals.

The Objective Cause-and-Effect Sequence

Sometimes, when we see a child feeling disappointed or sad, we may be tempted to interfere and rescue her from the consequences of her own actions. It is not, however, a useful practice for us to rescue children from the logical and natural results of their actions and choices as long as the consequences are reasonable and safe! We would never risk a child being run over as a natural consequence of running into the street, or allow a child to go hungry as a logical consequence of spilling food.

Tina arrived home after a family outing to a downtown movie-theater, and suddenly yelled, "Oh, no! I left my purse in the theater." Her dad fumed and sputtered, "Tina, why are you so careless. It'll take me a half hour to drive back downtown, and by then the purse will probably be stolen. You'd lose your head if it wasn't tied down." After yelling at Tina for twenty minutes while she sniffled and made ex-cuses for her behavior, he called the theater and drove back downtown alone to search for the purse.

Even though Tina's dad reprimanded her loudly and angrily, in actuality he rescued her from any responsibility for her forgetfulness. He was the one who made the phone calls, drove all the way back to the theater, and did the searching. Tina had nothing to do but feel miserable and stupid.

Tina's dad would have used natural consequences if he had said:

"Tina, I'm sure you feel awful about losing your purse. Can you think of anything we could do to find it? Would you like for me to help you look up the phone number of the theater? Would you like for me to drive you back to the theater so that you can look for it? I don't know if we'll find it or not. Purses left in public places are often stolen."

Tina's dad would have used logical consequences if he had said:

"Tina, it isn't fair for me to have to drive all the way back to town. Next time we go to the theater, you will have to leave your purse at home. When you're a little older, you can try again. Perhaps by then it won't be so hard for you to remember your things."

By helping Tina find ways to solve her problem (rather than solving it for her), Tina's father guides her to focus on her forgetfulness, not her father's anger, as the problem. She realizes that her discomfort results from the natural or logical consequences of her forgetfulness, not from someone trying to punish or embarrass her. She will become responsible when she learns to remember her possessions simply be-cause it is frustrating and inconvenient to lose them, not just to please her father. If Tina learns to behave appropriately only to please her father, she may be tempted to behave inappropriately just to annoy him when she is angry with him or feeling rebellious.

Punishment versus Discipline

Punishment is negative. It is intended to hurt, humiliate, or pay a child back for something she has done. The purpose of discipline, in contrast, is to teach children (assertively and respectfully) to behave appropriately. Discipline is a part of positive child guidance. Punishment is not.

Following are examples of punishment versus discipline as used with a preschooler:

Punishment

"Don't you dare touch that cake. Get away from here and go play. If I catch you fooling around with it, you're really gonna get it!"

"I saw you touch that cake. Get in the time-out chair and stay until I say you can get up. Everyone's going to see you sitting in the 'naughty' chair and know that you were being bad."

"I'd better not see you get up! If I see you try to get up, I'll make you stay twice as long."

Discipline

"This is Stephen's birthday cake. No one is allowed to touch it. It isn't fair to mess up Stephen's beautiful cake. You may look at it—but only if you keep your hands in your pockets."

"You seem to be having a hard time remembering to keep your hands in your pockets while you look at the cake. You need to come sit on the time-out chair until you feel *sure* you can remember our rule about not touching the cake. Come and tell me when you are sure you can look at the cake without touching."

"I like the way you are keeping your hands in your pockets while you look at Stephen's cake. Stephen will be so happy when he sees his beautiful birthday cake. Ummm, it smells good, doesn't it."

Punishment is used to bully or coerce children into behaving the way we want them to. Following are some of the ways adults *punish* children:

- Spanking, slapping, arm-yanking, and shaking.
- Biting, hair-pulling, or pinching (so he will know how it feels).
- Withdrawing affection, ignoring, avoiding eye contact, not speaking.
- Humiliating the child, putting her in a position to be ridiculed or laughed at.
- Endlessly lecturing, nagging, or harping on problems that are past history (they're done, the child can't undo them).
- Forcing the child to sit or stay somewhere for a set period of time regardless of whether the child is sincerely remorseful and ready to make amends.
- Arbitrarily taking away privileges, forbidding activities that the child particularly enjoys (especially privileges that are totally unrelated to the child's offense).

Following are some of the ways adults *discipline* children:

- Changing the surroundings to remove the likelihood or temptation for misbehavior.
- Focusing the child's attention on logical and natural consequences that will, or may, follow a specific behavior.
- Expressing concern for the child's feelings, but refusing to rescue the child from reasonable and safe consequences that are natural or logical results of his behavior.
- Carefully supervising the child in order to prompt or cue appropriate behavior and remind the child of rules.
- Firmly, but respectfully, redirecting the child's behavior away from inappropriate actions and substituting more appropriate activities.
- Decisively stopping or interrupting any behavior that is clearly dangerous or unfair, responding as firmly as necessary but as gently as possible.
- Physically removing a very young child from a conflict or during a tantrum (even if the child is kicking and screaming) when it is necessary to protect the child and the environment.
- Letting an older child know that you refuse to join her in her tantrum, but that you will be glad to talk when she is ready to speak calmly and respectfully.
- Assuring the child that he is loved and valued. Letting him know

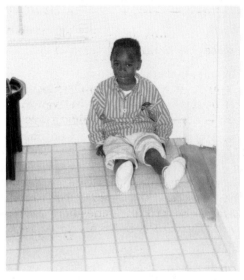

Figure 8–4 Sitting in time-out can feel lonely and embarrassing.

that you accept and respect his negative feelings, even if you *must stop* his negative action (it's okay to feel angry, but not okay to hurt others).

There is a very fine line, sometimes, between punishing and disciplining. A controversial concern for many early-childhood educators is whether or not to use something called "*time-out*" as a consequence for inappropriate behavior. In their efforts to avoid overtly negative punishments, many early-childhood professionals for years responded to misbehavior by having children sit in time-out, by "the thinking wall," or in "the thinking chair." More negative versions banished children to the "bad chair," the "baby chair," or the "naughty chair." Experts cautioned that children should not be required to sit any longer than three minutes for every year of the child's age (for example, nine minutes for a three-year-old, fifteen minutes for a five-year-old). In reality, it is not uncommon for children in some settings to be forced to sit many times that length of time.

Today, some experts say that time-out is a viable and positive method of guiding behavior while other experts insist that time-out just allows children uninterrupted time to plot their revenge. The real issue, however, is not whether a time-out chair is used or not used (or whether a penalty is imposed, or whether a privilege is denied). The concern lies in *how* the adult goes about her enforcement and *why* she does what she does. Following are several characteristics of punishment and discipline:

PUNISHMENT	DISCIPLINE
Lowers Self-Esteem	Builds Self-Esteem
Humiliates	Strengthens
Degrades	Respects
Hurts (physically or emotionally)	Heals
Angers	Gives Hope
Frustrates	Models Coping Skills
Thwarts Efforts	Enables Efforts
Embarrasses	Gives Confidence
Discourages	Encourages
Belittles	Enhances Self-Image
Socially Isolates	Facilitates Trust
Emotionally Abandons	Gives Emotional Support
Denies Affection	Is Loving and Caring

At this point, one might respond by saying, "Those lists are lovely, but when little Elroy draws on my freshly painted walls with his crayon, I'm furious. I don't care about enhancing his self-image, I just want to wring his little neck!" Actually, Elroy's infuriating behavior

Figure 8–5 "I am still a good person even if I sometimes break a rule." *(Photo courtesy of Montessori Country Day School)*

gives us an excellent opportunity to put our preaching into practice. We can *show* Elroy, through our own behavior, that feeling angry is natural and normal; but hurting, humiliating, or belittling others is simply not okay. Socially accepted rules for appropriate behavior do not apply only to children, they apply to all of us.

Having Elroy tediously scrub the crayon marks off the wall and taking the crayons away until he can be more carefully supervised are both assertive and effective disciplinary methods. They are a part of positive child guidance—but *only* if the adult's attitude is optimistic and assertive, rather than mean-spirited and punitive. Our attitude toward Elroy should be one of helping him succeed in behaving more appropriately in the future, not making him miserable to punish him for his bad deed.

Separating the Deed from the Doer

In order to be firm and fair in guiding children, deeds must be seen as separate from the person who did them. In other words, what a child did may have been dishonest, but that doesn't mean the child is now a dishonest person. Because children are prone to become what we tell them they are (remember the self-fulfilling prophecy), we must be very careful about *what* we tell children they are. It is helpful to tell a child, "Pouring water on a cat is a thoughtless and unkind thing to do. You are a kind and thoughtful boy. But, even kind, thoughtful boys make mistakes. I make mistakes too. The important thing is to do better next time."

Following are some helpful and some not-so-helpful phrases:

NOT HELPFUL	HELPFUL
"You are a naughty girl!"	"Spitting at people is not allowed!"
"Why are you so bad?"	"Why are you angry with your brother?"
"Don't act like a dummy."	"Think! What will happen if you put paint in the fish bowl?"
"You lazy thing! Look at your messy room."	"After your room is clean, *then* you may turn on the television."

Phrases that are not helpful do little more than stereotype children in negative roles (naughty, bad, stupid, lazy, etc.). Helpful phrases give children very specific information about what is expected, without labeling the child in a negative way. Children always appreciate being reminded, "I'm very upset with what you *did*, but I'm not angry with *you*. I still love *you* a whole lot, even when you make mistakes."

Figure 8–6 "Please swing carefully, so you don't bump anyone."

Overindulgence and Overprotection, Spoiling

Caring adults know how to say "no." The idea of positive child guidance is sometimes interpreted to mean that adults are slaves to children, that adults must somehow keep things happy, glowing, and idyllic for children at all times. This could not be further from the truth. We have an obligation to be fair, caring, and available, but we are *not* responsible to make sure that children are completely happy every moment of their lives.

Caring for and guiding children is physically demanding, emotionally draining, and intellectually taxing work. And, growing up is not an easy task for the children either. Adults and children will sometimes be at cross-purposes, so there are bound to be conflicts. Overindulgence and overprotection (sometimes referred to as spoiling) are not a part of positive child guidance. Not being firm enough is just as damaging as being too firm.

One mother says, "But I have to give Lindy ice cream while I'm preparing dinner. If I don't, she screams and holds her breath until she turns blue. I have no choice!" Of course, Lindy's mother *does* have a choice. She is the only one tall enough to reach the freezer!

Lindy's mother needs reassurance that it is perfectly okay for Lindy to cry. Lindy feels frustrated, and crying is her way of expressing herself. When Lindy was a helpless newborn, her mother had to respond quickly to her cries of hunger to instill in her a sense of trust. Now Lindy is older. She can delay gratification (wait a few minutes) for her needs to be met. In fact, she *must* learn how to delay gratification if she is to develop responsibility and self-control.

Her mother needs to feel more relaxed about Lindy's breath holding. Babies and toddlers automatically forget to breathe for a few seconds when they are very stunned or hurt. Parents often hear the loud thump of their toddler falling, then a moment of silence, and, finally, loud, howling cries. The toddler isn't holding her breath to be manipulative. That's just how her body works. If, however, a great deal of attention is paid to that pause in her breathing, the child might eventually learn to hold her breath just for dramatic effect. Even in an extreme case of breath holding, the worst that would be likely to happen is that Lindy would succeed in causing herself to faint, at which time she would automatically resume breathing.

The most effective way for Lindy's mother to deal with the child's behavior is to assertively and caringly acknowledge that wanting ice cream is okay, but that no ice cream will be served until after dinner. The mother could tell Lindy, "I know you wish you could have ice cream. It's all right to cry. Sometimes I cry when I'm mad or upset. You may cry as long as you need to. If you need to cry for a long, long time, then you must cry in your room so that you don't hurt other people's ears."

After Lindy finishes crying (remember, no child ever cried forever), her mother could redirect Lindy's hunger (present a compromise) by offering peanut-butter crackers or apple slices. Or, if she senses that bringing up the subject of hunger would cause another scene, she may wait and offer a nutritious treat the next time she anticipates a problem.

Before Lindy has a chance to mention ice cream, her mother can choose not to purchase ice cream for a while to reduce Lindy's temptation (as well as her own temptation to give in). Whatever she does, she must not give in to Lindy's tantrum and reinforce her inappropriate behavior by rewarding it with ice cream.

Giving in to Lindy's demand while at the same time yelling, complaining, or making her feel guilty is inappropriately overindulgent and very confusing. Lindy may not learn that the word "no" really means no. Or, she may come to view herself as an unlovable and spoiled brat, thinking badly of herself but not really knowing how to behave differently.

Making Choices Within Limits

Children need freedom within clear limits. Freedom without limits is not really freedom. Instead, it is chaotic and dangerous. Jesse's parents tried to give him complete freedom. Jesse rules the family with the total abandon of a dictator. Whatever is being served for breakfast is not what he wants. Even if asked in advance for his breakfast order, he goes through several changes of mind. His parents meekly pour out bowls of cereal and make waffles or throw away waffles and make oatmeal.

Whatever clothes Jesse's mother chooses for him to wear are almost never to his liking, either. He stamps down the hall like a little emperor and ceremoniously stuffs the clean clothing into the laundry hamper. His mother meekly offers alternate selections of clothes she hopes he will like. Sometimes Jesse goes to school wearing clothes that are totally inappropriate for the weather or the setting.

His parents wonder why he is so demanding. They are so proud of their beautiful little boy. They want so much for him to love them that they fail to use good judgement. They also hate to confront him and risk an ugly scene. They don't realize it, but what Jesse really wants and needs are strong, loving parents who are willing and able to help him grow up. Secretly, Jesse realizes that he is acting like a baby.

Jesse didn't become a dictator overnight, and he won't be able to change into a reasonable and polite person overnight. With time and patience, however, Jesse can learn to make choices within clearly defined, reasonable limits. Jesse can be given a choice between eggs and cereal, between the red shirt and the blue shirt; and he can be allowed to deal with the natural and logical consequences of refusing to accept the limits he has been given.

His parents can say, "Jesse, if you're not hungry enough to eat the corn flakes you asked for, then you're obviously not very hungry for breakfast." "You may have ten minutes to choose what you want to wear from these clothes. If you are not able to choose, then I will choose for you. If you are not dressed and ready for school on time, you will be tardy. I will not write a note to your teacher excusing your lateness." "If you stuff clean clothes in the laundry hamper, you will have to help with the extra laundry by sorting and folding clothes instead of watching television."

In order to enforce freedom of choice within reasonable limits, Jesse's parents will have to make a commitment to confront him, lovingly and persistently. Of course, in the long run, Jesse will be a happier, friendlier, more likeable person.

EXTERNAL REINFORCEMENT

Developing children's *inner* control and self-motivation for behaving acceptably are addressed throughout this text. Previous sections emphasized the concept that children must *want* to behave well, that they must assume conscious responsibility for their actions. Positive child guidance is not a gimmicky strategy to manipulate children into behaving according to our specifications, but a process of guiding children to become competent, confident, and cooperative human beings who behave well, not to win favors, but because behaving well is the right thing to do.

Now, however, it is time to look at the opposite side of the coin—techniques for refining *external* control. Some behaviors do not come from internal motivation. They are unconscious habits that are very resistant to even the most sincere desire for change. We know from our own experiences that *wanting* to quit smoking, lose weight, or exercise regularly is not always enough to make those things happen. I can want desperately to lose weight, but if I am unconsciously conditioned to open the refrigerator every time I pass it, I may be my own worst enemy.

Jeremy tells his mother that he doesn't want to practice the piano each day (as his piano teacher has asked him to do). Consequently, his mother delves into the Jeremy's inner motivations. She talks with him about his hope to become a famous piano player and his feelings of pride when he masters difficult pieces of music.

If Jeremy really has an *inner desire* to play the piano, and the lack of practicing is simply a matter of establishing new habits, giving him a cute little sticker as a reward each day that he practices may work wonders. If he doesn't practice because he *lacks* inner motivation, stickers will be a waste of time. In fact, they may be worse than a waste of time. Jeremy may make his decision not to practice based on the fact that he is only giving up a little sticker that really isn't very valuable anyway. Also, if Jeremy is coerced into practicing to get a reward, he may respond to future reminders of things he is supposed to do by saying, "What will you give me if I do it?"

In contrast, when Jeremy decides to train his pet chicken to "play the piano" for a county fair, he doesn't waste any time telling the hen how proud she will feel, he just drops a pellet of corn into her dish each time she inadvertently steps on the keyboard of the toy piano he has placed on the floor of her cage. Before long, Jeremy's chicken clucks loudly and pounds on the piano keyboard every time she sees him.

My placing coins in a candy vending machine every day may be every bit as mindless as the chicken's stepping on the toy piano keyboard to get pellets of corn. I may need to change my external surroundings to break my habit cycle. Perhaps I could walk a different route so that I don't pass the vending machines, think of a reward to give myself if I resist candy bars for a whole week, or even bring nutritious, low-calorie snacks with me as a substitute when I am tempted to eat candy. We can assist children in breaking undesirable habits in exactly this same way.

Supportive External Conditions for Appropriate Behavior, Unconscious Conditioning

Stephanie runs to her mother when her mother arrives to pick her up from her child-care center. Stephanie has a handful of drawings, and she dances around her mother squealing, "Mommy, look what I made! Look what I made!" Stephanie's mother is busy chatting with other mothers, so she ignores Stephanie. Finally, Stephanie throws the drawings down on the ground and yells, "I hate you, Mommy!" Instantly, her mother bends down and says (with a tone of disgust), "Stephanie, what do you want?"

Stephanie learned a lesson that her mother did not intend to teach her. When you want your mother's attention, be hateful and destructive because you will get attention faster than by just asking for attention.

Children generally do whatever they need to do to get their needs met. Many unconscious habits are formed simply because they work. We need to analyze our daily procedures very carefully to identify *how* children get the things they want and need in the environment.

Does the child who pushes and shoves the hardest always get to be

Figure 8–7 Children do whatever they need to do to get affection and attention. *(Photo courtesy of Cynde Miller)*

first in line? Does whining and arguing always succeed in extending bed time or television-viewing time? Does pitching a fit mean the child doesn't have to buckle her seat belt? Does the child who misbehaves the most during storytime get almost all of the adult's eye contact, verbal contact, physical contact, and name recognition? *Even negative attention is preferable to being ignored.*

We also need to consider the powerful effect of intermittent (occasional) reinforcers. People in Las Vegas don't need to get a reward *every* time they put money in a slot machine. They will feed money to "one-armed bandits" for hours just for a chance at one really big payoff. Children, likewise, can pester for hours on the chance that a disgusted adult will finally give in and reward their inappropriate behavior with the desired privilege or response.

Without realizing it, we may be reinforcing and rewarding dysfunctional and annoying behaviors on a daily basis. By consciously looking at what a child gets out of various behaviors and changing our own behaviors, we may take big steps in preventing and resolving many frustrating misbehavior patterns.

Appropriate Use of Behavior Modification

Behavior modification means observing a child's present behavior, identifying a desired future behavior, breaking the distance between the two behaviors into component parts ("bite-sized" bits), and systematically reinforcing (rewarding) each little step as the child moves closer to the desired action. Behaviorists see learning as a process of piecing together a chain, one link at a time. The process is external to the child because the adult chooses the skill to be learned and, then, rewards that behavior in the child.

Exceptional children (children with developmental delays, learning deficits, and language disabilities) may lack the ability to discuss or reflect on their inner motivations. Behavior modification may truly be a godsend for guiding these children.

Elinor is a beautiful little girl who is a victim of autism. She cannot speak and she constantly flutters around the room flapping her arms and making small grunting sounds. Pleading with her to stop these behaviors would only confuse her, making her so anxious that the behaviors would probably increase. Using behavior modification, however, would be an effective and caring way to shape her behavior into more socially accepted patterns.

Elinor's teacher, Thomas, simply ignores the flapping and watches carefully for the instant that Elinor stops to look at something. Immediately, Thomas gives Elinor a tiny paper cup of Cheerios, her favorite cereal and says, "Good girl, Elinor." Over a period of months, very quietly and unobtrusively, Thomas conditions Elinor to focus more of her attention on the toys and books in the classroom and to spend a great deal less time flapping and grunting. Very importantly, Thomas ignores Elinor's undesirable *behavior*. He never ignores or withdraws affection from Elinor herself.

Thomas's next task is to gradually wean Elinor from the cereal and replace that reinforcement with shiny plastic coins that he calls tokens. Eventually, he hopes that Elinor will comprehend that if she collects a certain number of tokens, she can trade them in for a special treat, privilege, or snack.

Behavior modification can be used very successfully with well-developing, even gifted, children. It is, however, essential to enlist the bright child's voluntary and active cooperation. Children and adults who are capable of examining their own motives and the motives of others will feel betrayed or coerced if they realize that their behavior was manipulated without their knowledge. If I, for example, suddenly realize that someone has rigged the candy-vending machine to steal my quarters (so that I will stop buying candy), I will feel furious. I may stubbornly eat even more candy just to assert my own autonomy.

Behavior modification works most effectively with bright children when adults are straightforward about their plan. An adult might say, "Ginger, let's make a little booklet to help you remember to go to the bathroom on time. I will set the timer for one hour, and each time it rings, if your pants are still dry, you may paste a special sticker in

Figure 8–8 "Thank you for remembering not to throw sand."

your book. Do you think that would help you remember? Would you like to try it?"

Obviously, the sticker booklet will only help if Ginger is wetting her pants simply because she has a habit of delaying visits to the bathroom. A young toddler won't suddenly be able to master toilet training just to get stickers. The strategy also won't work if Ginger has inner motivation problems (such as needing to be a baby to compete for attention with a new baby in her family). If, however, Ginger really wants to stop wetting her pants, and she just needs a little boost to break a bad habit, she is likely to cooperate fully and feel very proud of herself when she succeeds.

Behaviorism Oversimplified—Ignoring the Negative and Rewarding the Positive

Behavior modification is a powerful tool when used appropriately. A primary concern, however, is that ignoring inappropriate behavior may become an excuse to abdicate responsibility for children's unacceptable behavior. Tactfully overlooking certain inappropriate behaviors may be helpful in some situations, and reinforcing positive behaviors has a tremendous impact in many situations. There is a risk, however, that if used inappropriately, behaviorist tactics can become manipulative and aloof. Ignoring can become punitive and hurtful, and the adult can find herself working *on* the child rather than *with* the child.

As adults, we have a responsibility not to stand by passively while a child is labeled as "bad" or "wild," but to actively involve ourselves in making it easy for children to behave properly and very, very difficult for them to behave improperly. We may not always succeed, but, we *can* give our most persistent and energetic effort! Then, at least, a child with behavioral problems will know we care very much about her and that we will not give up on her, no matter what she does.

SUMMARY

We give subtle messages to children about how we expect them to behave by the surroundings we plan for them. We can prevent many behavior problems before they begin simply by careful planning, by understanding children's developmental needs, and by creating a match between their needs and the environment. Developmentally appropriate early childhood settings are neither overwhelming nor so simplistic as to be boring. Behavior problems are minimized simply because children are busy and excited about their accomplishments. By scheduling large blocks of time for child-directed (independent) activities, children feel freer to work and play at their own pace and are more likely to be cooperative and focused.

Additionally, our physical postures, movements, and gestures communicate a great deal of information to children. Infants and young children rely heavily on nonverbal communication to interpret moods and expectations in their interactions with others. Adults must consider nonverbal expressions whenever they attempt to communicate with children. Nonverbal communication must match verbal communication. If nonverbal cues are too playful or casual, children will assume that they don't have to comply. If cues are too threatening and intrusive, children bristle and resist the commands. If they are assertive, caring, confident, and respectful, children are likely to comply quickly and willingly.

A primary goal for early childhood development is the growth of personal responsibility and independence in children. In order to become socially competent, children need to master active negotiation skills so that they can successfully resolve at least some of their own problems. There are occasions when children should not be rescued from the unpleasant (but reasonable and safe) consequences of their own actions. To foster independence, children should be *helped* to do as much for themselves as they can reasonably be expected to handle successfully.

Toddlers behave aggressively primarily because they lack the verbal ability to express themselves otherwise. In positive child guidance, children are taught ways to communicate feelings honestly and assertively without having to resort to verbal aggression. We should never push children into being so "nice" that they hold their emotions inside. Our goal is to channel their emotional expression into words and actions that *inform* rather than words and actions that *hurt*.

No child should be forced to say she feels something that she really doesn't feel. Insisting that children apologize, whether or not they feel regret, is neither an honest nor effective way to guide children. Sharing should also be voluntary. We can encourage generosity most by protecting a child's property rights, so that he feels it is safe to invite others to share. The more vulnerable the child feels about losing his possessions, the more tightly and greedily he will guard them.

Children learn skills and information through active involvement in their day-to-day environment. They learn by watching others, by being told things, and (most importantly) by experiencing life. In life, actions are often followed by logical or natural consequences. Punishment is negative. It is intended to hurt, humiliate, or pay a child back for something she has done. Discipline is optimistic and assertive rather than mean-spirited and punitive. In discipline, the adult's attitude is one of helping children succeed in behaving more appropriately in the future, not making them miserable to punish them for past deeds.

In order to be firm and fair in guiding children, deeds must be seen as separate from the person who did them. Also, caring adults must know how to say "no." Not being firm enough is just as damaging as being too firm.

Children need freedom within clear limits. Freedom without limits is not really freedom: instead, it is chaotic and dangerous. Positive child guidance is not a gimmicky strategy to manipulate children into behaving according to our specifications. Instead it is a process of guiding children to become competent, confident, and cooperative human beings who behave well, not to win favors, but because behaving well is the right thing to do.

Some behaviors, however, do not come from internal motivation. They are unconscious habits that are very resistant to internal desire for change. It may be necessary to change external surroundings in order to break a mindless habit cycle. Children generally do whatever they need to do to get their needs met. Many unconscious habits are formed simply because they obtain for children the attention or objects they want. We need to analyze our daily procedures very carefully to identify the behaviors children use to get the things they want and need in the environment.

Behaviorists see learning as a process of piecing together a chain, one link at a time. The process is external to the child because the adult chooses the skill to be learned and then rewards that behavior in the child.

Exceptional children (children with developmental delays, learning deficits, and language disabilities) may lack the ability to discuss or reflect on their inner motivations. Behavior modification may be the most humane and effective strategy for guiding these children. Behavior modification can also be used very successfully with well-developing, even gifted, children, if the adult succeeds in enlisting the children's active, voluntary cooperation. Children and adults who are capable of examining their own and the motives of others will feel betrayed or coerced if they realize that their behavior has been manipulated without their knowledge.

Behavior modification is a powerful tool when used appropriately, as long as it does not become an excuse to abdicate responsibility for children's unacceptable behavior. There is a risk, however, that if used inappropriately, behaviorist tactics can become manipulative and aloof. Ignoring can become punitive and hurtful, and the adult can find herself working *on* the child rather than *with* the child.

PRACTICAL APPLICATION/DISCUSSION

The Big Boys and the Very Muddy Day

Mrs. Belk taught first-graders in a neighborhood public school for several years. She already had her undergraduate degree in early-childhood education but decided to upgrade her skills by taking a graduate course in psychology at a nearby university. She was enrolled in the class for only a few weeks, but the professor already lectured on various methods for reinforcing positive behaviors rather than focusing only on inappropriate behaviors. What a great idea, she thought. Ignore the negative and reinforce the positive.

Mrs. Belk was eager to try some new disciplinary techniques on several of her more difficult children, especially Chad, who tended to be her group's ring leader for inappropriate behavior. Chad was tall for his age and wiry. He appeared to be a thin child, but he was surprisingly muscular. His calf muscles were rock-hard and bulged conspicuously on his skinny legs. Mrs. Belk thought that he probably worked off every ounce of fat by being in a constant state of motion.

For two years, he had been taking daily prescription doses of a medication for hyperactivity (which his doctor referred to as hyperkinesis or attention-deficit disorder). His parents and teachers agreed that the medication helped him to function at home and at school, but he still had a difficult time dealing with the limits that adults set. And, adults had a difficult time coping with his frenetic level of activity and wildly impulsive behavior.

The past week was particularly stressful for Mrs. Belk. Chad was even more out of control than usual. It rained for so much of the week that the children did not once play outside. Mrs. Belk felt as if the classroom were shrinking and the children multiplying.

She looked out the window. The sun was out and the only problem with the playground was that there were still some very large mud puddles here and there. Mrs. Belk flipped the light switch on and off several times to signal the children that it was time to put away their work and gather on the rug for story time. When the room was clean and the children were all sitting around on the floor in a big circle, Mrs. Belk said, "How would you like to go outside to the playground?"

To their gleeful shouts of, "Yes, yes, yes!" Mrs. Belk answered, "We can go outside on one condition. Everyone has to agree only to play on the dry areas. There are mud puddles and you must remember to walk around them." The children eagerly agreed to stay on dry land. Chad and his buddies were so excited that they could hardly contain themselves, but they promised Mrs. Belk that they would not forget about the mud puddles.

Mrs. Belk opened the door and was stampeded by squealing, laughing children. As Mrs. Belk walked out into the bright sunlight, she took a deep breath of fresh air and felt a great sense of relief to be outside the stuffy classroom.

After only a few seconds, she saw Chad running backwards to catch a ball, and—splatt—he stepped right into the mud. Mrs. Belk stood with her hands on her hips, glaring at Chad and thinking whether or not to have him sit down on the bench for ten minutes for breaking a class rule. She knew that it was a real effort to keep Chad sitting for ten minutes. Mrs. Belk dreaded a confrontation and decided that she just didn't have the energy to deal with Chad at the moment.

She thought about what her professor said about ignoring inappropriate behavior. And besides, she thought, maybe his stepping in the mud was really an accident. She looked the other way and decided to ignore Chad. Within seconds several children were pulling at her shirt sleeves saying, "Mrs. Belk, Mrs. Belk, look. Chad is in the mud!" Mrs. Belk told them, "Go play, and don't pay any attention to Chad."

Within minutes, two of Chad's favorite cohorts, Eddie and John, hollered as Chad stamped his foot in the mud, splattering mud on them. They found it necessary, of course, (after they nervously looked back to make sure Mrs. Belk's back was still turned) to stamp their feet in the mud, splattering Chad from head to toe. The chase was on with half the class frantically telling Mrs. Belk, "Look, look at Chad!" and the other half squealing and laughing as the three boys chased and slid in the mud.

Mrs. Belk saw that her strategy was not working. With the look of daggers in her eyes she shouted, "Okay, everybody line up at the door to go inside." All of the children (except Chad, Eddie, and John) hurried to the door and made a straight line. In a loud voice, Mrs. Belk stared straight at the three boys and said, "I'm waiting. Not everyone is ready to go inside." She thought, "There is no way I am going to chase those three around in this mud. They are just doing this to get attention. They'll come as soon as they think we are really going inside." Mrs. Belk opened the door and said, "Everyone walk quietly in the hall, please." While the group of children were led inside, they nervously glanced back and forth at Mrs. Belk and the three boys running around outside. They knew the three boys were in a lot of trouble, and they knew Mrs. Belk was angry. The three boys chased and played in the mud, pretending not to notice that the others were going inside, and trying to look tough and macho. By this time, their shoes and clothes were caked with mud and they were beginning to feel very uncomfortable.

As soon as Mrs. Belk ushered her line of children inside, she asked another teacher to watch her class while she stood behind the door where the boys couldn't see her and watched them through the glass. The other teacher's mouth dropped open as she saw the mud-covered boys. Mrs. Belk said, "They're just doing this for attention, so the best thing is to ignore it. I'm sure they'll get tired of it in a few minutes when they realize they don't have an audience, and then they'll be begging to come inside."

Within five minutes, a teacher whose room overlooked the playground ran down the hall and said, "Mrs. Belk, you've got to get those boys inside! They've taken off all their clothes and they are on top of the fort throwing mud balls at the building and at cars."

The playground was a mess. The building and cars were a mess, and the boys were a mess. The situation was no longer salvageable. The boys had to be forcibly brought inside. The principal called their horrified parents to come and get them. There was no easy way for the boys to make amends for their behavior or to save face in front of their peers, parents, and teachers. They had engaged in an open rebellion, a serious and scary step for a child, and a damaging precedent for future behavior.

QUESTIONS FOR DISCUSSION

1. What are some possible reasons for Mrs. Belk's ignoring the muddy boys. Evaluate those reasons.
2. List some ways that you think these problems could have been

avoided. What could Mrs. Belk have done that might have prevented or stopped the inappropriate behavior?

3. What do you think the muddy boys were thinking and feeling throughout this episode? What do you think the rest of the children were thinking and feeling?

4. How would you have responded if you were the principal? The parents? Another teacher in the building?

5. If you were Mrs. Belk, what would you say or do when the boys came back to school the next day?

Figure 9-1 Healthy, well-developing children are supposed to be lively and full of silliness.

9

Guidelines for Effective Discipline

Maintain and Express Confidence that Problem Will
   Be Resolved
Protect the Child's Dignity and Privacy
Be Willing to Start Over—To Forgive and Forget

OBJECTIVES
   This chapter will assist you in:

- Developing specific strategies for effective discipline.
- Formulating guidelines for responding to inappropriate behaviors.
- Identifying methods to shape positive behavior.
- Specifying techniques for assertive redirection and follow-up.

IGNORE MILDLY ANNOYING BEHAVIOR THAT IS NEITHER HARMFUL NOR UNFAIR

Children are not helped by intrusive and overwhelming attempts to change too much of their behavior at one time. Adults do well to focus disciplinary actions on urgent priorities, while overlooking mildly annoying behaviors that are neither harmful nor unfair to others. In dealing with a child who behaved aggressively and who also bites her fingernails and rocks her chair back and forth, an adult should initially focus attention only on the aggression. A mental note could be made to address the other problems in a more subtle and indirect manner at a later time, well after the aggression is been resolved. We adults sometimes have a tendency to "unload all barrels," overwhelming children with too many demands, especially when we are angry and upset.

Focus Attention Elsewhere

When a child does something that is mildly annoying or embarrassing (but not unacceptable), the adult may resolve the problem simply by focusing the child's attention elsewhere. A baby who bangs a spoon on a metal highchair tray in a restaurant may be distracted by a parent who plays peek-a-boo or dangles a softer, quieter toy. A thumb-sucking toddler may be distracted from the sucking by an interesting toy. A curious preschooler may be distracted from handling items on shelves in the grocery store by being allowed to help push the grocery cart or to help arrange foods in the basket as they are selected.

Discreetly Redirect Slightly Inappropriate Behavior to More Positive Substitute Behavior

Slightly annoying behaviors can also be redirected by involving the child in an activity that replaces (cannot be done simultaneously with) the undesirable behavior. For example, a child who picks at his nose can be directed to use a tissue to blow his nose. Without even mentioning the nose picking, the adult can explain how using a tissue, throwing away the tissue, and then washing hands may keep others from catching a cold.

In order to redirect slightly inappropriate behaviors, adults can identify activities that involve the part, or parts, of the child's body he is currently using in the undesirable action, and substitute an alternative action involving those body parts. For example, a child who is using her *hands* to feel the blossoms of a neighbor's delicate and expensive garden plants could be shown how to put her hands behind her back or in her pockets while she leans over to smell the wonderful fragrance of the gardenias. She could also be redirected to use her hands to gather interesting leaves and acorns from the ground.

This helps the child know that it is okay to explore and enjoy nature but not okay to damage another person's property. Snapping, "Don't touch those plants!" discourages curiosity—a key factor in the child's long-term ability to develop intellectually. Of course, standing by passively while one's child damages a neighbor's prized gardenias would be rude and disrespectful.

Another method for gently redirecting minor misbehaviors involves focusing the child's attention on the positive outcome of more desirable

Figure 9-2 "Baby William smiles when you show him a toy."

behaviors. The adult gives information to the child. The adult might say, "If you put your glass of milk on the top corner of your place mat, it will be safely out of your way until you want to drink it." A teacher might say, "If you erase mistakes slowly and lightly, your paper will look very nice." A toddler can be told, "I like to hear 'thank you.' Oh, how nice! Brett remembered to say 'thank you.' "

IMMEDIATELY INTERRUPT BEHAVIOR THAT IS HARMFUL OR UNFAIR

Children rely on adults to enforce rules and protect individual rights. Children will be willing to "play by the rules" only if they believe that rules are meaningful. Consistency and fairness in the enforcement of rules help children learn to trust authority figures. Behaviors that are harmful or unfair must be interrupted immediately by a responsible adult.

Adults do *not* help children become cooperative and respectful by passively watching them fight, saying, "They'll just have to learn to stand up for themselves. When Jimmy has enough of Gerald hitting him, he'll learn to hit back." We also fail to help children when we say, "Don't come tell me that someone hit you. I don't want to hear about it!" Children *can* be helped to resolve their own disagreements, but they must know that adults will reliably stop unacceptable, hurtful behavior.

Intervene as Firmly as Necessary, as Gently as Possible

When adults find it necessary to stop an unacceptable behavior, they should always proceed as firmly as necessary to stop the unacceptable action, but as gently as possible to remind the child that he is accepted and respected as a person even if his behavior must be ended.

For example, Miss Melanie firmly pries a toddler's clenched fingers one-by-one out of another screaming toddler's hair, she says with a tone of urgent concern (not anger) in her voice, "Ouch! Pulling hurts. No pulling. Touch gently please!" After the toddlers are safely separated, she softly strokes each toddler's hair saying, "Gentle, be gentle. Please touch hair gently." Miss Melanie has interrupted a harmful behavior as firmly as necessary but as gently as possible.

Roger grabs a little car from his friend Chris and runs away. Chris yells and starts to cry. Mr. Reese follows Roger (persistently but without chasing him), saying in a deeply concerned tone, "Stop, please. Roger, I need you to stop so that we can talk about Chris's car." When Roger finally pauses for a second, Mr. Reese says, "Thank you for

Figure 9–3 Enforcing fair rules protects the rights of all the children.

waiting. Let's sit down and talk about Chris's car. You like Chris's car, don't you. It's really a neat car isn't it."

Mr. Reese does not immediately attempt to snatch the car away from Roger. He patiently asks, "What should you do if you want to see someone else's toy? Should you ask, 'May I play with your car?'" Roger hung his head and said, "But if I ask him, he might say '*no*'." Mr. Reese answered, "You're right. He might say 'yes' or he might say 'no'. Would you like for me to come with you so you can ask? If he says 'no', I will help you find a different toy to play with. Remember, taking things without asking is not allowed. When you choose a toy, no one will be allowed to take *your* toy away without asking you first, right?"

Roger's unfair action was stopped, firmly but gently, and Roger had a chance to learn a very important lesson. Although rules sometimes stop him from doing what he wants to do, they also assure that his own rights are protected.

Maintain Objectivity

Marilyn's three-year-old daughter, Stephanie, waited patiently (although she became very bored) while her mother shopped for new towels in a department store. Stephanie saw a little boy about her age shopping with his mother on the other side of a large pillow display. Stephanie peeked around the edge of the pile of pillows to get a better look at the little boy. He grinned at her. Embarrassed, she quickly scrambled back from behind the pillow display. Unfortunately, in her haste, she dislodged the display and an avalanche of pillows piled down on top of her.

Two sales persons rushed over (looking very annoyed) and several other shoppers stared at the mess. Marilyn was startled and horrified to see what Stephanie had done. She grabbed Stephanie by the arm and marched her off to the ladies' lounge to have a "few words." Marilyn didn't manage to stay objective about her daughter's behavior. She took her own feeling of embarrassment out on Stephanie. She could be more helpful to Stephanie if she were able to maintain a more objective and less emotional perspective.

Adults can greatly assist the development of self-control in children by staying focused on the reality of a situation rather than on feelings that are not relevant to the child's problem, preconceived notions, and biased attitudes that don't relate directly to what the child has done. Marilyn's guidance will be more effective if she can push aside her feelings of humiliation (and apprehension that complete strangers will think she is a bad mother). Marilyn should focus on the objective reality of the situation. Stephanie was trying to wait patiently. She didn't intentionally do anything wrong, and she was obviously feeling upset and embarrassed herself.

Positive child guidance is basically an educational process. As in any educational process, powerful emotions such as anger, disgust, or the threat of harm, *damage* rather than *assist* the process of learning.

Figure 9–4 Even a child who has misbehaved deserves to know she is still loved. *(Photo courtesy of Rod Smalley)*

People, children included, are better able to concentrate and absorb information when they are reasonably calm and relaxed. A terrified child may remember vividly the look of daggers in a parent's eyes but completely forget the whole point of the reprimand and not be able to recall what behavior caused the problem in the first place.

It is perfectly normal and healthy for us to feel waves of sheer fury now and again. Because of our size and power, however, it is appropriate for us to release most of those feelings of frustration and rage away from young children. We can jog, punch and knead bread dough, or pound out melodies on a piano. It is not fair or helpful to blow children away with powerful and scary expressions of anger. We can be honest without being overpowering.

Remove the Child from a Problem Situation

Removing a child from the scene of a conflict allows a cooling-off period for the adult and child, removes whatever temptation the child has difficulty with (out of sight, out of mind), and assures that a gawking or giggling audience is not watching and triggering further misbehavior. Although compromise should never be considered during the heat of a full-blown tantrum, compromise *after* the child has gained control may serve as a powerful reinforcer in teaching the child to talk rather than scream to get what she wants.

Occasionally, adults have no choice but to pick up a young child, who may be kicking and screaming, and haul the child (as gently as possible but as firmly as necessary) away from the scene of a conflict. A preschooler who is having a tantrum in a grocery store because she can't have the candy bar she wants should probably be escorted, or, if necessary, picked up and carried out of the store. She can be helped to understand that she has two, and *only* two, choices. She can sit and cry for a long, long time in the car with her patient but assertive father, or she can return to the grocery store and continue the shopping trip, accepting the fact that there will be no candy bar.

If the father, through consistent verbal and nonverbal communication, convincingly indicates to his daughter that he will not become angry or argumentative, but that he will also absolutely *not* back down, the little girl will soon recognize the futility of a long, dramatic, exhausting fit of crying. She will learn that that sort of thing simply doesn't work.

When she seems ready to throw in the towel, recognizing that she can't bully or manipulate her father he should give her an opportunity to "save face." At this point, restraint, tactfulness, empathy, and perhaps an appropriate compromise (letting her choose a nutritious snack to take home) would prevent a winner-and-loser situation. The little girl's future cooperativeness will hinge on her feeling confident that she can be cooperative without losing her dignity and autonomy, and without having her past mistakes thrown in her face.

ASSERTIVELY SHAPE POSITIVE BEHAVIOR

When a child must be subjected to an unpleasant occurrence, the situation should be discussed squarely and honestly to give the child a chance to cooperate voluntarily. The situation should not, however, be allowed to stall or become a stalemate if the child refuses to cooperate. When a scraped knee requires medication, the adult should quickly and matter-of-factly explain what must be done, and then get the unpleasant task over even if the child is unwilling. The longer discussion, whining, and arguing are tolerated, the more unpleasant and stressful the task of applying medicine will become.

Separation is a good example of a necessary but unpleasant occurrence in the lives of toddlers. Before a separation, parents should have all the time they want to visit with their child and express affection.

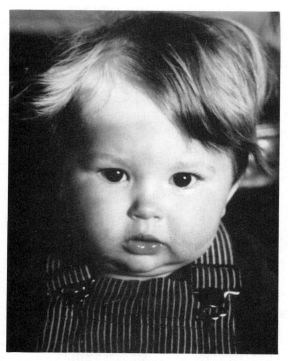

Figure 9–5 Saying good-bye to Mommy and Daddy may be very difficult at times. *(Photo courtesy of Gary Peters)*

A parent should not be rushed but should clearly indicate to the caregiver when she is ready to leave (and willing to actually walk out the door). At this decisive moment of separation, a skilled caregiver will firmly but lovingly state, "Mommy needs to leave now. You may give Mommy a hug, and then wave bye-bye through the window. Or, if you need, I can hold you while Mommy leaves." If the child is clearly not willing to hug mommy and wave good-bye, then the parent and caregiver can move quickly and assertively to get the separation over with, even if the child resists loudly and has to be held.

The caregiver can express empathy, "Yes, you love your Mommy. You miss her when she leaves. Sometimes I miss my Mommy too. Did you know I have a Mommy? Let's go see the dolls. Would you like to feed a bottle to our baby doll? Which baby doll do you want?" One can shape positive behavior by making sure that it happens. Adults can often help children avoid situations in which they may experience failure by quickly and decisively making the right thing happen, and then rapidly moving on to happier activities. The adult can do this without giving an appearance of frustration, anger, guilt, or disgust with the child's inability to actively cooperate or comply. Children's negative feelings should be acknowledged and accepted, but they don't necessarily need to be dwelled upon for a lengthy period of time.

Teach Ground Rules

Children need to know exactly what is expected of them. Simple, consistently enforced guidelines help children learn to respect and abide by rules. Children, however, must have adult help in order to understand and remember ground rules.

Following are several ways adults can actively teach children about rules.

Role Play

Give children a chance to "act out" or practice correctly following rules. For preschoolers, switch roles so that the child can see and experience an appropriate response. Pretend to be the child and allow the child to pretend to be the adult, or pretend to be the child's troublesome friend. For example, "I will pretend to be Bert. Let's pretend I just pulled your hair. Can you point your finger at me, make a frown, and say, 'Don't pull my hair. That hurts!' "

Repetition

Children need many opportunities to hear a rule repeated before knowledge of that rule fully reachs the child's long-term memory bank. Any adult who experienced an electrical power failure but mindlessly continued attempting to turn on appliances and lights knows that having knowledge of a thing doesn't necessarily bring about an immediate change in habit behaviors. We have to remind ourselves over and over, "Oh, yes, I can't listen to the radio . . . .Oh, the electric can opener won't work . . . .Oh, the clock is not right." Children need and deserve patient reminders of rules and expectations so that they will be encouraged to change their habit patterns.

Discussion

Rules have much more *meaning* for children who really understand reasons for the rules. Adults should remove from their vocabulary that age-old phrase, " . . . because I said so," which is often used as a blanket explanation for all rules and regulations issued by adults. Positive guidance requires that adults explain things to children simply and honestly. For example, "You must use the blunt knife instead of the sharp knife. I don't want you to get cut." "You may not open the gate without permission, because the street is busy and dangerous." "You must wash your hands with soap and water before you eat. Your hands are dirty and you could get sick from getting germs in your mouth."

Figure 9–6 "Can you remember our rule about using words instead of hitting?" *(Photo courtesy of Lynne Aiken)*

Clarify Expectations

If we want children to follow our instructions, we must make sure that they really understand what we intend for them to do. Adults often speak in vague, general terms. They say things such as, "Be good." "Be nice." "Act like a big boy (or girl)." What children need are simple but specific statements of our expectations. For example, we might say such things as:

> "Sit down please. Make sure your bottom is *in* the chair and your feet are *on* the floor."
> "Please hold your milk with *both* hands."
> "Please wait at the *bottom* of the slide until the person in front of you has gone down the slide. Then, you may climb up and have *your* turn."
> "I need for you to use a *soft, slow* voice to talk to me about your sister. I don't like to listen to whining and screaming."

Additionally, adults sometimes assume that children automatically know how objects are intended to be used. Instead, children over the age of three need to be told specifically what various objects are for. Babies and toddlers put bowls on their heads, try to eat decorative plastic fruit, and attempt to pull tee shirts on like underpants. One can gently guide them toward the proper use of objects, but they need a great deal of freedom to explore safe objects thoroughly, using all their senses and muscles to discover their world. If a baby or toddler stands up in a chair that could fall, she should tactfully be redirected to a safer place to climb. Or, the chair should simply be removed. A child past three, however, can be told, "A chair is for your seat, not your feet."

Figure 9–7 "Please hold your milk with both hands."

Figure 9–8 "A shovel is a tool for digging."

Children past three can be taught the difference between toys, tools, and weapons. For example, "A toy is something you can play with, a tool is something useful to help you, and a weapon is intended to hurt someone. At school we use toys and tools but not weapons." A ball can be used as a *toy* to play catch, or it can be used as a tool to knock a kite out of a tree; but it must not be used as a weapon to hit someone in the face. A fork should be used only as a *tool* to pick up food, not as a toy to wave around, or as a *weapon* to poke at another child. Older children are especially capable of comprehending and identifying categories of objects. They will spontaneously point out to one another, "That pencil is a tool. It's for writing. You mustn't use it like a toy or a weapon!"

Maintain Consistency

In order for children to behave appropriately, there must be consistency, with a reasonable level of flexibility, in the adult's expectations and enforcement of rules. Discipline should not be based on the adult's mood or coincidental circumstances. For example, it would be inconsistent to indicate to a young child (through our actions), "You can walk around the house eating and dropping crumbs, except when I am too tired and crabby to clean up after you, or when we have company." There should either be a consistent rule that eating takes place at the table, or that eating at various places in the house is allowed, as long as each family member cleans up after himself or herself.

Older children, who have a clear understanding and acceptance of specific rules, can deal with occasional exceptions to those rules. They can understand that family members are expected to eat in the kitchen, even though on special, *designated* occasions food may be eaten in the living room in front of the television.

Toddlers and young preschoolers, on the other hand, do not have a full grasp of rules. They view the world in very literal, black-and-white terms. An action either *is* or *is not* allowed. They become very frustrated and confused and tend to ignore a rule altogether if it seems to them to be inconsistently enforced. For example, little ones should not ever be allowed, even once, to ride in a car without being properly buckled into an appropriate car seat. If they believe that there is absolutely no chance that the car will move until they are seat belted, they will accept the car seat as a fact of life rather than something to be negotiated through whining and resisting.

In order to be consistent, adults should make very sure that a child's behavior is not laughed at on one occasion and reprimanded on another. Bathroom terms that brought giggles at home may not be nearly so funny at church or synagogue, or announced loudly at a family gathering. The toddler with spaghetti in his hair may be adorable the first time, but if he receives a great deal of attention (laughter, photographs, calling the neighbors to come see), he may be inclined to repeat the behavior on a regular basis, which will not be nearly so entertaining to harried parents the second, third, or fourth times.

In the early childhood setting, consistency, with reasonable flexibility, is *essential*. Marty, a toddler teacher, tried to teach her eighteen-month-olds not to climb on the low, redwood picnic table on their playground. Toddlers who climbed on the foot-high plank table were removed and placed on a foot-high, redwood plank deck nearby for a "time-out." Marty knew that decks were to walk on and tables were not. To the toddlers, however, the rule about climbing seemed inconsistent. Both structures looked about the same. They were removed from one and placed on the other as a negative consequence. Being on the second structure was intended to teach them not to get on the first structure. Of course, the toddlers were never able to make sense of Marty's rule. So, for the most part, they simply ignored it.

Remove Possible Causes of Problem Behavior

It is almost always *easier* to change the circumstances surrounding a child than it is to change the child. Additionally, it is more nurturing and less stressful for everyone involved if adults focus on setting the stage for proper behavior, rather than on reprimanding children after they behave improperly. For example, if children run in the classroom, it is better and easier to change the room arrangement to make run-

Figure 9–9 Positive guidance means that adults work diligently to help children behave appropriately—not just to correct them after they have behaved inappropriately.

ning difficult than to endlessly remind children to walk. If toddlers persist in spilling their milk, they can have smaller cups with only an ounce of milk at a time. That way, if they do have a spill, very little milk is wasted and very little effort is needed to clean it up.

Rather than yelling to get the attention of rowdy children, an adult can use a dramatic whisper. Children will almost always pay more attention to a whisper than to a bellowing voice. If children in a preschool program consistently become tired and irritable on field trips, perhaps field trips can be rescheduled to a different time of day or to a shorter time period, or perhaps they can be made less often to more carefully chosen locations.

When confronted with troublesome behavior problems, adults should ask themselves, "Instead of trying to change the child, is there any way I can reasonably change the child's environmental surroundings, my own actions, or attitudes to ease the problem."

Offer Assistance and Encouragement

Children thrive on positive attention. They usually become very compliant when adults say, "How can I help you remember this rule?" "What can *we* do to make it easier for you to get to bed on time?" "Let's practice the words you should say when you feel angry." Positive guidance means that adults work very, very diligently to help children

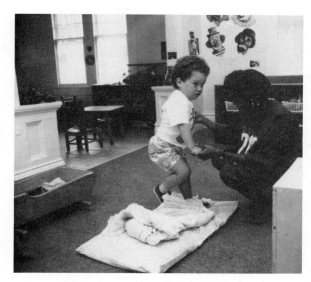

Figure 9–10 "Jeremy, it's time for nap."

behave appropriately. Their goal is not just to punish children for behaving inappropriately, but instead to make the right thing happen.

Give Undivided Attention

Children immediately recognize whether an adult is serious enough about what he is saying to stop and see that a request is followed. Even toddlers and preschoolers know that instructions don't mean much when they are given by an adult casually glancing back across his shoulder, making an offhanded comment across a room, "Come on now, put those toys away."

In contrast, children sense that instructions mean a great deal when the adult stops what he is doing, walks to the child, bends down to eye level, gently touches the child's shoulder, and looking directly into the child's eyes, says in a gentle but firm tone, "Sherrie, I need you to stop now and put the blocks away." A half-hour of nagging and threatening from across the room will not have the impact of one quiet statement made eye-to-eye, using the child's name.

Undivided attention has a powerful effect on children. In positive child guidance, attention focused directly on children will be assertive, positive, and self-esteem building rather than negative, angry, and destructive of pride and confidence.

The following four actions can be carried out in a positive way to show children that they have our undivided attention and that we really care about their behavior:

Eye Contact

Move close and try to establish eye contact. A shy child or a child who has experienced eye contact as part of threatening, angry interactions will feel compelled to look away. Don't force the child to look you in the eye, but rather attempt to win the child's trust by associating eye contact with positive, loving interactions. If the child does look you in the eye, sincerely commend him, "Thank you for listening so well."

Body Positioned at Child's Level

Bend down to the child's eye level. Staring down one's nose at a child tempts the child to look away. Being stared down on may also seem cold, threatening, or belittling to the child (a little like being formally grilled by an FBI agent).

Appropriate Touch

Gently placing a hand on a child's shoulder or arm, or lightly holding one or both of the child's hands helps focus attention. If the child is sitting on the floor, gently touching a foot or knee will obtain the child's attention and communicate caring concern. Appropriate touching is never grabby or forced. Follow the child's signals. Children usually make it very clear whether they find the adult's touch aversive or comforting.

Use of Child's Name

Using a child's given name or accepted nickname is more personal and appropriate than general terms of endearment such as "sweety" or "honey." Adults in early care and education settings must learn every child's name very quickly in order to be effective. Sadly, some young children hear their names yelled so often as a reprimand that they fail to respond as we would expect when their name is used in a positive context. They don't recognize their name as a symbol for who they are, but only as a word that means they are in trouble.

Redirect Inappropriate Behavior Firmly and Respectfully

An adult who must stop a child's inappropriate behavior can gain cooperation and avoid resentment simply by offering the child an acceptable, alternate activity. A child who pours milk back and forth from cup to bowl during a meal may be told, "You may not play with your food. *After* lunch (or after nap), I will show you a *good* place for pouring." The child could then be directed at an appropriate time to pour, squirt, dribble, and splash to her heart's content with dishes and toys at a sink, a bathtub, a commercial water table, an outdoor wading pool, or a plastic basin placed within her reach with an inch or two of water.

When children feel angry, they hit, kick, pinch, scratch, etc. These typical aggressive behaviors must be stopped. The child's anger should, however, be given an appropriate outlet. When a child is told, "Hitting hurts, no hitting is allowed," the adult should also add, "Use words. Tell Jessica you don't like it when she steps on your fingers. Show Jessica your fingers and tell her how much they hurt."

Common sense and knowledge of the basic principles of behavior modification will guide the effective use of redirection. Miss Kimberly, a toddler caregiver in a child-care center, was concerned about the biting that was happening almost daily her room. She thought that perhaps the toddlers were biting because their gums were uncomfortable with teething and they needed strong oral stimulation. She decided to offer hard crackers for the toddlers to bite as a substitute for biting each other. Within a few days, she discovered, to her dismay, that the toddlers were attacking and biting each other whenever they felt hungry for crackers. They became conditioned to expect crackers in response to biting.

Clearly Express Appropriate Feelings

Although it is very appropriate for adults to be honest in their expression of feelings to children, an adult's expression of *anger* can be too overwhelming for a young child to handle. Rage has no place in posi-

Figure 9–11 "Thank you for touching the plant so gently and carefully." *(Photo courtesy of Wilmer Roberts)*

tive child guidance. When confronted by a large, snarling, furious grownup, a young child has two possibilities: recoil in fear and try to stay out of the grownup's way, or fight back by being rebellious and insubordinate. Neither of those options help the child become a more confident, competent, and cooperative person.

Rather than focus on feelings of anger, the adult can identify the underlying feelings that caused the anger. The adult can ask, "Am I feeling angry because I was startled, disappointed, worried, frightened, or frustrated?" Instead of saying, "I am furious with you," the adult can say, "I felt really *frightened* when I didn't know where you were. I was *afraid* you were hurt or lost. I was so *upset* I felt like crying."

Following are several other examples of appropriate verbal expressions of adult feelings that give the child information but don't directly attack anyone:

- Surprise, Disbelief—"I can't believe this beautiful plant has its leaves torn off. Plants can die if their leaves are harmed."
- Sadness, Disappointment—"I feel very sad when I find books with the pages torn out. Books are beautiful and fun to read, but they aren't of any use when they are ripped apart."
- Concern, Worry—"I feel worried when I see you scratching your mosquito bite. Scratching may cause it to become infected and sore. Let's cover it with a Bandaid."
- Apprehension, Fear—"I feel very frightened when I see you climbing on the top rail of the fort. You must stay off the rails or else choose a different place to play on the playground."
- Distress, Frustration—"I feel very frustrated to find the door left open. We can't keep our house warm and comfortable inside when a door is left open. Please check the door each time you go out to make sure it's properly closed."

Explain the Potential Consequences of Unacceptable Behavior

Children past the age of three are usually perfectly capable of mentally connecting the cause-and-effect relationship between their conscious actions and potential consequences. If simple, polite, assertive statements of rules and expectations do not bring about an appropriate response from children, it is time to discuss potential consequences. Explaining potential consequences is *not* the same as bribing, intimidating, or giving idle threats. It is intended to inform the child, to give an honest, sincere warning of an impending consequence. It is not intended to manipulate, coerce, or trick the child into behaving a certain way, but rather to give the child honest, reasonable choices. "If you do this, *this* will happen. If you do that, *that* will happen." We should only give children reasonable choices that we know we will be comfortable carrying out. It is not acceptable to say, for example, "If you don't come with me this instant, I will leave you here in the store by yourself."

The old cliche that you can lead a horse to water, but you can't make him drink, fits children quite well. We can offer a well-balanced

Figure 9–12 The nurturing adult resolves conflicts assertively but respectfully. *(Photo courtesy of Cynde Miller)*

meal to a young child, but we cannot presume to force the child to eat it if she chooses not to. What we can do is say, "You may eat your vegetables and meat if you feel hungry. If you are not hungry enough to eat your dinner, then you may wait until breakfast to eat. I will put your plate in the refrigerator in case you change your mind." This statement is assertive, confident, and reasonable, but *not* threatening or punishing. It is merely a recognition that the child has choices about her own body, and the adult has choices and responsibilities about what foods are healthy and appropriate to offer.

Provide Persistent Follow-up

A motto to be emblazoned in the memory of all adults who deal with children is, "Say what you mean, and mean what you say." There is no magic wand or bag-of-tricks in positive child guidance—only persistence, persistence, persistence! Adults who persevere in firm, assertive, respectful, and caring discipline will surely see positive results in the children they care for and teach. Children may be very persistent in their patterns of misbehavior. We, as adults, however, must be even *more* persistent in our supervision, follow-up, and enforcement of reasonable, logical consequences.

The consistency of small but persistent nudges toward appropriate behavior are far more effective than erratic and inconsistent explosions of anger, harsh punishments, or intimidating threats. *The gentle, rippling stream etches deep patterns in solid rock. Pounding on rocks with sledge hammers changes the shape of the rocks but risks a lot of damage in the process.*

Emphasize Unconditional Caring and Affection

Unconditional caring, giving affection without any strings attached, is the foundation on which good discipline is built. Unconditional caring lets children know that they don't have to perform or achieve or submit to be loved and respected. We may disagree with things they do and work hard to change them, but we will still love and care for them. Adults should create an environment that tells children verbally and nonverbally (Clarke, 1978):

> "You have a right to be here. I'm glad you are who you are."
> "It is okay for you to have needs."
> "You don't have to be cute (sick, sad, mad, or scared) to get attention and approval."
> "It's okay to be smart, curious, and inventive and still get support and protection at the same time."
> "I'm glad you are growing up."
> "I'm not afraid of your anger."
> "You can express your feelings honestly, openly, and respectfully."

Figure 9–13 The nurturing adult listens and reflects the children's feelings, then helps them resolve their problems in a fair way.

Figure 9–14 "I'm glad I'm me!"

"You can be independent and still have needs."
"You can think before you make a rule your own."
"You can trust your feelings to help you know."
"It's okay to disagree."
"You don't have to suffer to get your needs met."
"I love you."

Maintain and Express Confidence

Guiding children can be frustrating and distressing at times. We look at our children and shake our heads, wondering if they will ever gain self-control and self-discipline. We must, however, firmly maintain and express confidence that specific problems will be resolved and our children will learn to behave appropriately, at least *most* of the time. Our confidence will strengthen children and convince them that control over their own behavior is a reachable goal.

Protect the Child's Dignity and Privacy

When positive, but assertive, disciplinary measures are necessary, children should be afforded the dignity of being talked to in private. They are humiliated by being corrected in front of their friends, or even in front of other adults. Adults should refrain from discussing in front of a child all the careless, immature, and improper things the child might have done. Adults should refrain from talking about and laughing about the child's past mistakes. And, most of all, adults should treat children the way they themselves like to be treated—with dignity and respect.

Be Willing to Start Over

In positive child guidance, adults should do the best they know how to do and, then, never look back. Worrying about the past, carrying grudges, or keeping mental lists of past misdeeds all undermine positive child guidance. For young children, every day is a new day. No matter what happened yesterday, today can be a good day and a successful day. When children know that adults are willing to forgive and forget, they will be more compliant and more willing to admit it when they know they are wrong. Forgiveness encourages honesty in children and motivates them to try harder to meet adult expectations.

SUMMARY

Children are not helped by intrusive and overwhelming attempts to change too much of their behavior at once. Adults should focus disciplinary actions on urgent priorities and overlook mildly annoying behaviors that are neither harmful nor unfair to others.

Mildly annoying behaviors can be resolved by simply focusing children's attention elsewhere, by involving the child in an activity that replaces the undesirable behavior, or by focusing the child's attention on the positive outcome of more desirable behaviors.

Consistency and fairness in the enforcement of rules help children learn to trust authority figures. Behaviors that are harmful or unfair must be interrupted immediately by a responsible adult. Adults should always proceed as firmly as necessary to stop an unacceptable action, but as gently as possible to remind the child that he is accepted and respected as a person even if his behavior must be ended.

Adults can greatly assist the development of self-control in children by staying focused on the reality of a situation, rather than on unrelated feelings, preconceived notions, and biased attitudes that don't relate directly to what the child has done. Positive child guidance is an educational process in which anger, disgust, or the threat of harm will damage rather than *assist* the process of learning.

Removing a child from the scene of a conflict allows a cooling-off period for the adult and child, removes whatever temptation the child is having difficulty with, and assures that having others watching is

Figure 9–15 Children's negative feelings should be acknowledged but not dwelled upon. *(Photo courtesy of Cynde Miller)*

not triggering further misbehavior. Compromise should only be considered *after* the child gains control. The development of compliance and cooperativeness hinges on children feeling confident that they can be cooperative without losing dignity and autonomy.

When a child must be subjected to an unpleasant occurrence, the situation should be discussed squarely and honestly to give the child a chance to cooperate voluntarily. A situation should not be allowed to become a stalemate if the child refuses to cooperate. Adults can help children avoid failure by quickly and decisively making the necessary action happen, and then rapidly moving on to more pleasant activities. Children's negative feelings should be acknowledged and accepted but not dwelled on.

Children need to know exactly what is expected of them. Simple, consistently enforced guidelines help children learn to respect and abide by rules. Children are helped to understand and remember ground rules through role play, repetition, and discussion.

Children past the age of three should be told what various objects are intended for. They can be taught the difference between toys, tools, and weapons. They can be told that a toy is something you can play with, a tool is something useful to help you, but a weapon is intended to hurt someone. At school we use toys and tools, but not weapons.

In order for children to behave appropriately, there must be consistency, with a reasonable level of flexibility, in the adult's expectations and enforcement of rules. The enforcement of discipline should never hinge on the adult's mood or coincidental circumstances. Toddlers and young preschoolers do not have a full grasp of rules, so they become especially frustrated and confused if rules are inconsistently enforced.

There are many situations in which it is easier and better to change the circumstances surrounding the child than it is to change the child.

Children thrive on positive attention. Adults should not just punish children for poor behavior but rather assertively shape positive behavior.

Undivided attention has a powerful effect on children. Attention focused directly on children should be assertive, positive, and promote self-esteem, rather than negative, angry, and destructive of pride and confidence.

The following four actions can be carried out in a positive way to show children that they have our undivided attention: eye contact, body positioned at child's level, appropriate touch, and use of the child's name.

When a child's inappropriate behavior must be stopped, the caregiver can gain cooperation by offering the child an acceptable alternate activity. Children's aggression should be redirected to more socially acceptable expressions of anger or distress.

Common sense and knowledge of the basic principles of behavior modification will guide the effective use of redirection. Redirecting children into especially rewarding or pleasurable activities may inadvertently reinforce the inappropriate behavior that triggered the redirection.

Rage has no place in positive child guidance. Rather than focusing on feelings of anger, adults can identify the underlying feelings that caused them to be angry (such as disappointment, worry, fear, or frustration). Adults can find appropriate ways to express surprise, disbelief, sadness, disappointment, concern, worry, apprehension, fear, distress, or frustration without overpowering children with anger or inducing guilt.

Children past the age of three are capable of mentally connecting the cause-and-effect relationship between their actions and potential consequences. Explaining potential consequences is not the same as bribing, intimidating, or giving idle threats. It informs the child of an impending consequence. It does not manipulate, coerce, or trick the child into behaving a certain way, but rather gives the child reasonable choices.

Figure 9–16 Unconditional caring means affection with no strings attached. *(Photo courtesy of Lynne Aiken)*

Adults who persevere in firm, assertive, respectful, and caring discipline will see positive results in the children they care for and teach. The consistency of small but persistent nudges toward appropriate behavior are far more effective than erratic and inconsistent explosions of anger, harsh punishments, or intimidating threats.

Unconditional caring is the giving of affection without any strings attached. It lets children know that they don't have to perform or achieve or submit to be loved and respected. They can be loved just because they are themselves (even though we may persist in attempting to change certain of their behaviors).

Adults should firmly maintain and express confidence that specific problems will be resolved and that children will learn to behave appropriately. Our confidence will strengthen children's confidence that they can gain control over their own behavior.

When assertive disciplinary measures are necessary, children should be afforded the dignity of being talked to in private. Children are indeed full-fledged human beings and, as such, should be treated with the respect we give to and expect from other people we admire and care deeply about.

Adults must be willing to let go of past events and look toward the future.

PRACTICAL APPLICATION/DISCUSSION

Will and the Cream-Cheese Wonton

Renee and Tom are loving and assertive parents. They taught their children—Amy, who is ten, and Will, who is five—to respect the rights of others. They consistently provided firm guidance tempered with unconditional love.

One evening the entire household was aflutter with excitement. The children's grandparents arrived for a short visit. Because Renee and Tom both worked, Renee picked the children up from child care and Tom picked up Chinese food for dinner from a favorite restaurant. Tom made sure to include an order of cream-cheese wontons. The children weren't too wild about Chinese food, but they both especially loved the restaurant's specialty—cream-cheese wontons.

The children helped set the table with festive place mats and napkins and even a candle. Everyone sat around the table chatting and enjoying dinner. Will sat up on his knees in the big dining chair so that he could see better. He listened attentively to every word of conversation as he slowly nibbled at the food on his plate.

As the family members finished eating, they pushed back their plates and continued to sit at the table, laughing and talking, catching up on family news and funny stories about the children and all their great adventures and escapades. When Tom finished eating, he leaned back in his chair, stretched out his long legs and draped an arm across the back of Will's chair. Tom really enjoyed these family get-togethers. As he laughed and talked, he happened to glance at Will's almost empty plate. He noticed one last cream-cheese wonton pushed to the back of the plate. Absent-mindedly, he picked up a fork, stabbed the wonton, and popped it into his mouth.

The instant Tom swallowed the wonton, he saw a stricken look fall across Will's face, and he knew he had made a big mistake. Will leaned close to his dad's ear and whispered intently, "Dad, we have to go to a lonely place and talk." Quietly, Tom got up from the table and followed Will to the bathroom. Tom sat down on the side of the bathtub while Will ceremoniously closed the bathroom door and then, with big tears sliding down his cheeks, said, "Dad, you're not supposed to take other people's things without asking. That was the only cream-cheese wonton left and I was saving it for last. You did a wrong thing."

Tom lifted Will into his lap and they hugged each other long and hard. Tom said, "You're right, son. I did do a wrong thing and I apologize." Tom almost had tears in his own eyes, but his heart was filled with pride that his son had been able to stand up for his rights but also had made a special effort to spare his dad's dignity—by asking to talk in a "lonely place."

QUESTIONS FOR DISCUSSION

1. Why do you suppose Tom ate Will's wonton? Have you ever inadvertently hurt a child's feelings? How did the child respond?
2. How do you think Will learned to resolve problems the way he did? Why do you think he asked for a "lonely place" to talk with his father?
3. How would it make you feel if a child responded to you the way Will responded to his father? How do you imagine Will's father felt? What do you suppose he was thinking during his conversation with Will?

Section 5

What Should I Do When Nothing Else Seems to Work?

Figure 10–1 Feelings of self-worth make it possible for a child to learn acceptable behavior. *(Photo Courtesy of Rod Smalley, Montessori Country Day School)*

10

Dealing with Patterns of Chronic Misbehavior

Locating Community Resources
Meeting Adult Needs

OBJECTIVES

This chapter will assist you in:

- Identifying chronic patterns of dysfunctional behaviors.
- Categorizing problem behaviors in terms of their misguided purpose.
- Defining the typical characteristics of problem behaviors.
- Recognizing various hidden reasons for children's misbehavior.
- Listing steps to resolve conflicts between adults and children.
- Defining strategies for meeting special needs.
- Identifying appropriate resources for problem-solving.

REACTING TO NEEDS—MASLOW'S HIERARCHY

Human beings—children and adults—behave in many complicated ways in order get their emotional needs met. At the heart of almost any behavior lies the desire to acquire something, whether an object, an experience, or just a feeling. Although some behaviors may be directed toward frivolous whims, many behaviors focus on basic human needs. Maslow (1943) developed a theory of human motivation. He proposed that basic needs are arranged in a hierarchy, a pyramid in which each overriding level of need has been met before successive levels of need can be addressed. Following is Maslow's list of emotional needs that motivate behavior arranged in the order in which they must be met. People need:

1. Freedom from discomfort—to have food, water, shelter, etc.
2. Physical safety, to feel secure from danger.
3. A sense of belonging, to feel loved.
4. Self-esteem, to feel valued and self-sufficient.
5. To stretch intellectually, to know and understand.

In other words, a child who is starving will not be concerned about anything other than sheer survival. A child who is frightened and insecure will show little interest in making friends or building castles with blocks. A child who feels unloved will not be able to function independently and confidently. In fact, very young children will tend to do whatever seems to work to get their needs met, no matter how

Figure 10–2 After physical comfort and safety needs are met, children's most pressing need is for a sense of belonging.

annoying or uncivilized their behavior seems to the adults around them, because they haven't yet developed the ability to inhibit their impulses. Only after their basic emotional needs are met can we expect them to be calm, cooperative, and curious learners.

The Role of Self-esteem in Chronic Misbehavior

Unmet needs are a hidden cause of chronic patterns of dysfunctional behavior in children. In order to behave well, children must have a strong sense of self-esteem. Many behavior-disordered children seem to be walking around with a big, black hole inside them where their self-esteem ought to be. Self-esteem has become more and more emphasized over the past few decades as a characteristic that seems closely tied to school success and social adjustment (Kokenes, 1974). Early-childhood educators especially focused on activities intended to foster self-esteem. Children, unfortunately, don't suddenly become equipped with a sense of self-worth simply because we have them sing a cute song about themselves and color in between the lines on a ditto sheet that says, "I am special."

Supporting the Child's Development of Self-esteem

The perceptions of value children place on themselves tend to be fairly accurate reflections of the values important others place on them (Coopersmith, 1967). If parents and caregivers see a child as lovable,

Figure 10–3 If adults consistently see a child as lovable, capable, and worthwhile, then the child will probably feel high self-esteem. *(Photo courtesy of Lynne Aiken)*

capable, and worthwhile, then the child will probably have a high level of self-esteem. Children begin to develop self-esteem from birth. But, they acquire self esteem only if their needs are met by attentive caregivers, they feel safe and loved, and they are consistently treated with respect (even while they are being disciplined). Although it may be possible to rebuild damaged self-esteem, it is much easier to support the development of a positive self-concept from the very beginning.

If a child's early experiences were damaging to her sense of self, it is essential to begin fostering self-esteem and to teach her functional ways to get her needs met. With a great deal of support and patience, children can unlearn old, dysfunctional behaviors that were the only way they knew to get their needs met in a confusing or unsupportive environment. Chronic cycles of dysfunctional behavior are difficult to handle, and adults easily fall into behaviors that are as dysfunctional as that of the children they are trying to help.

A key to success in dealing with children with habit patterns of inappropriate behavior is for the adult to persistently pull the child up to a more acceptable level of behavior, rather than allowing the child to pull the adult down to the child's level of immature and inappropriate interaction. This advice is easy to give but never easy to put into practice. It is amazing how quickly a tantruming two-year-old can bring a sedate and mature thirty-year-old down to the level of a screaming, irrational toddler.

THE NO-LOSE METHOD OF CONFLICT RESOLUTION

Often, children and adults become locked in a struggle over who will be in control. These power struggles become win-lose situations in which the only way the adults get their needs met is for children to submit to control, and the only way for children to get their needs met is for adults to submit to control. This tug-of-war pits adults and children against each other. Typically, this results in misbehavior patterns becoming chronic and well-established. Antagonism between adults and children can also begin to interfere with the pleasurable, nurturing interactions that strengthen self-esteem and are a critical part of daily life for children. Adults find themselves chronically annoyed with children, and children become more and more resistant and noncompliant.

The no-lose method of conflict resolution is a strategy for avoiding power struggles and for adults and children working together to solve problems positively and cooperatively. Following are six steps to use in resolving conflicts (Gordon, 1970; Dinkmeyer & McKay, 1982):

Figure 10–4 Nurturing adults are assertive but not punitive.

Step 1—Use reflective listening to clarify feelings.
Adult: "Joel, it sounds like you're angry because Amy keeps pulling at your book."

Step 2—Generate possible solutions by brainstorming.
Adult: "What are some ways you could let Amy know she is bothering you besides screeching?" "You could use words to tell Amy you are upset, or maybe you could move back away from her."

Step 3—Evaluate the probable consequence of possible solutions.
Child: "If I move back, Amy will still grab my book."

Step 4—Choose the best possible solution.
Adult: "I see. Perhaps it would be best for you to tell Amy how angry you feel when she takes your book. If she doesn't listen, then you can ask me for help."

Step 5—Decide how to carry out the solution; make a commitment to action.
Adult: "Would you like for me to come with you so that you can talk to Amy right now?"

Step 6—Evaluate how well the solution worked.
Adult: "Joel, do you feel better now? Do you think you will be able to remember about talking instead of screeching?"

After this interaction, Joel should feel that the adult is really on his side, that the adult is really trying to assist him rather than just take control of him. This guidance interaction is positive because it fosters self-esteem and helps the child feel more confident, competent, and self-reliant. Joel had an opportunity to participate actively in the decision making and to think through the process of problem solving.

DREIKURS' MISTAKEN GOALS

Taking steps to involve a child in conflict resolution is important, but in order to break a chronic cycle of dysfunctional behavior, the care giver must also simultaneously take steps to see that the child's emotional needs are met. Adler (1931), a colleague of Freud, theorized that dysfunctional behavior stemmed from inadequate early guidance. He believed that some children were kept from developing a sense of competence and self-worth by doting or dominating parents who saddled them with an inferiority complex, causing them to adopt inappropriate ways to exert control and feel competent.

Dreikurs (1974) further developed this idea for teachers and parents by proposing four mistaken goals that he hypothesized to be the root of long-standing, habitual patterns of dysfunctional behavior. He theorized that children behave inappropriately because of their overwhelming urge to:

- Get attention from others.
- Gain a sense of control.
- Get revenge for their own perceived hurts.
- Remove themselves from frightening or painful situations.

Each of the mistaken goals is directed toward getting an emotional need met. These include the need for recognition, the need for a sense of control over one's life, the need for fairness, and the need to avoid stressful and frightening situations. Unfortunately, each behavior listed above may seem to make the child feel a little better temporarily, but it actually compounds and worsens the problem in the long run. There is a snowball effect in which the child's inappropriate responses increase the negativity and hostility in her environment, which in turn increases her emotional neediness and the likelihood of her behaving more and more inappropriately in the future.

Oddly, a very natural reaction is to respond in a way that is precisely *opposite* to the response actually needed by the child. For example, we are tempted to ignore the child who is acting out to get attention, but that will cause him to have even more need to act out. We are tempted to get into a stern power struggle with the controlling child, "to show her who's boss," but this makes her feel even more powerless and out of control. We are sorely tempted to inflict pain on the aggressive child who bites or hurts another child, but angry aggression on our part can make the child even more resolved to get revenge. Additionally, we are tempted to shrug our shoulders and give up altogether on the withdrawn child who hides under a table, twisting his hair or bumping his head on the wall, but our abandonment only allows him to sink deeper and deeper into his isolation.

In order to bring about real change, we must cure (or at least

Figure 10–5 Sometimes children need to learn new ways to get their emotional needs met. *(Photo courtesy of Cynde Miller)*

relieve) the problems that cause chronic patterns of dysfunctional behavior, and retrain children in appropriate methods to get their emotional needs met. It is usually not very effective to tackle inappropriate behaviors as if they existed in a vacuum. When behavior is chronically dysfunctional, the child's misbehaviors can be thought of

Figure 10–6 Feelings of positive self-esteem blossom in young children as they live and play in a nurturing environment.

as superficial external symptoms, and the child's emotional neediness as an underlying disease. Suppressing behavioral symptoms without paying attention to the emotional well-being of the child may only result in the eruption of new or different symptoms.

Healing can only take place when the child feels she is an accepted and worthwhile group member, she has some sense of control over her life, she is treated fairly and respectfully, and she feels optimism that she can succeed in whatever is expected of her. If these feelings blossom in the child, then we can say that she has self-esteem, and the four key reasons for chronic misbehavior no longer exist. The child will no longer need to rely on misbehavior for emotional survival and can begin to break habit patterns and learn more effective ways to get along with others.

ATTENTION-SEEKING BEHAVIOR

Clinging, Feigning Ineptness

Human babies are born helpless and vulnerable. It makes sense that they become emotionally attached to caregivers, that they are most comfortable and secure when they can feel, see, or hear the caregiver's closeness. In a more primitive society, an infant's very survival could depend on staying close to a caring adult. As soon as infants are able to identify and distinguish among family members, caregivers, and strangers, they generally show signs of stranger anxiety and separation anxiety. A baby who always cooed, gurgled, and smiled for anyone will suddenly cry when a stranger leans close to admire her and tickle her chin. A one-year-old who usually toddles around the house getting into everything may become subdued and clingy while a visitor is in the house.

This bonding is a healthy and normal phase of development. Attachment to a dependable caregiver is an essential factor in the development of trust. We do no favor to babies and toddlers when we push them too early to break away from the adults who care from them. Babies who are allowed to develop secure, loving bonds with responsive caregivers become friendlier, more independent, and more successful preschoolers later (Bretherton and Waters, 1985) and Lamb, et. al. 1985). Close attachment in infancy does *not*, as parents often worry, cause children to become spoiled, clingy, attention-seekers.

Clingy children who pretend they can't do anything without help suffer from poor self-esteem. They have not been "loved" too much, although they may well have been overindulged and overprotected in ways that stunted their long-term development of healthy confidence and independence. Overindulgence and overprotection are poor excuses for real love, which is respectful and matched to a child's needs, rather than being intrusive or overwhelming. In some cases, clingy children may have been given too little attention and attachment. Their need to bond may never have been fully satisfied, and so they cling to baby behaviors. Clingy children only feel comfortable and loved when they are being fussed over and cared for. They long for the adult to cuddle them and to rescue them from their responsibilities.

Artificial Charm, Competitiveness

Children who are insecure in their sense of belonging often adopt an artificial charm. Younger children learn how to play the role of the adorable and irresistible child, while older children gush with insincere compliments. This niceness may vanish instantly, however, whenever the child feels threatened by attention directed toward someone else. The child may swing from absolute charmer to cold competitor in seconds. Adults may need to focus on developing the child's sense of security and self-esteem by giving sincere affection and encouragement at appropriate times. They may also need to set firm limits and help the child know that she is loved for herself, not for her fake charm.

Clowning, Acting Out, Silliness

Children use clowning, acting out, and silliness to get attention, not only from adults, but also from other children. Some children only seem to feel sure that they are loved and appreciated when they are at the center of attention, with everyone looking at them and either laughing or chiding. Children may be especially likely to get silly when they feel embarrassed or pushed into a corner. For some children, being a clown is a way of saving face and protecting damaged self-esteem.

Adults need to take care to allow clowning children to save their dignity. They should be corrected privately and respectfully when their acting out is unacceptable. It is also essential that they be given opportunities for responsibility and leadership in positive settings, as well as chances to entertain others in appropriate ways. For example, a child might be encouraged to plan a skit for classmates, chosen to pass out napkins or refreshments during a celebration, or allowed to sing, dance, or act out a story at group time.

Laziness, Compulsiveness, Obnoxiousness

Lazy, compulsive, or obnoxious behaviors may be a child's unconscious way of forcing adults to pay attention. They also signal a lack of self-esteem in the child. The child labeled as lazy may receive negative

Figure 10–7 Children who feel good about themselves feel comfortable behaving in a natural and spontaneous way, but they also are able to accept reasonable limits. *(Photo courtesy of Cynde Miller)*

attention when adults nag, take over the child's responsibilities, or insist that other children help or do the child's work for him. Children who overeat, bite their nails, tease, or purposely disgust other children and adults are also giving strong indications that they don't feel good about themselves.

Persistent, assertive, and loving guidance will build the child's respect for herself by helping her know that the adult cares deeply enough to become actively involved in redirecting her inappropriate behaviors. For example, a child who persists in running around the playground terrifying other children with bugs and worms could be *firmly* redirected from poking the creatures in others' faces to constructing a terrarium for the science center out of an old aquarium, some rocks and dirt, and a few little plants. There the insects and earth worms could be displayed in a socially acceptable manner that doesn't frighten or disgust others.

CONTROLLING BEHAVIOR

Manipulativeness, Vengefulness

Manipulative means trying to trick someone into doing something that he or she really doesn't want to do. Adults often role model this behavior in their attempts to gain control of the child's behavior. We tell children things such as, "Eat your bread crusts because they will make your hair curly," or, "Bend over, this shot won't hurt a bit!" We should not be surprised to hear a kindergartener say, "Give me your candy bar and I'll be your best friend forever."

Sometimes manipulativeness can become excessive and vengeful as children struggle to gain control of the children and adults around them. Adults need to define clear limits and help children become

Figure 10–8 Adults can help children become aware of the feelings of others. *(Photo courtesy of Cynde Miller)*

aware of the feelings and reactions of those around them. Adults can recognize and verbalize feelings. For example, "Sallie, I know you really want Alvie's doll, but the doll belongs to Alvie. Alvie doesn't like to play with you when you try to take her doll. You may choose a different toy, or you may play by yourself."

Pouting, Stubbornness

Children who want control but fail to get their way with others may react by pouting, stubbornly refusing to participate, or "causing a scene." The toddler who wants (but doesn't get) ice cream for dinner, for example, may push her plate off the highchair tray, kick her feet, scream, shake her head, and generally refuse to have anything to do with carrots and roast beef. .

Adults do no favor either by giving in to the toddler (and thus encouraging her controlling behavior) or by forcing nutritious food on her against her will. They can, however, avoid a power struggle by simply removing the toddler from the highchair and allowing her to express her anger. The adults can express sincere empathy, but allow the child to be stubborn without showing a great deal of attention or concern.

For example, the adult may say, "It's okay to cry. When you feel better, you can have dinner." When she finishes screaming, she may or may not want dinner. Either way, she will not starve before the next meal. The child's need for a sense of control can be met by allowing her to choose when she is ready to eat, not by letting her succeed in demanding things that are not in her best interest. Between the lines, the adult is saying, "You may make your own choices—within reasonable limits—but you must also deal with the consequences of your choices."

Bullying, Rebelling

Some children, when failing to gain control by other means, resort to bullying or rebelling. They gain control over smaller children by overwhelming them physically with their size and strength. Grownups are not usually so easy to bully, because size and strength advantages fall to the adult. A child, consequently, might be tempted to control adults by being so rebellious, so out of control, that adults feel totally helpless. It is important, however, that adults not allow themselves to lapse into feelings of inadequacy. The child needs strong, reliable adult support in order to give up dysfunctional behaviors and form new habits.

It is also essential for adults to avoid power struggles with the bullying or rebelling child. Head-to-head confrontation will trigger in-

Figure 10–9 It is most important for the child to discover that he is loved and respected. *(Photo courtesy of Cynde Miller)*

creases in angry rebellion and will not solve the problem. Aggressive, bullying behavior on the part of adults further establishes the role model for this undesirable behavior.

Instead, adults must find ways to build a positive relationship with the child and to help the child feel a sense of belonging. Clear limits are essential, as well as logical consequences, but the most important step is for the child to discover that he is loved, respected, and appreciated. Then he will be able to relax and relinquish his tight-fisted attempt to control those around him.

DISRUPTIVE BEHAVIOR

Destructiveness, Aggressiveness

Children whose self-esteem is lacking may deteriorate into disruptive habit patterns of destructiveness and aggression. These behaviors tell us that the child feels a sense of hopelessness. She may believe that she has already been rejected by others so that it really doesn't matter what she does. Nobody will like her no matter how she behaves. These feelings discourage her from developing self-control over her impulses.

The destructive or aggressive child must know that she will be stopped, that others' rights will be protected. Adults must not be afraid to do whatever has to be done to keep a child from harming others. A caregiver in a child-care facility who feels helpless and intimidated by a child does great harm to that child by allowing her to bite, kick, shove, pinch, and scratch other children and destroy shared toys. The caregiver must believe that he has two responsibilities:

- To befriend the child during non-crisis times and rebuild her feelings of self-esteem.
- To take steps to interrupt outbursts of aggression and protect other children and the physical environment.

The caregiver may need to ask for help from another staff member or administrator or from the parents. However tempting it may be for an adult to make excuses (no one will help me, I'm a single parent, my director is too busy, there is nowhere else for the child to be, psychologists are too expensive), the adult must not stop until he or she finds the support that is needed. Although it will probably not be necessary to call in the National Guard for help with a fifty-pound child who is throwing rocks, the caregiver *must have confidence* that if one strategy for stopping the child from hurting others doesn't work, then other strategies *will* be tried until something does work. The adult must be willing, in a crisis situation, to physically restrain the child as firmly as necessary but as gently as possible.

In dealing with a very difficult child, behavior modification may be an essential and effective tool for regaining a manageable relationship with the child. A reinforcer, or token reward, must be selected that is meaningful and desirable to the child. The specific desired behavior-goal must be identified in concrete terms, and a schedule of when, how, and under what circumstances the reinforcement will be given should be planned with the child. Reinforcement must always be immediate. As the child makes little steps of progress towards the desired behavior, she is instantly reinforced with a reward (a trinket or sticker) or a token (a plastic disk or checks on a chart) that can be exchanged at a predesignated number for special privileges or treats.

Behavior modification will be most successful (especially with an older child) if she enthusiastically agreed to participate in the plan. If the child likes and respects the adult and really wants to change some behaviors and habits she knows are unacceptable, she may be surprisingly willing to participate in a voluntary behavior modification plan—at least during the brief periods in which she is calm and logical.

During the entire process of behavior modification, the child must be helped toward the eventual weaning from external control to internal control. She can be told from the very beginning, "Changing bad habits is very, very hard for anyone! These little prizes will help you remember to use words instead of hitting. After a while though, you

Figure 10–10 Healthy emotional development hinges on the development of basic trust. *(Photo courtesy of Rod Smalley)*

won't need little prizes anymore. You'll remember to use words so that people will like you and want to play with you."

Contempt, Mistrust

Contempt and mistrust in children sadden and dismay us. The child filled with contempt has so much mistrust of others that he seems to despise everyone. We may find it necessary to backtrack and work on the basic development of trust. Just as a first-grader who lacked visual discrimination and vocabulary would need remedial work before he could learn to read, the child who feels contempt must relearn the essential lesson of infancy—to trust others, to believe that adults are reliable, predictable, and accepting—before he can learn to behave appropriately.

A child who feels that he received a great deal of hurt and unfair treatment in his life will not easily place his trust in adults. Adults will have to earn that trust through consistent fairness and sincere interest in the child's well-being. Adults can facilitate the development of trust in the child by modeling trust. They can find opportunities to place trust in the mistrustful child by situations in which the child is very likely to succeed and in which a failure to live up to the adult's trust can safely be overlooked.

Fits of Anger, Tantrums, Defiance

Children who regularly indulge in fits of anger, tantrums, and defiance need to know that the adults who care for them are not cowed by these behaviors, but they also need to know that adults will not explode into their own fits of anger. Angry, defiant behaviors may unconsciously be intended to strike back at adults who are perceived to be enemies. Adults, consequently, must take steps to build a cooperative relationship with the defiant child, to become the child's ally and friend while refusing to participate in inappropriate interactions with the child.

Adults can help children let go of explosive behaviors by responding matter-of-factly and steadfastly to the child's eruptions. An adult may be forced to remove or restrain the child in extreme circumstances, but the adult should be very sure the child recognizes that there is no anger or punitiveness in those actions, just firmness and resolve. Also, the adult can avoid overreacting to expressions of defiance such as vulgar language or spitting.

No adult wants to be spit at or to see other children spit on, but our own angry or violent outburst will make the child's problem worse, not better. Instead, a patient but very firm adult might say, "If you need to spit, you may spit in the sink. Spitting in the sink is fine. Spitting on people is not allowed, though. It makes them angry and it could get germs on them. If you spit, you can't play. You'll need to sit here by me until you are sure you are through spitting."

The child needs to learn that defiant tantrums are really a waste of time because they have no effect on the adult. The tantrums will not bring about special favors, and they will not succeed in "driving the adult up the wall." Because chronically disruptive behavior is unconsciously intended to hurt others as the child feels she has been hurt, the child may delight in seeing adults frustrated, angry, and helpless.

WITHDRAWN, PASSIVE BEHAVIOR

Cyclical Self-Stimulation

When a child is overwhelmed by fear, stress, and anxiety, she may withdraw into her own little world. Although most children do things to make themselves feel better from time to time, the chronically withdrawn child may sink into constant self-stimulation. This pattern is referred to as cyclical, because the child repeats the behavior cycle over and over. The cycle may consist of excessive thumb sucking, nail biting, hair twisting, overeating, head banging, masturbating, or any number of other self-stimulating actions.

Adults frequently find these behaviors very embarrassing and may focus on forcing the child to end the behavior without addressing the cause of the behavior at all. These behaviors tell us that the child is feeling too stressed and overwhelmed to participate in usual activities. By focusing on reducing stress in the child's life and drawing the child into pleasurable, nonthreatening activities, the child may be eased into more active involvement with things and people around him.

Rejection of Social Interchange

The severely withdrawn child may avoid eye contact, refuse to talk or play, and stay apart from others most of the time. Adults may mistakenly focus all of their guidance efforts on children whose inappropriate behaviors are active and annoying. Teachers, parents, and caregivers may view the child who is a loner as a good child who never bothers anyone. In reality, the child who is a loner may be more at risk emotionally than the difficult, loud, aggressive child. Self-esteem, trust, and a sense of belonging are all essential to building contact with the child who seems to have no interest in others.

Internalization of Stress

Chronically inhibited children sometimes turn all their bad feelings inward. Fear, anger, and frustration are not expressed. They are held inside, and may chip away at the child's sense of competence and self-worth. These children need opportunities to learn that they don't have to be perfect, it's okay to disagree, and they have a right to be who they are. As they develop stronger self-esteem, they will feel more

Figure 10–11 Children need to learn socially acceptable ways to express negative feelings. *(Photo courtesy of Cynde Miller, Montessori Country Day School)*

Figure 10–12 Even bright, cooperative, well-developing children have trouble coping sometimes. *(Photo courtesy of Patty Knowlton)*

comfortable expressing their feelings and actively standing up for themselves.

Children need opportunities to learn socially acceptable ways to express negative feelings. They need assertive role models and the freedom to say what they feel honestly (but respectfully). Adults should avoid telling children that their feelings are not real or valid, by saying such things as "That scratch doesn't hurt," "There's nothing to cry about," or "You have no reason to be mad!" Children must be allowed to feel what they feel, even though they must *also* learn to express negative feelings without hurting, harassing, or humiliating others. When children know an acceptable way to express themselves, they are likely to feel much freer about exposing their inner feelings.

Display of Ineptness and Hopelessness

Feelings of depression are not the exclusive territory of adolescents and adults. Even very young children can show signs of depression. Overwhelming disruption in the child's daily life may contribute to her listlessness and display of ineptness and hopelessness. These children do not involve themselves in spontaneous play or creative expression. They seem to have no energy. They may sleep too much or too little. They are clearly at risk and need special guidance to rebuild self-esteem and give them the spark of hope that fuels healthy curiosity, spontaneous play, and active involvement with others.

SCREENING FOR DEVELOPMENTAL "RED FLAGS"

All children behave very inappropriately from time to time—no matter how well they seem to be developing and how cooperative, competent, and confident they are generally. Some children, however, behave inappropriately often enough to cause serious concern. It is essential that we consider the possibility of physical causes for severe, chronic misbehavior. Various cues or signals could be taken as "red flags," or warning indicators, that something may be awry. Parents, teachers, and caregivers should never attempt to diagnose physical ailments or developmental delays. They should, however, watch carefully for indications that a child needs further evaluation by a physician or other expert to rule out or confirm physiological or psychological problems.

Can hearing problems affect behavior?

The ability to hear properly has an important influence on a child's ability to comply with adult instructions. A child who suffers from frequent nasal congestion, ear infections, and sinus drainage is a prime candidate for hearing difficulty. A young child may have occasional bouts of partial hearing loss or long, persistent periods of hearing difficulty due to these upper respiratory problems. Partial hearing loss can be surprisingly difficult for parents, teachers, and caregivers to notice. Because children pay close attention to body language and

Figure 10–13 Partial hearing loss can be surprisingly difficult to notice. *(Photo courtesy of Lynne Aiken)*

nonverbal gestures, they may appear to hear and understand more than they really do.

There are, of course, many other possible causes for partial or full loss of hearing as well. Medical evaluation and treatment may, in some cases, restore the child's hearing completely or at least make adults aware that a communication problem exists. Red flags signalling the possibility of a hearing problem include such things as:

- Pulling, tugging, poking at, or rubbing the ears.
- Slowness in learning to speak compared to age-mates.
- Muffled or garbled pronunciation of words.
- Consistent failure to follow even simple instructions.
- Appearance of being socially isolated in group settings.
- Unresponsiveness to group activities, such as story reading.

What Other Physical Conditions Affect Behavior?

Because irritability and discomfort are both likely causes for misbehavior, any number of physical illnesses or conditions could result in behavior changes. Muscular disabilities could hamper a child's ability to carry out tasks that might be expected, or developmental delays could make it impossible for a child to live up to typical adult expectations. Parents, teachers, and caregivers can assist medical personnel in evaluating a child who seems to be displaying signs of difficulty by observing and keeping records of behaviors on a daily basis that seem unusual for a child at a given age.

Child Abuse or Neglect

A very serious potential cause of developmental and behavioral problems can be abuse or neglect in a child's life. Although virtually any normally-developing child can experience a rare incident of abusive or neglectful treatment, children who lead lives filled with abuse and neglect are profoundly affected by that experience, even if they are not maimed or killed. Every aspect of their development is affected— intellectual, physical, social, and emotional (Dean, Malik, Richards, and Stringer, 1986; Hoffman-Plotkin and Twentyman, 1984; Kempe and Kempe, 1978; Lamb, Gaensbauer, Malkin, and Schultz, 1985).

Abused and neglected children's behaviors tend toward extremes. There seems to be no happy middle for these children. They may be diagnosed as learning disabled or they may be compulsive overachievers. They may be hyperactive or lethargic. They may be physically inept weaklings or street-smart, death-defying daredevils. They may either cling relentlessly to others or shun all social interaction. They may appear either dirty and unkempt or rigidly and spotlessly

scrubbed, starched, and pressed. They may either defy authority altogether or compulsively try to please everyone at all times, in all ways.
They may always play the role of victim or brutally victimize others.

The one characteristic that is shared by all abused and neglected
children is their lacking or stunted sense-of-self. They do not have that
essential component of all fully functional human beings, the positive
feeling of self-worth that comes with self-esteem.

> Childhood Remembrance
>   When the image leaves the retina,
>   The pictures remain in your mind,
>   Some longer than others.
>   There's a lot of scar tissue on my brain
>   From specific incidents . . .
>   Like when I was a young child in a big green swivel chair near the
>   window,
>   And I would spin around and around, getting toeholds on
>   The window frame with which to spin the chair.
>   I went to place my foot, as I was slowing down, in an attempt to gain
>   more momentum.
>   My foot slipped, and went clear through the glass.
>   My father, watching football two yards away, had told me to "Stop doing
>   that. You're gonna break out a window,"
>   So he leapt across the den, pulled me out of the chair,
>   Flipped me over, ripped his belt off and began whipping me in a Contra-
>   like manner.
>   I don't remember if my foot bled or not,
>   But that doesn't matter anymore, I suppose.
>   My mind is left with many indelible images.
>   One of them is the look on that face.
>   (Michael Sicinski, 1988. Unpublished poem.)

LOCATING COMMUNITY RESOURCES

Adults caring for children who have chronic misbehavior problems
need help. Once possible causes for behavior problems are identified, a
search for appropriate community resources should take place. Families, schools, and child-care facilities all have the potential to serve as
resources for each other, to share ideas and methods and to give each
other emotional support and encouragement. Parents can learn a great
deal from teachers and caregivers, and they can learn a great deal
from parents. Additionally, almost any community setting offers a
wealth of potential resources such as the following:

- *The Medical Community*—Physicians, Psychologists, and other
  therapists.
- *Governmental Agencies*—Child protective service workers, child-

care licensing specialists, health departments, social workers, Head Start, and Title XX funded programs.

- *Religious Entities*—Churches, synagogues, temples, priests, ministers, counselors, and congregational support groups.
- *Non-Profit Organizations*—Self-help groups, child care resource and referral organizations, associations focused on specific problems such as diabetes or hyperactivity, and parenting classes or seminars.
- *Treatment Centers*—Special schools, testing clinics, or therapy facilities such as schools for the blind or physical therapy facilities for such things as cerebral palsy.
- *Public School Systems*—Educational programs for exceptional children, early intervention programs for children at risk, school psychologists, and counselors.

Parents often need help in overcoming feelings of pain and denial when they discover that their child has developmental, physical, or behavioral problems. They may hold an idealized image of their child and resist the notion that their child is, in fact, human and imperfect, having both strengths and weaknesses. They may need to be reminded that there is no shame in having a disability or an imperfection. There is only shame in not dealing with reality and not taking steps to help the child function as well as possible. Many potentially disabling conditions can be prevented or alleviated if they are identified and treated during infancy or earliest childhood. Therefore, early screening for special problems has special importance.

MEETING ADULT NEEDS

Children definitely have needs, but adults have needs, too. Caring for children is demanding, exhilarating, frustrating, and rewarding—and it is also exhausting. Adults can best care for children if their own social, emotional, physical, and intellectual needs are met. We must set aside time for our own rest and recreation, and we must be able to admit to ourselves at times that we are not able to deal with children in a positive and productive manner. If children are dealt with in a caring and respectful manner most of the time, they will be likely to cope well and respect our own need when we say, "I'm too frustrated and angry to talk about this right now. I just want to be alone for a few minutes."

We can be patient and reasonable with ourselves, recognizing that we, too, are imperfect. It is easy to sit down and think carefully about an ideal response to a misbehaving child, but it is not so easy to respond perfectly when the response is instantaneous and in the heat of a conflict with that child. It is important for adults to be supportive, calm, respectful, and consistent, but it is most important for them to do something! Children must know that adults care enough to do something, even if it isn't the best possible thing to do.

When we attempt to change our ways of dealing with children, we go through the same stages of learning that children go through when they learn new behaviors. For example, a toddler who has no concept of toileting will simply show no awareness when she makes a puddle on the floor. When she develops a recognition of the desired behavior but lacks practice carrying it out, she will make a puddle, look down, smile sweetly, and say, "Go potty!" Of course, it will be too late to go to the potty. Finally, when she has fully developed both the awareness and the skill to carry out the new behavior, she will notice the sensation of a full bladder and do what needs to be done to successfully use the toilet.

We go through the same process of learning. At first, we may be totally unaware of the negative, destructive, and hurtful things we say or do with youngsters in the name of disciplining them. As we discover more productive and effective ways to guide them, we begin for the first time to hear ourselves saying or doing negative things. We feel frustration because we only seem to become aware of these actions after we have done them. We become aware of our inappropriate actions, but only after it is too late. Gradually, however, with persistence and practice, we are able to anticipate and respond more skillfully and appropriately. Eventually, our new behaviors become so natural to us that we can behave as we wish with almost no thought or effort.

Positive child guidance is a tool that can be used to help mature, caring adults teach young children the skills they need to lead productive, happy lives.

Treat people as if they are what they ought to be,
and you help them to become what they are capable of being.
(Johann Wolfgang von Goethe. German poet, 1749-1832.)

SUMMARY

At the heart of almost any behavior lies the desire to acquire something (an object, an experience, or a feeling) in order to meet some need. Maslow proposed that basic needs are arranged in a hierarchy of successive levels of needs.

Unmet needs are a hidden cause of chronic patterns of dysfunctional behavior. In order to behave well, children must have a strong sense of self-esteem.

Seeing children as lovable, capable, and worthwhile supports the growth of self-esteem. Children begin to develop self-esteem from birth if their needs are met by attentive caregivers and they are taught functional ways to get their needs met.

The no-lose method of conflict resolution is a strategy for avoiding power struggles between adults and children.

Dreikurs proposed four mistaken goals that he hypothesized to be the root of long-standing, habitual patterns of dysfunctional behavior. He theorized that children misbehave to get attention from others, gain a sense of control, get revenge for their own perceived hurts, or remove themselves from frightening or painful situations.

Suppressing behavioral symptoms without paying attention to the emotional well-being of the child may result in the eruption of new or different symptoms. Healing can take place only when the child feels she is an accepted and worthwhile group member, she has some sense of control over her life, she is treated fairly and respectfully, and she feels optimism that she can succeed in things that are expected of her.

Attachment to a dependable caregiver is an essential factor in the development of trust. Clingy children have not been "loved" too much (although they may well have been overindulged and overprotected in ways that stunted their long-term development of healthy confidence and independence). Instead, they may have been given too little appropriate attention and attachment.

Children who are insecure in their sense of belonging may adopt an artificial charm or gain excessive attention by clowning. It is essential that these children be given positive opportunities for responsibility and leadership in positive settings as well as chances to entertain others in appropriate ways.

Lazy, compulsive, or obnoxious behaviors may be a child's unconscious way of forcing adults to pay attention. They may excessively overeat, bite their nails, tease, or purposely disgust other children and adults.

Sometimes manipulativeness can become excessive and vengeful as children struggle to gain control of the children and adults around them. Adults need to define clear limits and help children become aware of the feelings and reactions of those around them.

Children who want control but fail to get their way with others may react by pouting, stubbornly refusing to participate, or "causing a scene." Adults can deal with this by being assertive and fair.

Some children, when failing to gain control by other means, resort to bullying or rebelling. The child needs strong, reliable adult support in order to give up dysfunctional behaviors and form new habits.

Children whose self-esteem is lacking may deteriorate into disruptive habit patterns of destructiveness and aggression. The destructive or aggressive child must know that she will be stopped, that others' rights will be protected. In dealing with a very difficult child, behavior modification may be an essential and effective tool for regaining a manageable relationship with the child. Contempt and mistrust in children indicate a need for a basic development of trust. Adults must earn trust through consistent fairness and sincere interest in the child's well-being.

Children who regularly indulge in fits of anger, tantrums, and defiance need to know that the adults who care for them are not cowed by these behaviors, but they also need to know that adults will not explode into their own fits of anger.

Although most children do things to make themselves feel better from time to time, the chronically withdrawn child may rely on constant self-stimulation. Adults frequently find these behaviors embarrassing and may focus on forcing the child to end the behavior without addressing the cause of the behavior at all.

The severely withdrawn child may avoid eye contact, refuse to talk or play, and stay apart from others most of the time. Self-esteem, trust, and a sense of belonging are all essential to building contact with the child who seems to have no interest in others.

Figure 10-14 With persistence and practice, we can learn to respond to children more skillfully and appropriately.

Chronically-inhibited children sometimes turn all their bad feelings inward. Fear, anger, and frustration are not expressed, they are just held inside.

Overwhelming disruption in children's daily lives may contribute to their feeling listless, inept, and hopeless. These children are clearly at risk and need special guidance to rebuild self-esteem.

Adults must watch chronically-misbehaving children for indications that underlying problems may be contributing to their misbehavior. Communities offer many resources to help parents, teachers, and care-givers deal effectively with physical or developmental problems.

Abuse and neglect have a profoundly negative effect on children's overall development and ability to comply with adult expectations.

Adults must recognize their own needs and imperfections in order to be effective in child guidance.

PRACTICAL APPLICATION/DISCUSSION

"Thank Heavens for Sarah"

Sarah taught and cared for a small group of children in her own home. She felt strong commitment to her work and believed that she made a difference in children's lives. She took great pride in operating her home-based child-care program in a professional and responsible manner. She bristled at the term babysitter, and she referred to herself as a teacher, because that's what she believed she did with the babies, toddlers, and preschoolers in her care.

Robert was three. Sarah had care for him for several months and became very concerned about his behavior. He always seemed to be in conflict with the other children, and he never seemed to listen or follow even the simplest of Sarah's directions. Sarah began to wonder if Robert had some problem that was causing him to misbehave. She watched him carefully and wrote down her observations about when, where, and why he seemed to get into trouble.

Sarah began to suspect that Robert couldn't hear as well as he should. She noticed that while all the other children ran to the window each morning when they heard the garbage truck, Robert either didn't respond at all or was the last to look up and run to the window. One day, Sarah stood quietly behind Robert and said very softly, "Robert, it's time for lunch." Although other children quickly responded, Robert never even looked up from his puzzle.

Sarah approached Robert's parents about the problem on several occasions. She said, "I'm not an expert in hearing problems, but I wonder if Robert could have a hearing problem. Has his pediatrician ever tested his hearing?" Robert's father said, "That's ridiculous. He hears whatever he wants to hear. He just chooses to ignore grownups most of the time." Robert's mother said, "His doctor hasn't ever mentioned a problem and I don't see any reason to think anything is wrong."

Sarah continued caring for and working with Robert, but she still had a nagging feeling that his behavior was just not up to par for a child who seemed very bright in other ways. She noticed that his relationship with his parents had deteriorated and that he was almost constantly in trouble with adults or other children. Finally, she set an appointment to sit down privately to talk with Robert's parents.

Sarah, with kindness and respect in her voice, said "I know that you have to do whatever you think is right for Robert, but I have to do what is right for me and for the other children in my care. I have become very attached to Robert. He is so full of creative energy. However, much of the time his behavior is out of control, and I don't know if I am doing the right thing for him. I worry that he may not be able to hear, and I wonder if that is part of the problem. I just don't feel comfortable caring for him without some kind of screening to at least rule out the possibility of a hearing problem."

Robert's father blurted out, "Fine! We'll just find someone else to care for him. We are not about to set out on some wild-goose chase, looking for problems that don't exist." Sarah responded, "I understand. You have every right to do only what you believe is best for your child. I'm sure that I would do the same myself. I need you to understand, though, that I am having real difficulty with Robert's behavior, and I just don't feel comfortable caring for him if I'm not sure I'm doing the right thing for him and for the other children. I am willing to accept your decision, and I'll do anything I can to help with the transition to a different child-care situation. The important thing is for each of us to feel comfortable with what we do."

Robert's mother was not eager to find new child-care for Robert. She really liked the way Sarah cared for the children. Robert's mother had several long discussions with her child's doctor and with her husband and finally convinced her husband that Robert should have his hearing tested in a medical clinic that specialized in that kind of thing.

A few weeks later, Robert's father stopped by to talk to Sarah. He said, "You know, I was so sure that nothing was wrong with Robert's hearing that I really resented you insisting on a hearing test. I can't believe it, but the doctor says he has a seventy-five-percent hearing loss in one ear and a slight loss in the other. I just didn't know."

Sarah responded, "I could have been right or I could have been wrong. I'm no expert on hearing, but I do appreciate knowing more about why he may have been having such a hard time behaving. Thank you for being so tolerant of my questions and concerns. I think we can all work together now much more effectively to help Robert get his act together."

As Robert's father turned to leave, he patted Robert's head and said softly, "Thank heavens for Sarah."

QUESTIONS FOR DISCUSSION

1. Do you think Sarah's actions were within her role as a caregiver?
2. Do you think Sarah went too far in insisting that Robert's hearing be checked?
3. How do you think this story would have ended if nothing had been wrong with Robert's hearing?
4. Specifically what things did Sarah say or do that made her assertiveness more tolerable to Robert's parents?
5. What would you have done?

Figure 10–15 Within every child is an adult in-the-making—and within every adult is a child who has just gotten older.

Appendix

CURRENT STUDY OF YOUNG CHILDREN

Recent studies affirm the special importance of environmental factors during the first years of life. A growing body of research on early socialization processes (Adlam, 1977; Anyon, 1983; Bernstein, 1975; Berlak and Berlak, 1981) holds that environmental factors may help or hinder a child's later progress in school and in other situations that give her a chance to succeed in later adult endeavors and gain access to desired careers.

Because of the present social climate (feminism, more employed mothers, and more single-parent homes) the role of fathers in caring for young children is a very popular topic for study. The cultural stereotype of father as aloof disciplinarian and provider is now considered oversimplified, if not incorrect (Cordell, 1978 and Russell, 1980). Although several studies found that very few fathers share responsibility for child-care equally with their wives (Kotelchuck, 1976; Richards, Dunn, and Antonis, 1977), fathers are definitely more interested and involved in actively caring for babies and young children than they were a generation ago (Kammerman, 1980).

This extra involvement from fathers offers many benefits for children, as well as pleasure and fulfillment for parents. There are strong indications that infants who receive ample quantities of care and attention from involved "daddies" are more curious, more confident in exploring the environment, more secure, and even more advanced in motor development (Biller, 1982).

Additionally, recent studies document continued increases in parents' reliance on some form or other of day-care. While provisions for help with child care were a fact of life for centuries, proprietary- and publicly-funded day-care centers were used primarily by relatively small numbers of blue-collar families twenty years ago. Only recently dramatically increasing numbers of doctors, lawyers, and business people began placing their young children in early childhood programs instead of, or in addition to, care by housekeepers, babysitters, and nannies. Today, child care in group settings is becoming more and more attractive to families of modest to affluent means, for children of all ages.

However, for the care of infants and toddlers under the age of three, care by relatives or care by small-group providers in licensed, registered, or often "underground," family day-homes is the primary mode for care. In 1982, private-home care accounted for seventy-seven percent of infant/toddler care. By 1985, only sixty-nine percent of infants and toddlers in care were kept in private homes. Forty-five percent of these children under the age of three were cared for by a relative (twenty-seven percent of those in their own homes and eighteen percent in the home of the relative) and twenty-four percent were cared for in family home care facilities. Almost ten percent were cared for in group-care centers (Committee for Economic Development, 1987). Infants and toddlers unaccounted for in these figures include those taken to work by their parents.

In 1985, more than one-fourth of all impoverished mothers with children under the age of six were in the labor force. Their marital status (single or married) made little difference in whether or not they worked outside the home.

Increasing Reliance on Child Care

Twenty-five years ago, economic opportunities limited career choices available to women. Social mores dictated that women who could afford to should stay home to care for young children while their husbands provided financial support. Mothers who had to work looked to relatives and friends for child care. Those who could afford in-house care for their children hired maids or nannies to assist in the care of young children.

Because domestic work was one of the few employment avenues open to low-income women, a pool of cheap labor was readily available. Today, steps to equalize job opportunities for women have decreased the number of women interested in low-paying domestic jobs, while at the same time luring ever-increasing numbers of women into the work force. This trend confronts many parents with a new dilemma—how to take advantage of rewarding dual-career opportunities without sacrificing whatever care and guidance children need to develop well (Kamerman, 1985, 1983; Kamerman and Kahn, 1981; and Waldman, 1983).

The number of children who now have mothers in the labor force is growing. By the early 1990s, twice as many mothers of children under six are expected to be employed as in 1970 (Children's Defense Fund,

1986). By 1995, two-thirds of all children under age six and three-quarters of school-age children are projected to have working mothers (Hofferth and Phillips, 1987). A number of experts now agree with Weiser's (1982) statement:

> The traditional family, in which the husband worked out of the home and the wife stayed in the home with the children, is part of the historical past and now describes less than a tenth of the families with young children (p. 35).

Parents' Concerns About Child Care

For those parents who are new consumers of day care, the big question looming on the horizon is: "Can I go back to work without hurting my child in some way?" For these parents, "hurting" transcends basic physical care and safety. It broadens to include the constellation of experiences that prepare a child to live a responsible, successful, and fulfilling life (Lamb, 1978). Parents want to be assured that their children will receive proper guidance.

Special Concerns About Infants and Toddlers

In the past few years, popular magazines and newspapers featured major stories on child care and early learning. Experts and pseudo-experts abound, offering a rainbow of advice and warning to parents. The present accumulation of infant/toddler day-care research offers little clear information about the long-term effects of group care for babies, except that quality day-care does not appear to disrupt the attachment between mothers and their infants (Maccoby and Feldman, 1972; Kagan, Kearsley, and Zelazo, 1978; Levy-Shiff, 1983; Farran, Burchinal, Hutaff, and Ramey, 1984 Ainslie and Anderson, 1984) and that quality child care has neutral or positive effects on cognitive development (Belsky, Steinberg, and Walker, 1982; Clarke-Stewart and Fein, 1983).

Child-development experts who hold solid research credentials seem to have espoused positions for or against infant day-care based on personal experience and intuition rather than hard evidence. Burton White, (1973), an infant learning researcher, has steadfastly disapproved of day care for infants and toddlers:

> But assuming the most common situation of a loving, reasonably well-put-together family . . . it is my considered opinion that attending just about any day-care installation full time, is unlikely to be as beneficial to the child's early educational development as his own home during these first three years (White, 1975, pp. 253-254).

Researchers and educators were interviewed by journalists writing for the popular press. This media attention becomes significant because of its impact on public opinion. Psychologist Lee Salk, an outspoken critic of day care, was quoted by Stein (1984, p. 149) as saying that the youngest children in day care are "walking time bombs" and that parents who cannot take time off from work to provide home care simply should not have children.

T. Berry Brazelton, popular author, Associate Professor of Pediatrics at Harvard Medical School, and chief of the Child Development Unit at Children's Hospital in Boston, is one of the professionals who endorse infant/toddler day care. However, his description of acceptable day care is well beyond that managed by many providers. In a recent interview for a popular magazine (Minsky, 1984), Brazelton is quoted as saying:

> One worker for every four children is the absolute minimum, and ideally it should be a one-to-three ratio. The workers should be well trained and should not be competitive with the parents in a relationship with the child (p. 156).

Brazelton notes that this kind of day care is probably only available to parents with hefty incomes. He also notes that a great deal is expected from child-care workers who are among the very lowest paid of all personnel in the field of education.

Ambiguity and uncertainty exist in both the academic and popular literature concerning day care for infants and toddlers. While there are questions about day care at all age levels, the most pressing concern is focused on the most vulnerable of all child care recipients—the child from birth to three years of age—whose future happiness and productivity may to some extent depend on skills, habits, and attitudes established early in life (Willis, 1981; Apple, 1982; and Giroux, 1983).

It is clear that many babies and toddlers are in child care now, and many more will probably be in child care in the future. The continuing old debate about whether mothers "ought to" stay home and accept all responsibility for child care, therefore, appears less important than the new debate about how society can best assure that all child care is of sufficient quality to support healthy growth. There is good evidence that care for children under three, by adults other than parents, can be healthy and supportive for babies and a godsend for their parents. However, care of these youngest children is a tremendous responsibility that must be taken with deepest respect for the vulnerability and potential for harm that exists in sub-standard settings.

References

Adlam, D. 1977. *Code in Context*. London: Routledge and Kegan Paul.

Adler, A. 1931. "Compulsion Neurosis." In H.L. Ansbacher and R.R. Ansbacher (eds.), *Superiority and Social Interest*. Evanston, IL: Northwestern University Press, 1964.

Ainslie, R.C., and Anderson, C.W. 1984. "Day Care Children's Relationships to Their Mothers and Caregivers: An Inquiry Into the Conditions for the Development of Attachment." In R.C. Ainslie (ed.), *Quality Variations in Daycare* (pp. 98–132). New York: Praeger.

Ainsworth, M.D.S. 1973. "The Development of the Infant–Mother Attachment." In B.M. Caldwell & H.N. Ricciuti (eds.), *Review of Child Development Research* (Vol. 3, pp. 1–94). Chicago: University of Chicago Press.

Alley, T. 1981. "Head Shape and the Perception of Cuteness." *Developmental Psychology, 17*, 650–654.

Altenor, A., Kay, E., and Richter, M. 1977. "The Generality of Learned Helplessness in the Rat." *Learning & Motivation, 8*, 54–61.

Anyon, J. 1983. "Intersections of Gender and Class: Accommodation and Resistance By Contradictory Sex–Role Ideologies." In S. Walker and L. Barton (eds.), *Gender, Class and Education* (pp. 21–37). London: Falmer.

Apple, M. 1982. *Cultural and Economic Reproduction in Education: Essays on Class, Ideology and the State*. London: Routledge and Kegan Paul.

Aries, P. 1962. *Centuries of Childhood*. New York: Random House Inc.

Bagley, C., Verma, G.K., Mallick, K., and Young, L. 1979. *Personality, Self-esteem and Prejudice*. Westmead, Farnborough, Hants, England: Saxon House.

Bandura, A. 1977. *Social Learning Theory*. Englewood Cliffs, NJ: Prentice-Hall.

Belsky, J., Steinberg, L., and Walker, A. 1982. "The Ecology of Daycare." In M. Lamb (ed.), *Childrearing in Nontraditional Families* (pp. 71–116). Hillsdale, NJ: Erlbaum.

Berlak, A., and Berlak, H. 1981. *Dilemmas of Schooling: Teaching and Social Change.* London: Methuen.

Bernstein, B. 1975. *Class, Codes and Control*, Vol. 3, *Towards a Theory of Educational Transmissions.* London: Routledge and Kegan Paul.

Biller, H.B. 1982. "Fatherhood: Implications for Child and Adult Development." In B.B. Wolman (ed.), *Handbook of Developmental Psychology* (pp. 707–720). Englewood Cliffs, NJ: Prentice Hall.

Bloom, B.S. 1964. *Stability and Change in Human Characteristics.* New York: John Wiley & Sons, Inc.

Bowlby, J. 1958. "The Nature of the Child's Tie to His Mother." *International Journal of Psychoanalysis*, 39, 350–373.

Brazelton, T.B., Koslowski, B., and Main, M. 1974. "The Origins of Reciprocity." In M. Lewis & L. Rosenblum (eds.), *The Effect of the Infant on Its Caregiver.* New York: Wiley-Interscience.

Bredekamp, S. (Ed.) 1987. *Developmentally Appropriate Practice in Early Childhood Programs Serving Children From Birth Through Age 8.* Washington, D.C.: National Association for the Education of Young Children.

Bremner, R. H. (ed.) 1970–1974. *Children and Youth in America: A Documentary History*, Vols. 1–3. Cambridge: Harvard University Press.

Bretherton, I., and Waters, E. 1985. "Growing Points of Attachment Theory and Research." *Monographs of the Society for Research in Child Development*, 209 (50).

Bruner, J. 1978a. "Learning the mother tongue." *Human Nature*, September, 11–19.

――――― 1978b. "Learning How to do Things with Words." In J.S. Bruner & A. Garton (eds.), *Human Growth and Development: Wolfson College lectures.* Oxford: Clarendon Press.

Cairns, R.B. 1979. *Social development: The Origins and Plasticity of Interchanges.* San Francisco: Freeman.

Children's Defense Fund 1986. *A Children's Defense budget: An Analysis of the FY 1987 Budget and Children.* Washington, DC: C.D.F.

Chomsky, N. 1965. *Aspects of the theory of syntax.* Cambridge: M. I. T. Press.

Clarke, J.I. 1978. *Self-Esteem: A Family Affair.* New York: Winston Press.

Clarke-Stewart, A. 1978. "Popular Primers for Parents." *American Psychologist*, 33, 359.

Clarke-Stewart, A., and Fein, G.G. 1983. "Early Childhood Programs." In P.H. Mussen (series ed.); M. Haith and J. Campos (vol. eds.), *Handbook of Child Psychology: Vol. II, Infancy and Developmental Psychobiology* (pp. 917–1000). New York: Wiley.

Cole, L. 1950. *A History of Education.* New York: Rinehart and Co.

Committee for Economic Development 1987. *Children in Need: Investment Strategies For the Educationally Disadvantaged.* New York: C.E.D.

Condon, W.S., and Sander, L. 1974. "Neonate Movement is Synchronized With Adult Speech: Interactional Participation and Language Acquisition." *Science,* 183, 99–101.

Cook-Gumperz, J. 1973. *Social Control and Socialization.* London: Routledge and Kegan Paul.

Coopersmith, S. 1967. *The Antecedents of Self-esteem.* San Francisco: W.H. Freeman & Co.

Cordell, A.S. 1978. *The Father–Infant relationship.* Unpublished Doctoral Dissertation, University of Chicago.

Costley, D., and Todd, R. 1987. *Human Relations in Organization* (3rd ed.). New York: West.

Corsaro, W.A. 1981. "Friendship in the Nursery School: Social Organization in a Peer Environment." In S.R. Asher and J.M. Gottman (eds.), *The Development of Children's Friendships.* New York: Cambridge University Press.

Cotton, N. 1984. "The Development of Self-Esteem and Self-Esteem Regulation." In J.E. Mack and S.L. Ablon (eds.), *The Development and Sustaining of Self-Esteem in Childhood.* New York: International Universities Press.

Cunnington, P., and Buck, A. 1965. *Children's Costume in England.* New York: Barnes and Noble, Inc.

Dean, A.L., Malik, M.M., Richards, W., and Stringer, S.A. 1986. "Effects of Parental Maltreatment on Children's Conceptions of Interpersonal Relationships." *Developmental Psychology,* 22, 617–626.

DeCasper, A.J., and Fifer, W.P. 1980. "Of Human Bonding: Newborns Prefer Their Mothers' Voices." *Science,* 208, 1174–1176.

Dennis, W. 1960. "Causes of Retardation Among Institutional Children: Iran." *The Journal of Genetic Psychology,* 96, 47–59.

——— 1973. *Children of the Creche.* New York: Appleton-Century-Crofts.

Dewey, J. 1966. *Experience and Education.* New York: Collier.

Dinkmeyer, D., and McKay, Gary, D. 1982. *Systematic training for effective parenting: Parent's handbook.* Circle Pines, MN: American Guidance Service, Inc.

Douglas, J., and Kerr, K. 1987. "Abuse and Death: Did the System Fail 2-Year-Old Jesse Wheeler." *The Houston Post,* May 9, 1–14 A.

Dreikurs, R., and Cassel, P. 1974. *Discipline Without Tears* (2nd ed.). New York: Hawthorn Books.

Eisenberg, R.B. 1976. *Auditory Competence in Early Life.* Baltimore: University Park Press.

Eisenberg-Berg, N. 1979. "Development of Children's Prosocial Moral

Judgment." *Developmental Psychology*, 15, 128–138.

Erikson, E. 1959. "Identity and the Life Cycle." *Psychological Issues*, 1 (1), Monograph 1.

————— 1963. *Childhood and Society* (2nd ed.). New York: W.W. Norton & Co.

————— 1982. *The Life Cycle Completed: A Review*. New York: W.W. Norton & Co.

Faegre, M., and Anderson, J. 1930. *Child Care and Training* (3rd ed.). Minneapolis Institute of Child Welfare: University of Minnesota Press.

Farran, D.C., Burchinal, M., Hutaff, S.E. and Ramey, C.T. 1984. "Allegiances or Attachments: Relationships Among Infants and Their Day Care Teachers." In R.C. Ainslie (ed.), *Quality Variations in Daycare* (pp. 133–158). New York: Praeger.

Ferguson, T.J., and Rule, B.G. 1982. "Influence of Inferential Set, Outcome Intent, and Outcome Severity on Children's Moral Judgments." *Developmental Psychology*, 18, 843–851.

Field, T.M. 1982. "Affective and Physiological Changes During Manipulated Interactions of High-Risk Infants." In T. Field & A. Fogel (eds.), *Emotion and Early Interaction*. Hillsdale, NJ: Erlbaum.

Finkelstein, N.W., and Ramey, C.T. 1977. "Learning to Control the Environment in Infancy." *Child Development*, 48, 806–819.

Fleming, P., Baum, A., and Singer, J.E. 1984. "Toward an Integrative Approach to the Study of Stress." *Journal of Personality and Social Psychology*, 46, 939–949.

Froebel, F. 1887. *The Education of Man: The Art of Education, Instruction and Training*. New York: D. Appleton and Co.

Gazda, G.M., Asbury, F.S., Balzar, F.J., Childers, W.C., and Walt, R.P. 1984. *Human Relations Development* (3rd ed.). Boston: Allyn & Bacon.

Gerbner, G., & Gross, L. 1980. "The Violent Face of Television and Its Lessons." In E.L. Palmer and A. Dorr (eds.), *Children and the Faces of Television: Teaching, Violence, Selling*. New York: Academic Press.

Gesell, A., Halverson, H.M., Thompson, H., and Ilg, F. 1940. *The First Five Years of Life: A Guide to the Study of the Preschool Child*. New York: Harper & Row.

Giroux, H. 1983. *Ideology, Culture, and the Process of Schooling*. Philadelphia: Temple University Press.

Glubok, S. (ed.) 1969. *Home and Child Life in Colonial Days*. New York: Macmillan Publishing Co., Inc.

Gordon, T. 1970. *Parent Effectiveness Training*. New York: Peter Wyden.

Grusec, J.E., Kuczynski, L., Rushton, J.P., and Simutis, Z. 1979.

"Learning Resistance to Temptation Through Observation." *Developmental Psychology*, 15, 233–240.

Harding, C.G., and Golinkoff, R.M. 1979. "The Origins of Intentional Vocalizations in Prelinguistic Infants." *Child Development*, 50, 33–40.

Harlow, H., and Zimmerman, R. 1959. "Affectional Responses in the Infant Monkey," *Science*, 130, 421–432.

Hartshorne, H., and May, M.A. 1928. *Studies in the Nature of Character*, vol. 1. New York: Macmillan.

Hess, E. 1972. "Imprinting in a Natural Laboratory." *Scientific American*, 227, 24–31.

Hess, R., and Shipman, V. 1967. "Parents as Teachers: How Lower and Middle Class Mothers Teach." In C.S. Lavatelli and F. Stendler (eds.), *Readings in Child Behavior and Development* (3rd ed.). New York: Harcourt Brace Jovanovich, 436–446.

Hofferth, S., and Phillips, D. 1987. "Child Care in the United States, 1970 to 1995." *Journal of Marriage and the Family*, 49 (3), 559–571.

Hoffman, M.L. 1979. "Development of Moral Thought, Feeling, and Behavior." *American Psychologist*, 34, 958–967.

Hoffman-Plotkin, D., and Twentyman, C.T. 1984. "A Multimodal Assessment of Behavioral and Cognitive Deficits in Abused and Neglected Preschoolers." *Child Development*, 55, 794–802.

Honig, A.S. 1986. "Stress and Coping in Children (Part 2): Interpersonal Family Relationships." *Young Children*, 41 (5), 47–60.

Hunt, J. 1976. "The Psychological Development of Orphanage-Reared Infants: Interventions with Outcomes (Teheran)." *Genetic Psychology Monographys*, 94, 177–226.

Kagan, J., and Moss, H. 1962. *Birth to Maturity*. New York: Wiley.

Kagan, J. 1971. *Change and Continuity in Infancy*. New York: Wiley.

Kagan, J., Kearsley, R.B., and Zelazo, P.R. 1978. *Infancy: Its Place in Human Development*. Cambridge, MA: Harvard University Press.

Kagan, J., Lapidus, R., and Moore, N. 1978. "Infant Antecedents of Cognitive Functioning: A Longitudinal Study." *Child Development*, 49, 1005–1023.

Kammerman, S., and Kahn, A. 1981. *Child Care, Family Benefits, and Working Parents*. New York: Columbia University Press.

Kammerman, S. 1980. *Parenting in an Unresponsive Society: Managing Work and Family Life*. New York: The Free Press.

———— 1983. "Child Care Services: A National Picture." *Monthly Labor Review* (December), 106, 35–39.

———— 1985. "Child Care Services: An Issue for Gender Equality and Women's Solidarity." *Child Welfare* (May–June), 3, LXIV, 259–271.

Katz, P. A. 1982. "Development of Children's Racial Awareness and Intergroup Attitudes." In L. Katz (ed.), *Current Topics in Early Childhood Education* (Vol. 4). Norwood, NJ: Ablex Publishing Corp.

Kaye, K. 1982. *The Mental and Social Life of Babies.* Chicago: University of Chicago Press.

Kempe, R.S., and Kempe, C.H. 1978. *Child Abuse.* Cambridge, MA: Harvard University Press.

Kohlberg, L. 1966. "A Cognitive-Developmental Analysis of Children's Sex-Role Concepts and Attitudes." In E. E. Maccoby (ed.), *The Development of Sex Differences.* Stanford: University Press.

_____ 1969. "Stage and Sequence: The Cognitive-Developmental Approach to Socialization." In D. Goslin (ed.), *Handbook of Socialization Theory and Research.* Skokie, Ill.: Rand-McNally.

_____ 1976. "Moral Stages and Moralization: The Cognitive-Developmental Approach." In T. Lickona (ed.), *Moral Development and Behavior.* New York: Holt, Rinehart and Winston.

Kokenes, B. 1974. "Grade Level Differences in Factors of Self-Esteem." *Developmental Psychology,* 10, 954–958.

Kotelchuck, M. 1976. "The Infant's Relationship to the Father: Experimental Evidence." In M.E. Lamb (ed.), *The Role of the Father in Child Development* (pp. 329–344). New York: Wiley.

Kuhl, P.K. 1981. "Auditory Category Formation and Developmental Speech Perception." In R. Stark (ed.), *Language Behavior in Infancy and Early Childhood.* New York: Elsevier.

Lamb, M.E. 1978. "Infant Social Cognition and "Second-Order" Effects." *Infant Behavior and Development,* 1, 1–10.

_____ 1981. *The Role of the Father in Childhood Development* (2nd ed.). New York: Wiley.

Lamb, M.E., Gaensbauer, T.J., Malkin, C.M., and Schultz, L.A. 1985. "The Effects of Child Maltreatment on Security of Infant–Adult Attachment." *Infant Behavior and Development,* 8, 35–45.

Lamb, M.E., Thompson, R.A., Gardner, W., and Charnov, E.L. (eds.) 1985. *Infant–Mother Attachment: The Origins and Developmental Significance of Individual Differences in Strange Situation Behavior.* Hillsdale, NJ: Erlbaum.

Landreth, C., and Johnson, B. 1953. "Young Children's Responses to a Picture Inset Test Designed to Reveal Reactions to Persons of Different Skin Color." *Child Development,* 24, 63–80.

Lefkowitz, M.M., and Tesiny, E.P. 1980. "Dejection and Depression: Prospective and Contemporaneous Analyses." *Developmental Psychology,* 20, 776–786.

Levy-Shiff, R. 1983. "Adaptation and Competence in Early Childhood: Communally Raised Kibbutz Children versus Family-Raised Children in the City." *Child Development,* 54, 1606–1604.

Locke, J. 1699. *Some Thoughts Concerning Education* (4th ed.). London: A. and J. Churchill.

Lorenz, K. 1966. *On Aggression*. New York: Harcourt, Brace & World.

Lubeck, S. 1985. *Sandbox Society: Early Education in Black and White America*. London: Falmer.

Maccoby, E.S. 1972. "Mother-Attachment and Stranger-Reactions in the Third Year of Life." *Monographs of the Society for Research in Child Development*, 37 (1, serial No. 146).

Maslow, A.H. 1943. "A Theory of Human Motivation." *Psychological Review*, 50: 370–396, July.

McGraw, M. 1941. *The Child in Painting*. New York: Greystone Press.

Miller, D. 1986. *Infant/Toddler Day Care in High, Middle, and Low Socio-Economic Settings: An Ethnography of Dialectical Enculturation and Linguistic Code*. Unpublished Doctoral Dissertation.

Minsky, T. 1984. "Advice and Comfort for the Working Mother." *Esquire*, November–December, pp. 153–157.

Montessori, M. 1968. *Reconstruction in Education*. India: Theosophical Publishing House.

———— 1971. *Peace and Education*. India: Theosophical Publishing House.

Morland, J. 1972. "Racial Acceptance and Preference in Nursery School Children in a Southern City." In A. R. Brown (ed.), *Prejudice in Children*. Springfield, IL: Charles C. Thomas.

Mussen, P.H., and Eisenberg-Berg, N. 1977. *Roots of Caring, Sharing and Helping*. San Francisco: Freeman.

Osborn, D. 1980. *Early Childhood Education in Historical Perspective*. Athens: Education Association.

Papousek, H. 1967. "Conditioning During Postnatal Development." In Y. Brackbill and G.G. Thompson (eds.), *Behavior in Infancy and Early Childhood* (pp. 259–284). New York: Free Press.

Parillo, V. 1985. *Strangers to These Shores: Race and Ethnic Relations in the United States* (2nd ed.). New York: John Wiley & Sons.

Parke, R.D., and Slaby, R.G. 1983. "The Development of Aggression." In E.M. Hetherington (ed.), *Handbook of Child Psychology: Socialization, Personality and Social Development*, (4th ed.), vol. 4, 537–643. New York: Wiley.

Peterson, L. 1983. "Influence of Age, Task Competence, and Responsibility Focus on Children's Altruism." *Developmental Psychology*, 19, 141–148.

Phillips, D., Scarr, S., and McCartney, K. 1987. "Dimensions and Effects of Child Care Quality: The Bermuda Study." In D. Phillips (ed.), *Quality in Child Care: What Does Research Tell Us?* Washington, DC: N.A.E.Y.C.

Piaget, J. 1952. *The Origins of Intelligence in Children*. New York: International University Press.

_____ 1962. *Play, Dreams, and Imitation in Childhood.* New York: W. W. Norton & Co.

_____ 1963. *The Origins of Intelligence in Children.* New York: W.W. Norton & Co.

_____ 1965, originally published 1932. *The Moral Judgment of the Child* (M. Gabain, trans.). New York: The Free Press.

_____ 1968. *On the Development of Memory and Identity.* Barre, MA: Clark University Press.

_____ 1970. *Science of Education and the Psychology of the Child.* New York: Orion Press.

_____ 1983. Piaget's theory. In P.H. Mussen (ed.). *Handbook of Child Psychology* (2th ed.). W. Kessen (ed.), *Vol.1: History, Theory, and Methods.* New York: John Wiley and Sons.

Richards, M.P.M., Dunn, J.F., and Antonis, B. 1977. "Caretaking in the First Year of Life: The Role of Fathers and Mothers' Social Isolation." *Child: Care, Health, and Development,* 3, 23–26.

Rosenblith, J. F., Sims-Knight, J. 1985. *In the Beginning: Development in the First Two Years.* Monterey, CA: Brooks/Cole Publishing Co.

Rosenthal, R., and Jacobson, L. 1968. *Pygmalion in the Classroom: Teacher Expectations and Pupils' Intellectual Development.* New York: Holt, Rinehart & Winston.

Rousseau, J. 1893. *Emile: Or Treatise on Education.* New York: D. Appleton & Co.

Russell, G. 1978. "The Father Role and Its Relation to Masculinity, Femininity and Androgyny." *Child Development,* 49, 1174–1181.

Rutter, M. 1976. "Family, Area, and School Influences in the Genesis of Conduct Disorders." In L. Hersov, M. Berber, and D. Shaffer (eds.), *Aggression and Antisocial Behavior Development.* Oxford: Pergamom Press.

Sameroff, J.J., and Cavanagh, P.J. 1979. "Learning in Infancy: A Developmental Perspective." In J.D. Osofsky (ed.), *Handbook of Infant Development* (pp. 344–392). New York: Wiley.

Sears, R.R., Maccoby, E.E., and Lewin, H. 1957. *Patterns of Child Rearing.* Evanston, IL: Row and Peterson.

Skinner, B. 1953. *Science and Human Behavior.* New York: Macmillan.

_____ 1974. *About Behaviorism.* New York: Alfred A. Knopf.

Sroufe, L.A. 1979. "Socioemotional Development." In J. Osofsky (ed.), *Handbook of Infant Development.* New York: Wiley.

Stein, H. 1984. "The Case for Staying Home." *Esquire,* November–December, pp. 142–149.

Stern, D.N. 1974. "Mother and Infant at Play: The Dyadic Interaction Involving Facial, Vocal and Gaze Behaviors." In M. Lewis and L. Rosenblum (eds.), *The Effect of the Infant on Its Caregiver.* New York: Wiley-Interscience.

Stott, L.H., and Ball, R.S. 1957. "Consistency and Change in

Ascendance-Submission in the Social Interaction of Children." *Child Development*, 28, 259–272.

Thomas, A., and Chess, S. 1977. *Temperament and Development*. New York: Brunner/Mazel.

Thomas, A., Chess, S., and Birch, H.G. 1970. "The Origin of Personality." *Scientific American*, 233, 102–109.

Toner, I.J., Parke, R.D., and Yussen, S.R. 1978. "The Effect of Observation of Model Behavior on the Establishment and Stability of Resistance to Deviation in Children." *Journal of Genetic Psychology*, 132, 283–290.

Toner, I.J., and Potts, R. 1981. "Effect of Modeled Rationales on Moral Behavior, Moral Choice, and Level of Moral Judgment in Children." *Journal of Psychology*, 107, 153–162.

Trehub, S. 1973. "Infants' Sensitivity to Vowel and Tonal Contrasts." *Developmental Psychology,* 9, 81–96.

Ulich, R. 1954. *Three Thousand Years of Educational Wisdom*. Cambridge: Harvard University Press.

Von Frisch, K. 1974. "Decoding the Language of the Bee." *Science*, 185, 663–668.

Waldman, E. 1983. "Labor Force Statistics from a Family Perspective." *Monthly Labor Review* (December), 106, 16–20.

Watson, J. 1930. *Behaviorism* (2nd ed.). Chicago: University of Chicago Press.

Watson, J.S. 1973. "Smiling, Cooing and The Game." *Merrill-Palmer Quarterly*, 18, 323–339.

Weiser, M. 1982. *Group Care and Education of Infants and Toddlers*. St. Louis: C. V. Mosby.

Weiss, C.D., and Lillywhite, H.S. 1976. *Communicative Disorders: A Handbook for Prevention and Early Intervention*. St. Louis: Mosby.

Werner, N. E., and Evans, I. M. 1971. "Perception of Prejudice in Mexican-American Preschool Children." In N.N. Wagner and M.J. Haug (eds.), *Chicano: Social and Psychological Perspectives*. St. Louis: C.V. Mosby Co.

White, B. 1975. *The First Three Years of Life*. New York: Avon.

White, B., and Watts, J. 1973. *Experience and Environment: Major Influences on the Development of the Young Child*, (Vol. 2). New Jersey: Prentice Hall.

White, B., Kaban, B., and Attanucci, J. 1979. *The Origins of Human Competence: The Final Report of the Harvard Preschool Project*. Massachusetts: Lexington Books.

Willis, P. 1981. *Learning to Labor: How Working Class Kids Get Working Class Jobs*. New York: Columbia University Press.

Wolff, P. 1963. "Observations on the Early Development of Smiling." In B. M. Foss (ed.), *Determinants of Infant Behavior* (Vol. 2). London: Methuen.

Index